IRELAND

Scale 1:200,000
3.16 miles to 1 inch
2km to 1cm

3rd edition January 2008

© Automobile Association Developments Limited 2007
Original edition printed 2004

Cartography:
All cartography in this atlas edited, designed and produced by
the Mapping Services Department of AA Publishing (A03356).

 This product includes mapping based upon
data licensed from Ordnance Survey of
Northern Ireland® reproduced by permission
of the Chief Executive, acting on behalf of the
Controller of Her Majesty's Stationery Office
© Crown copyright 2007. Permit number 70044. This product
includes RCDI by permission of Ordnance Survey of Northern
Ireland on behalf of the Controller of Her Majesty's Stationery
Office © Crown Copyright 2007.

Republic of Ireland mapping based on Ordnance Survey
Ireland. Permit number 8136. © Ordnance Survey Ireland and
Government of Ireland.

Published by AA Publishing (a trading name of Automobile
Association Developments Limited, whose registered office is
Fanum House, Basing View, Basingstoke, Hampshire
RG21 4EA, UK. Registered number 1878835)

ISBN-13: 978 0 7495 5606 8

A CIP catalogue record for this book is available from
The British Library.

Disclaimer:
The contents of this atlas are believed to be correct at the
time of the latest revision. However, the publishers cannot be
held responsible for loss occasioned to any person acting or
refraining from action as a result of any material in this atlas,
nor for any errors, omissions or changes in such material.
This does not affect your statutory rights. The publishers
would welcome information to correct any errors or omissions
and to keep this atlas up to date. Please write to the
Cartographic Editor, Publishing Division, The Automobile
Association, Fanum House, Basing View, Basingstoke,
Hampshire RG21 4EA, UK.
E-mail: *roadatlasfeedback@theaa.com*

Many place names in the main-map section of this atlas are
given in English and Irish. The names shown are those
approved by the Ordnance Survey of Northern Ireland and
Ordnance Survey Ireland.

Acknowledgements:
The AA would like to acknowledge the following bodies and
agencies for information used in the creation of this atlas:
The Environment & Heritage Service, Heritage of Ireland,
RSPB, Department of Agriculture & Rural Development,
An Roinn Gnóthaí Pobail, GaelSaoire, Tuaithe agus
Gaeltachta, Coillte Teoranta, The National Trust, An Taisce,
Roads Service and The National Roads Authority. Relief map
image supplied by Mountain High Maps ® Copyright © 1993
Digital Wisdom, Inc.

Printer:
Printed in Italy by Printer Trento srl, Trento, on Gardamatt
(made to ISO 9706 standards).

Atlas contents

Map pages	inside front cover
Route planning	II-VI
Route planner	II
Ferry ports	III
Distance chart	IV
The shape of the land	V
Language and dialects	VI
Key to map symbols	1
Road maps 1:200,000 scale	2-68
Town plans	69-75
Key to town plans	69
Motorways	76-80
Key to motorway maps	76
Index to place names	81-90
County and administrative areas	81
Freshwater fishing	inside back cover

Route planner

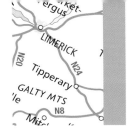

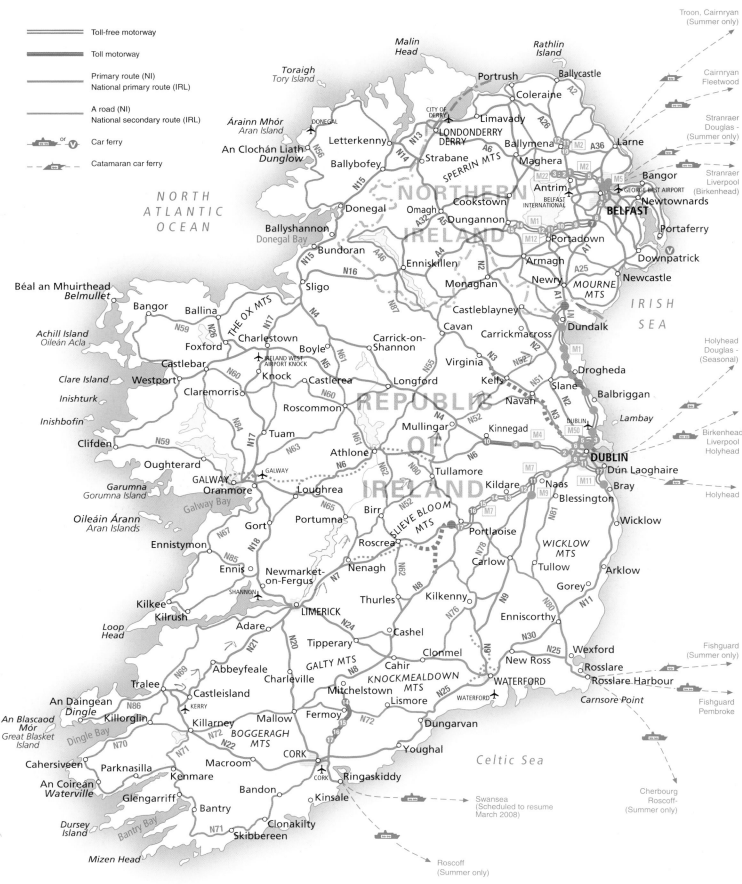

Toll-free motorway

Toll motorway

Primary route (NI)
National primary route (IRL)

A road (NI)
National secondary route (IRL)

Car ferry

Catamaran car ferry

NORTH ATLANTIC OCEAN

IRISH SEA

Celtic Sea

Troon, Cairnryan (Summer only)

Cairnryan Fleetwood

Stranraer Douglas - (Summer only)

Stranraer Liverpool (Birkenhead)

Holyhead Douglas - (Seasonal)

Birkenhead Liverpool Holyhead

Holyhead

Fishguard (Summer only)

Fishguard Pembroke

Cherbourg Roscoff (Summer only)

Swansea (Scheduled to resume March 2008)

Roscoff (Summer only)

| 0 | 10 | 20 | 30 | 40 | 50 miles |
| 0 | 20 | 40 | 60 | 80 km |

Ferry ports

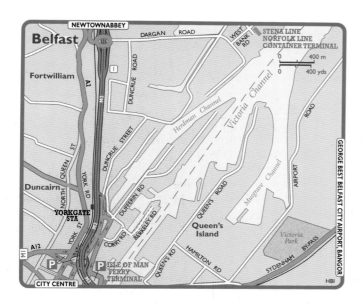

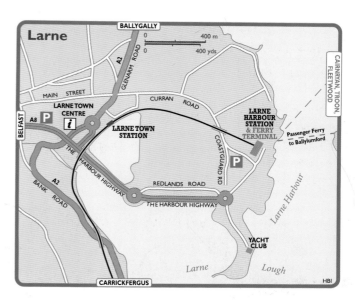

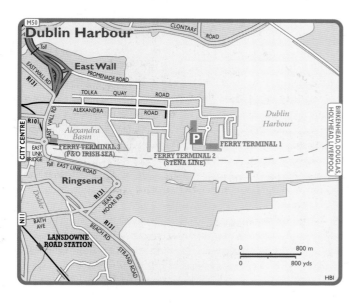

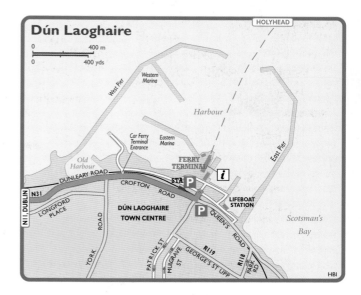

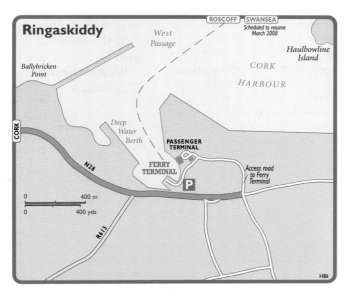

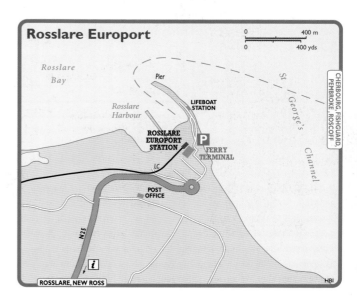

Distance chart

This chart shows distances, in both miles and kilometres, between two towns along AA-recommended routes. Using motorways and other main roads this is normally the fastest route, though not necessarily the shortest.

For example, the distance between Cork and Omagh is 395 kilometres or 245 miles (8 kilometres is approximately 5 miles).

To reflect the distances shown on road signs, distances shown on the road maps in this atlas are in miles in Northern Ireland and kilometres in the Republic of Ireland.

distances in miles

Antrim
Armagh
Athlone
Belfast
Béal an Mhuirthead Belmullet
Bundoran
Carlow
Cavan
Clifden
Cork
Donegal
Downpatrick
Dublin
Dundalk
An Clochán Liath Dunglow
Dún Laoghaire
Ennis
Enniskillen
Galway
Glengarriff
Kilkee
Kilkenny
Killarney
Larne
Limerick
Londonderry Derry
Mallow
Mullingar
Omagh
Portlaoise
Portrush
Roscommon
Sligo
Tipperary
Tralee
Tullamore
Waterford
An Coireán Waterville
Wexford
Wicklow

distances in kilometres

The shape of the land

Ireland at a glance
Area 84,433sq km (32,600sq miles)

▲ **Highest mountains**
Carrauntoohil, Kerry — 1039m (3,409ft)
Cnoc Bréanainn or
Brandon Mountain, Kerry — 950m (3,117ft)
Lugnaquilla Mountain, Wicklow — 924m (3,031ft)
Galtymore Mountain, Lim/Tipp — 919m (3,015ft)
Slieve Donard, Down, NI — 850m (2,789ft)

★ **World heritage sites**
Boyne Valley Mounds (Newgrange,
Knowth and Dowth), Meath
Giant's Causeway, Moyle, NI
Sceilg Mhichíl or Skellig Michael, Kerry

▲ **Highest cliff**
Croaghaun, Achill Island, Mayo — 668m (2,192ft)

Largest lake
Lough Neagh — 381sq km (147sq miles)

Longest river
Shannon — 259km (161 miles)

▼ **Highest waterfall**
Powerscourt Falls, Wicklow — 106m (348ft)

Teanga agus canúintí
Langue et dialectes
Sprache und Dialekte

Language and dialects

An Ghaeltacht

Gaeltacht is an Irish language term for those areas of Ireland where the Irish language is still spoken as a community language. When you see the road sign **An Ghaeltacht** you are about to enter a designated Irish (Gaeilge) speaking area where many road traffic signs are in Gaeilge only.

Within the Gaeltacht areas, in order to match the road signs on the ground, the place name spellings used in this atlas are in official Gaeilge. For example, 'An Daingean' is used in place of 'Dingle'. But, to help those unfamiliar with Gaeilge, the English version of the name is also shown on the maps and for ease-of-use both versions are listed alphabetically in the index.

More than 55,000 people in the Republic of Ireland speak Gaeilge. Many more learned it at school, but only in the west is it the first language of the majority of the population. It is an official language of central government and plays a large part in the educational system.

The English spoken in Ireland grew from a combination of Gaeilge and 17th century English. This Anglo-Irish has some dialect variations: the main dialect boundary separates the west and south with its Gaeilge influence from the north with its strong lowland Scottish element in vocabulary and markedly different vowel sounds. Some consider Ulster-Scots or Ullan as a separate language.

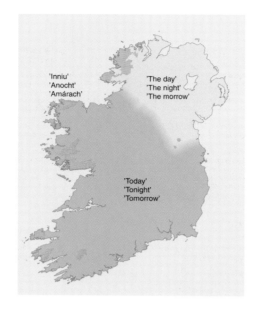

'Inniu'
'Anocht'
'Amárach'

'The day'
'The night'
'The morrow'

'Today'
'Tonight'
'Tomorrow'

GAELTACHT
Ceantair Ghaeltachta
La région Gaeltacht
Gaeltacht-Regionen

Scottish influence
Tionchar Albanach
Influence Ecossaises
Schottisches Beeinflusst

ANGLO-IRISH
Angla Éireannach
Anglo-Irlandaise
Anglo-Irisch

Gaeilge influence
Tionchar Ghaeilge
Influence Gaeilge
Gaeilge Beeinflusst

*Is téarma i nGaeilge í Gaeltacht do na ceantair sin in Éirinn ina bhfuil an Ghaeilge fós á labhairt mar theanga pobail. Nuair a fheiceann tú comhartha bóthair **An Ghaeltacht**, bíonn tú ar tí dul isteach go ceantar sainiúil ina labhraítear Gaeilge, áit a bhfuil go leor comharthaí bóthair ar fáil i nGaeilge amháin.*

Litrítear na logainmneacha atá laistigh de na ceantair Ghaeltachta de réir an chaighdeáin oifigiúil Ghaeilge chun teacht leis na comharthaí bóthair atá ina seasamh ar an talamh. Úsáidtear 'An Daingean' mar shampla in ionad 'Dingle'. Tá an leagan Béarla den logainm ar na léarscáil mar chúnamh dóibh siúd nach bhfuil taithí acu ar an nGaeilge agus ar son na soiléireachta tá an dá leagan liostaithe in órd abítearach san innéacs.

Labhrann sa bhreis ar 55,000 míle duine an Ghaeilge i bPoblacht na hÉireann. D'fhoghlaim go leor eile an Ghaeilge ar scoil, ach is san iarthar amháin a bhfuil sí ina teanga dúchais ag móramh an daonra. Is í an teanga oifgiúil í ag an rialtas lárnach agus tá páirt mhór aici sa chóras oideachais.

D'eascair an Béarla a labraítear in Éirinn as meascán de Ghaeilge agus Béarla na 17 aoise déag. Tá roinnt éagsúlachtaí canúna sa Bhéarla Angla-Éireannach deighleann an príomhteorainn canúna, an iarthar ón deisceart de bharr na tionchar atá air ó Ghaeilge an tuaiscirt agus eilimintí láidre de theanga na n-isealchríoch Albanach (Lallans) ó thaobh na foclóra agus ó thaobh fhuaimniú éagsúil na ngútaí de. Measann roinnt daoine gur teanga ar leith í Albainis Uladh nó Ultais.

Gaeltacht est un terme de la langue irlandaise pour les régions d'Irlande où l'irlandais est encore utilisé en tant que langue communautaire. Si vous voyez le panneau de signalisation **An Ghaeltacht** vous êtes sur le point d'entrer dans une zone irlandaise où l'on parle un irlandais spécifique (Gaeilge) et où de nombreux panneaux routiers sont uniquement en Gaeilge.

Pour avoir une correspondance avec les panneaux routiers se trouvant sur les lieux, les noms utilisés dans cet atlas pour les régions du Gaeltacht, sont donnés suivant le Gaeilge officiel. Par exemple 'An Daingean' est utilisé au lieu de 'Dingle'. Mais pour faciliter la tâche ce ceux qui ne connaissent pas le Gaeilge, la version anglaise du nom est également donnée sur les cartes et pour une utilisation plus aisée les deux versions sont données par ordre alphabétique dans l'index.

Plus de 55000 personnes parlent le Gaeilge dans la République d'Irlande. Ils sont bien plus nombreux à l'avoir appris à l'école mais c'est uniquement dans l'ouest du pays qu'il représente la première langue pour la majorité de la population. C'est une langue officielle du gouvernement central et elle joue un rôle important dans le système éducatif.

L'anglais parlé en Ireland est le résultat de la combinaison du Gaeilge et de l'anglais du 17ème siècle. Cette langue anglo-irlandaise comporte des variations dialectales-: la principale frontière du dialecte sépare l'ouest et le sud avec son influence Gaeilge, du nord où le dialecte comporte une forte caractéristique des terres basses écossaises pour le vocabulaire et des voyelles qui se prononcent nettement différemment. Certains considèrent l'Ulster-Scots ou l'Ullan comme une langue distincte.

Gaeltacht ist ein Begriff in der irischen Sprache für die Regionen in Irland, in denen die Irische Sprache noch gesprochen wird. Wenn Sie das Verkehrsschild **An Ghaeltacht** sehen, fahren Sie in ein Gebiet, in dem die offizielle Sprache Irisch (Gaeilge) ist und in dem viele Straßenschilder nur in Gaeilge beschriftet sind.

In den Gaeltacht-Regionen erscheinen in diesem Atlas die Ortsnamen mit ihrer offiziellen Gaeilge-Bezeichnung, damit sie den Ortsnamen auf den Verkehrsschildern entsprechen. Zum Beispiel wird 'An Daingean' anstatt von 'Dingle' verwendet. Um das Verständnis für diejenigen zu erleichtern, die des Gaeilge nicht mächtig sind, erscheint der englische Name ebenfalls auf den Karten und im Ortsregister sind beide Versionen in alphabetischer Folge aufgeführt.

In der Republik Irland wird Gaeilge heute von über 55.000 Personen gesprochen. Weit mehr haben die Sprache in der Schule gelernt, aber nur im Westen Irlands ist sie für den Großteil der Bevölkerung die erste Muttersprache. Gaeilge ist eine offizielle Regierungssprache und spielt im Bildungssystem eine wichtige Rolle.

Das Englisch, das heute in Irland gesprochen wird, hat sich aus einer Mischung aus Gaeilge und dem Englisch des 17. Jahrhunderts entwickelt. Innerhalb dieses Anglo-Irisch gibt es auch mehrere Dialekte: Die Hauptdialektgrenze trennt den Westen und Süden, die vom Gaeilge beeinflusst sind, vom Norden, in dem beim Vokabular und mit deutlichen Unterschieden bei den Vokallauten ein starkes schottisches Element vorherrscht. Von manchen wird Ulster-Schottisch oder Ullan sogar als eine separate Sprache betrachtet.

Major road ahead – give way to traffic on it

Comhartha tráchta ag ordú duit GÉILL nó GÉILL SLÍ roimh an trácht ar an bpríomhbhóthar romhat.

Panneau routier indiquant YIELD ou CEDER LE PASSAGE aux usagers de la route principale.

Bei diesem Verkehrsschild müssen Sie dem Verkehr auf der Hauptverkehrsstraße die VORFAHRT GEWÄHREN.

Key to map symbols
Eochair   Légende   Legende

Motoring information

Irish / French	Symbol	English / German
Mótarbhealach saor in aisce / Autoroute gratuite	M1	**Toll-free motorway** / Mautfreie Autobahn
Mótarbhealach le híoc / Autoroute à péage	M1	**Toll motorway** / Mautpflichtige Autobahn
Acomhal lán (1), srianta (2) / Échangeur (1), Échangeur partiel (2)	(1) (2) (1) (2)	**Full (1), restricted junction (2)** / Vollwertige (1), eingeschränkte Anschlussstelle (2)
Mótarbhealach á dhéanamh / Autoroute en construction		**Motorway under construction** / Autobahn in Bau
Carrbhealach dúbailte / Double voie		**Dual carriageway** / Straße mit getrennten Fahrbahnen
Carrbhealach singil / Une voie		**Single carriageway** / Straße mit einem Fahrstreifen
Bóthar á dhéanamh / Route en construction		**Road under construction** / Straße in Bau
Mionbhóthar / Route secondaire		**Minor road** / Nebenstraße
Droichead nó bóthar le híoc / Péage pont ou routier	Toll	**Bridge or road toll** / Brücken- oder Straßenmaut
Carrchaladh / Car-ferry	V or	**Car ferry** / Autofähre
Carrchaladh catamaran / Catamaran-ferry		**Catamaran car ferry** / Katamaran-Autofähre
Bealach iarainn, stáisiún, crosaire comhréidh / Voie de chemin de fer, gare, passage à niveau	×○	**Railway, station, level crossing** / Eisenbahn, Bahnhof, Bahnüber
Aerfort, aerpháirc / Aéroport, aérodrome	✈ ✈	**Airport, airfield** / Flughafen, Flugplatz
Cathair, baile mór, baile beag nó ceantar / Grande ville, ville, village ou localité		**City, town, village or locality** / Großstadt, Stadt, Dorf oder Ort
Airde i méadair, timpeall / Altitude en mètres, col	628 ▲ •	**Height in metres, pass** / Höhenangabe in Metern, Pass
Príomh cheann cúrsa (roghnaithe) / Destination primaire (sélectionnée)	CORK	**Primary destination (selected)** / Hauptziel (ausgewählt)
Bóthar príomha náisiúnta (IRL) / Route nationale (IRL)	N17	**National primary route (IRL)** / Nationalstraße erster Ordnung (IRL)
Bóthar tánaisteach náisiúnta (IRL) / Route départementale (IRL)	N56	**National secondary route (IRL)** / Nationalstraße zweiter Ordnung (IRL)
Bóthar réigiúnach (IRL) / Route communale (IRL)	R182	**Regional road (IRL)** / Regionalstraße (IRL)
Faid i gciliméadar (IRL) / Distance en kilomètres (IRL)	▼ 8 ▼	**Distance in kilometres (IRL)** / Entfernung in Kilometern (IRL)
Bóthar príomha (NI) / Route nationale (NI)	A4	**Primary route (NI)** / Straße erster Ordnung (NI)
Bóthar A (NI) / Catégorie A (NI)	A21	**A road (NI)** / Nationalstraße (NI)
Bóthar B (NI) / Catégorie B (NI)	B75	**B road (NI)** / Nebenstraße (NI)
Faid i mílte (NI) / Distance en miles (NI)	▼ 5 ▼	**Distance in miles (NI)** / Entfernung in Meilen (NI)
Tollán bóthair / Tunnel routier	═══════	**Road tunnel** / Straßentunnel
Teorainn idirnáisiúnta / Frontière internationale		**International boundary** / Staatsgrenze
Teorainn eile / Autre frontière		**Other boundary** / Andere Grenze
Trá, cladach eile / Plage, autre rivage		**Beach, other foreshore** / Strand, sonstige Uferbereiche
Abhainn, canáil, loch / Rivière, canal, lac		**River, canal, lough** / Fluss, Kanal, See
Uimhir leanúnach an leathanaigh / Numéro de continuation de page	23	**Page continuation number** / Nummer der Anschlussseite

Touring information

Irish / French	Symbol	English / German
Ionad eolais turasóireachta, séasúrach / Office de tourisme, saisonnier	i i	**Tourist information, seasonal** / Fremdenverkehrsamt, während der Saison
Ionad cuartaíochta / Centre pour visiteurs	V	**Visitor centre** / Besucherzentrum
Láithreán campála AA / Terrain pour camping homologué AA		**AA approved campsite** / Mit AA ausgezeichneter Campingplatz
Láithreán carbhán eile / Autre terrain pour caravanes		**Other caravan site** / Sonstiger Wohnwagenplatz
Mainistir, ardeaglais nó prióireacht / Abbaye, cathédrale ou monastère		**Abbey, cathedral or priory** / Abtei, Kathedrale, Priorei
Ballóg mainistreach, ardeaglais nó prióireacht / Ruines d'abbaye, de cathédrale ou de monastère		**Ruined abbey, cathedral or priory** / Abtei-, Kathedralen-, Priorei-Ruine
Caisleán, dún / Château, fortifications	♜	**Castle, hill-fort** / Schloss, Festung
Iarsmalann nó dánlann / Musée ou galerie	M	**Museum or gallery** / Museum oder Kunstgalerie
Gairdín, páirc tuaithe / Jardin, parc	❋ ⚘	**Garden, country park** / Garten, Landschaftspark
Zú, fiabheatha nó páirc éanlaithe / Zoo, réserve naturelle ou parc ornithologique		**Zoo, wildlife or bird park** / Zoo, Tier- oder Vogelpark
Dúlra, tearmann éin / Réserve naturelle, ornithologique	RSPB	**Nature, bird reserve** / Natur-, Vogelschutzgebiet
Slíbhealach le comharthaí / Promenade banalisée		**Waymarked walk** / Ausgeschilderter Weg
Ionad dearctha, láithreán picnicí / Panorama, aire de pique-nique		**Viewpoint, picnic site** / Aussichtspunkt, Picknick-Platz
Ar liosta AA, galfchúrsa eile / Terrain de golf homologué AA, non homologué AA	▶ ▶	**AA listed, other golf course** / Mit AA ausgezeichneter, sonstiger Golfplatz
Bealach radharcach / Itinéraire pittoresque		**Scenic route** / Landschaftlich schöne Strecke
Ceantair Ghaeltachta / La Gaeltacht région		**Gaeltacht (Irish language area)** / Gaeltacht-Regionen
Rásaí capall, ciorcad rásaí cairr / Hippodrome, circuit automobile		**Horse racing, motor-racing circuit** / Pferde-, Motorrennbahn
Lúthchleasaíocht idirnáisiúnta, aontas rugbaí / Événements athlétiques internationaux, rugby		**International athletics, rugby union** / Internationale Leichtathletik-, Rugby-Union
Gníomhaíocht sciála, bádóireacht / Activités nautiques, ski		**Boating, skiing activities** / Wassersport, Ski
Áitreabh Taisce Náisiúnta / Propriété du National Trust	NT AT	**National Trust property** / Eigentum des National Trust
Teach nó foirgneamh stairiúil / Bâtiment ou maison historique		**Historic house or building** / Historisches Haus oder Gebäude
Páirc Náisiúnta / Parc national		**National Park** / Nationalpark
Páirc Foraoise / Parc forestier		**Forest Park** / Parkwald
Foraois / Forêt		**Woodland** / Wald
Leacht réamhstairiúil / Monument préhistorique		**Prehistoric monument** / Prähistorisches Denkmal
Suim tionsclaíoch / Point d'intérêt industriel		**Industrial interest** / Industriedenkmal
Láithreán catha le dáta / Champ de bataille avec date	✕ 1690	**Battle site with date** / Schlachtfeld mit Datum
Leacht, áit eile suimiúil / Monument, autre lieu d'intérêt	⚹ ★	**Monument, other place of interest** / Denkmal, anderer interessanter Ort
Léiríonn comharthaí le boscaí tarraingtí laistigh de cheantair uirbeacha / Les symboles encadrés signalent un lieu d'attraction en zone urbaine	□	**Boxed symbols indicate attractions within urban areas** / Eingerahmte Symbole bezeichnen Attraktionen innerhalb der Stadtgebiete

Adrigole (4L)

Reen £95'000
1acre.

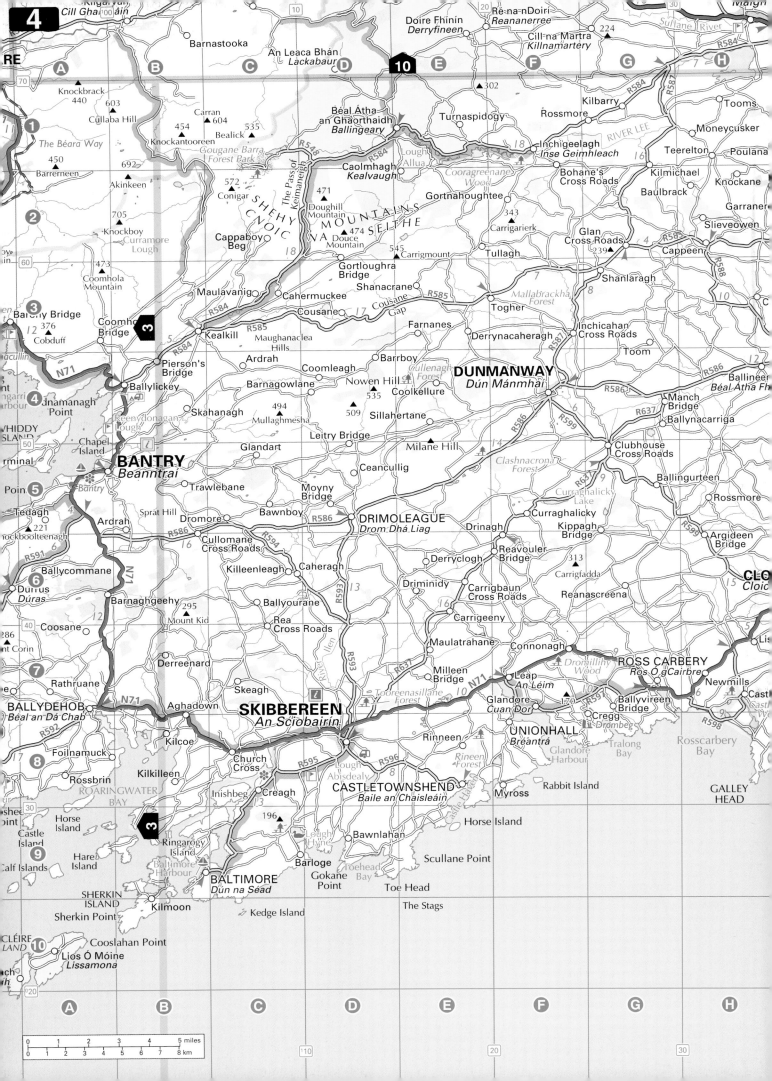

SEA

YOUGHAL BAY

DUNGARVAN
Dún Garbhán
Cuan Dhún Garbhán

YOUGHAL
Eochaill

ARDMORE
Aird Mhór

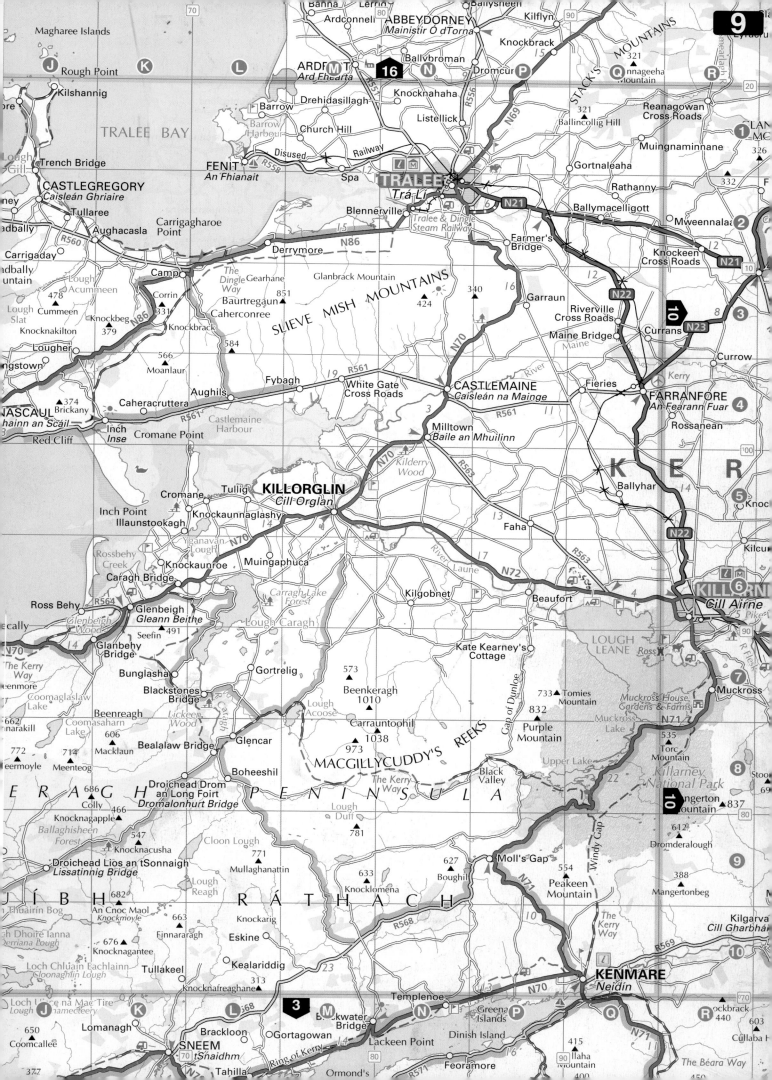

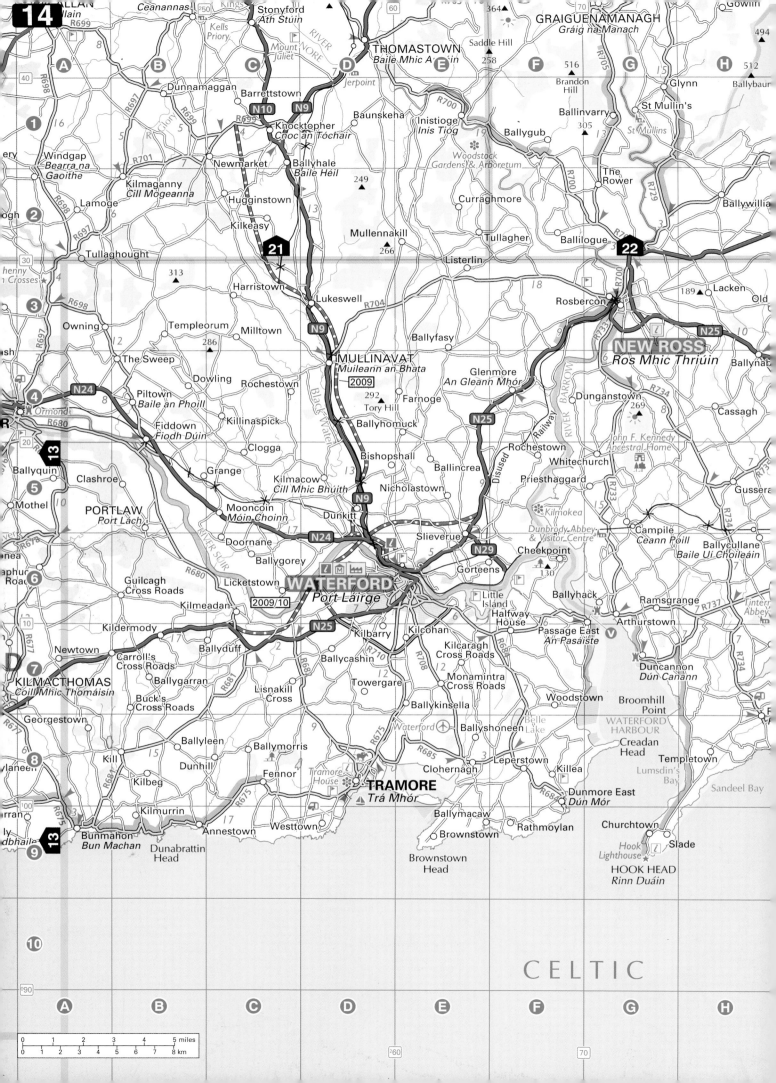

€29'000
∠7
Athea.

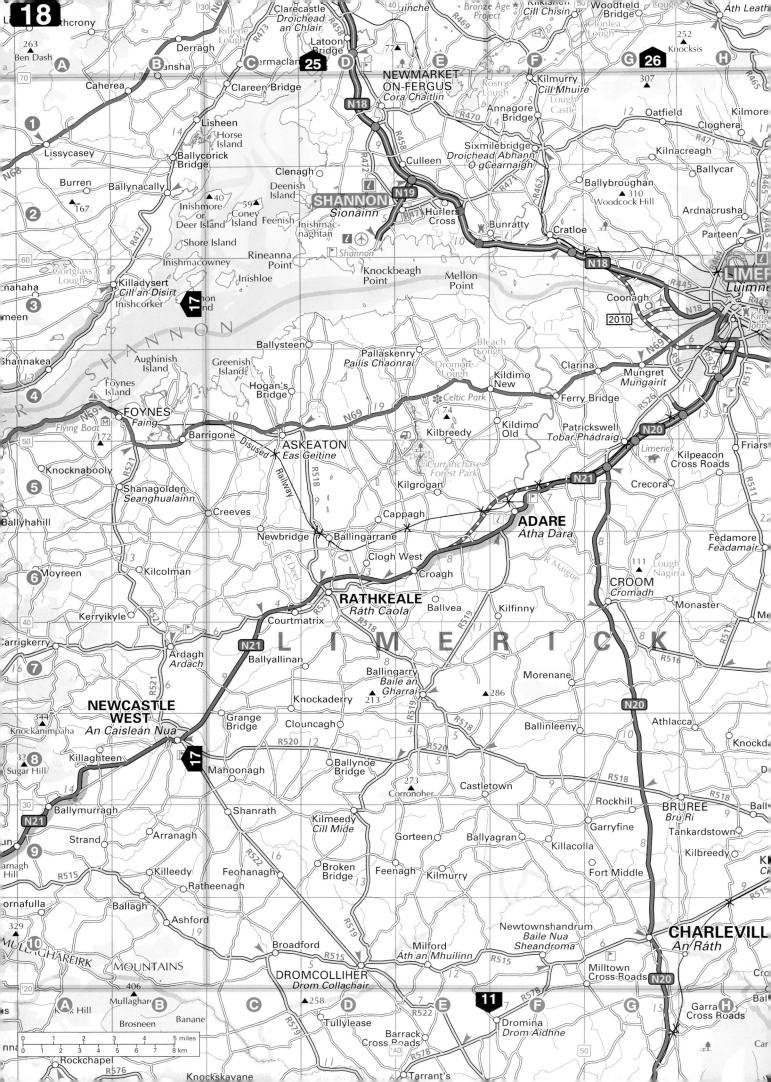

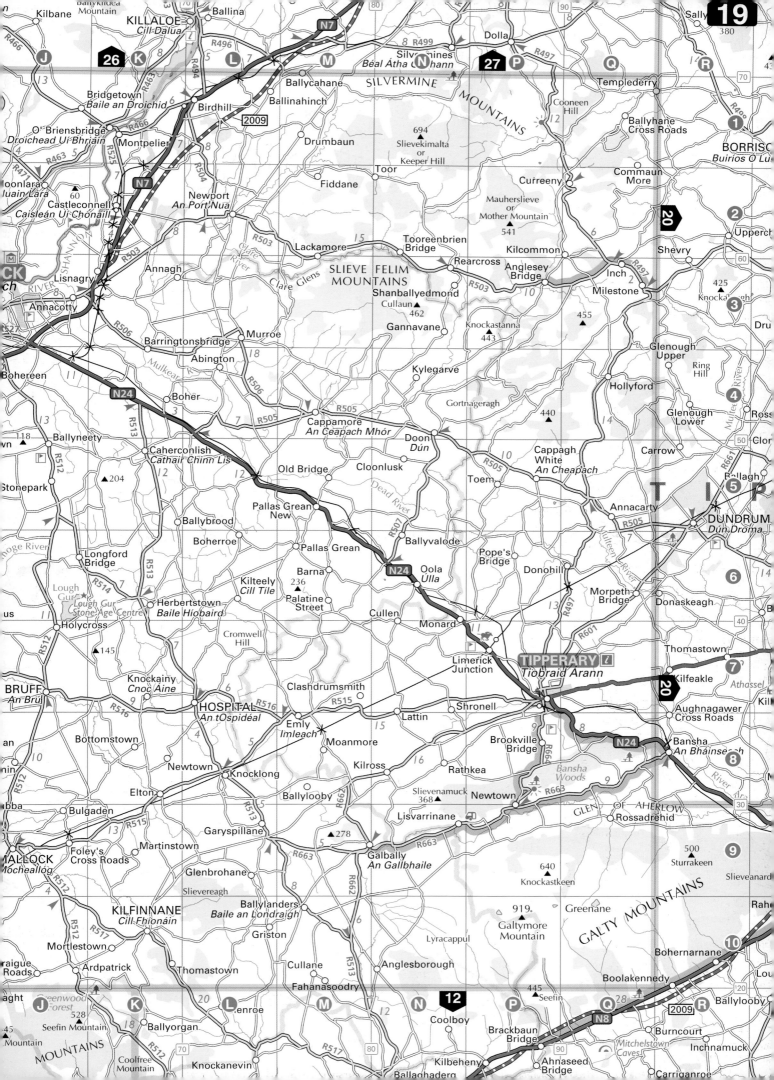

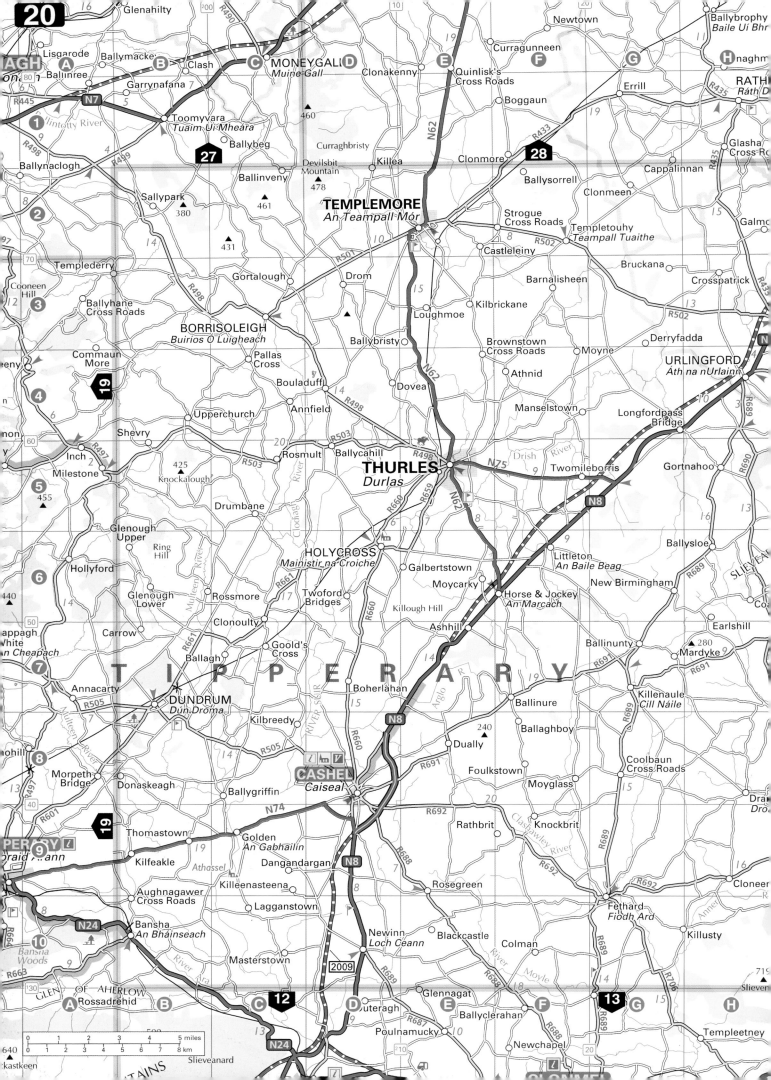

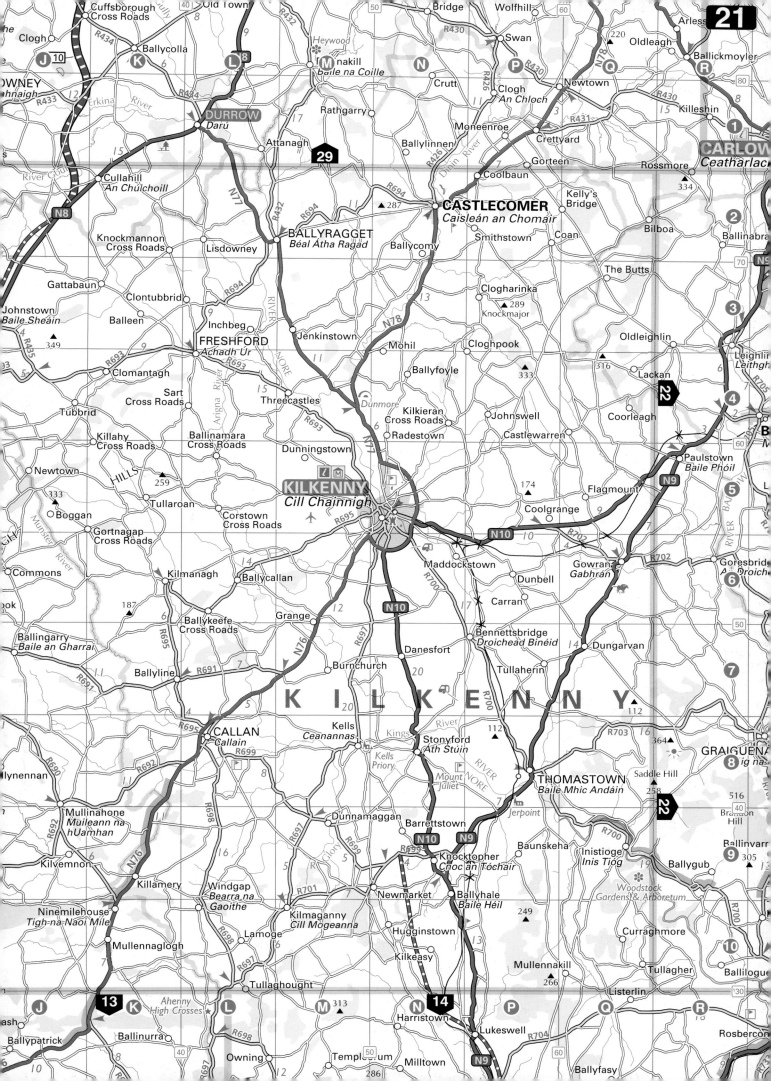

80 Inis Eirc
Island
90
Carraroe
12
100 An Tulaigh
Tully
R336
9
10

Leitir Mealláin
Lettermullan
Loch
Hirbirt
Loch
Bhaile
na Cille
Cuan an
Chasla
Cashla
Bay
Baile na
hAbhann
Ballynahown

Indreabhán
Inveran
An Lochán Beag
Loughaunbeg
AN S
Spidd

A Ceann Gólaim
Golam Head
B
Cuan an
Fhir Mhó
*Greatman's
Bay*
C
D
E och na
eibhinne
F Pointe an
Chaisleáin
Castle Point
G
H

1 ⬛ **32** ⬛ **33**

AN SUNDA Ó THUAIDH
NORTH SOUND

G A L W A Y   B A Y

An tOileán
Iarthach
Rock Is

2 Oileán
Dhá Bhranóg
Brannock Is
Eoghanacht
Onaght
Port Mhuirbhigh
Portmurvy
OILEAIN ÁRANN
ARAN ISLANDS
(Co Galway)
BLACK HE

▲105
Cill Mhuirbhigh
Kilmurvy
Fearann
an Choirce
Eochaill

Dún Aonghasa
▲123
CILL RÓNÁIN
ℹ *Kilronan*
Oileán na Tuí
Straw Island

3 Gort na gCapall
INIS MÓR
INISHMORE
Cuan Chill
Éinne
Ceann an Mhada
Dog's Head
INIS MEÁIN
INISHMAAN
Murroogh

Cill Éinne
Killeany
Sunda
Ghríora
*Gregory's
Sound*
Cra

Baile an Teampall
Slie
R477
30

4 ▲81 An Córa
An Sunda
Salach
*Foul
Sound*
Gob na
Cora
Ailladie

INIS ÓIRR
INISHEER

200

5 SOUTH SOUND
Knockfin
Cross Roads
R479
R477
L

Roadford
Doolin
4
N6

Fisherstreet
R479
Dúlainn

R478
202
▲
Knocknaiarabana

6 I5
Carrowduff
Kilsha

90
Cliffs of Moher
ℹ

7 Hags Head
Derreen
O'Brien's
Bridge
4

Cancregga
Liscannor
Lios Ceannúir
LAHINCH
An Leacht

LISCANNOR
BAY
Knockpatric

8 Rinneen
10
N67
Knockatulla

80
Cream Point
203
▲

9 MAL BAY
MILLTOWN MALBAY
Sráid na Cathrách
R460
Letter

Spanish Point
Rinn na Spáinneach
R482
R474
Caherogan
Shanavogh
East
Slie

Caherrush Point
17

Emlagh
Point
Annagh
Cross Roads

10 Quilty
Coillte
Mutton Island
Oileán Caorach
Kilmurry
Mullagh
Knockna

7
Doo Lough

170
Carrowmore
Point
Lough
Donnell
Knocknahila
Drummin
Glenmor

A **B** **C** **D** ⬛ **16** **E** **F** N67
7
5
R483
ghaun
▲174
Cahermurphy
G
H

Killard
Creegh
R484
Greygrove

0 1 2 3 4 5 miles
0 1 2 3 4 5 6 7 8 km

Ball 090 Bay
Donegal Point
Doonbeg
Mountrivers
Creegh River
Leitrim
10

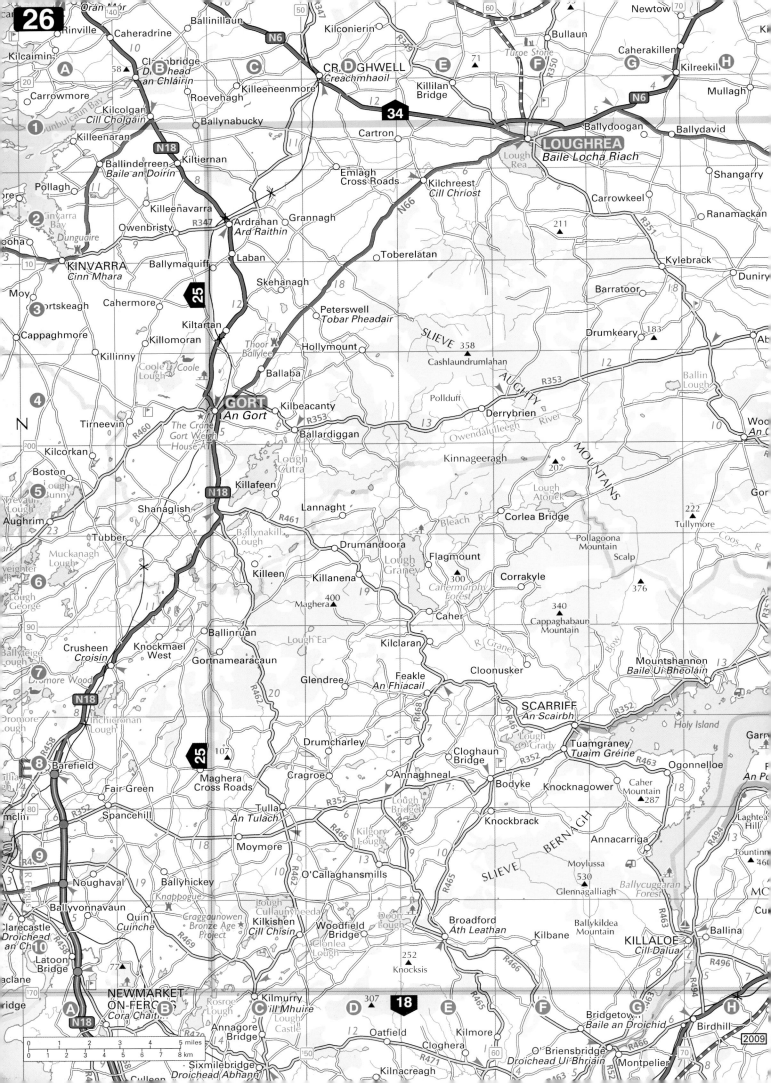

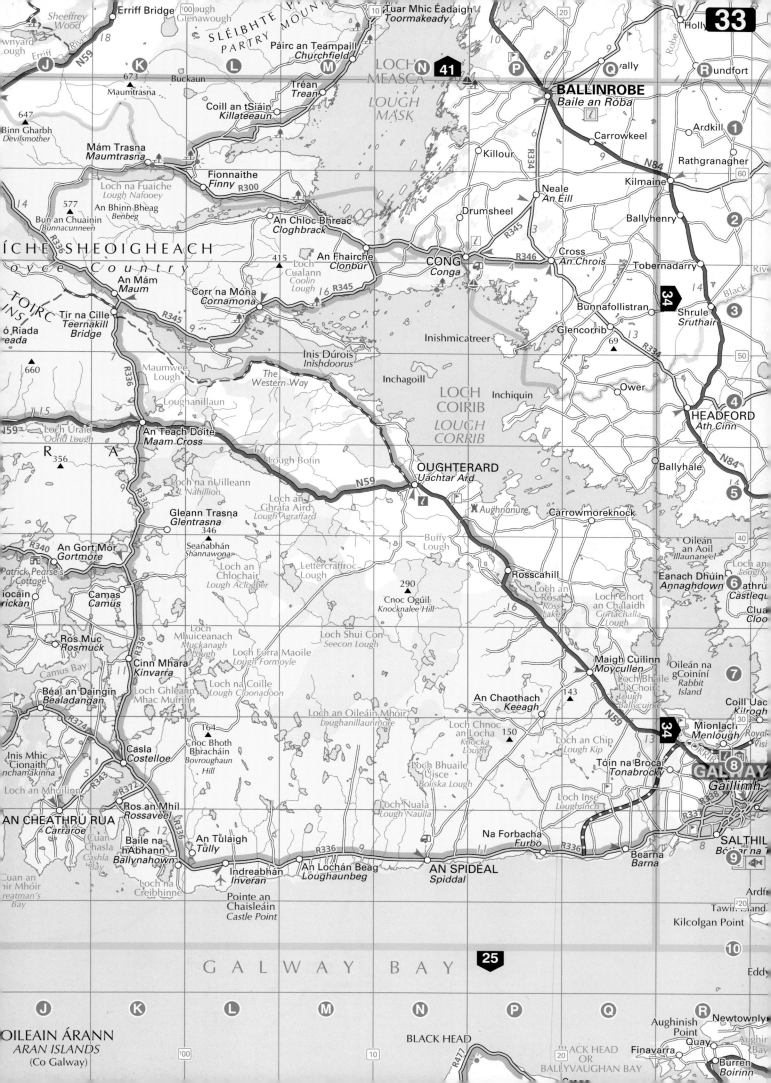

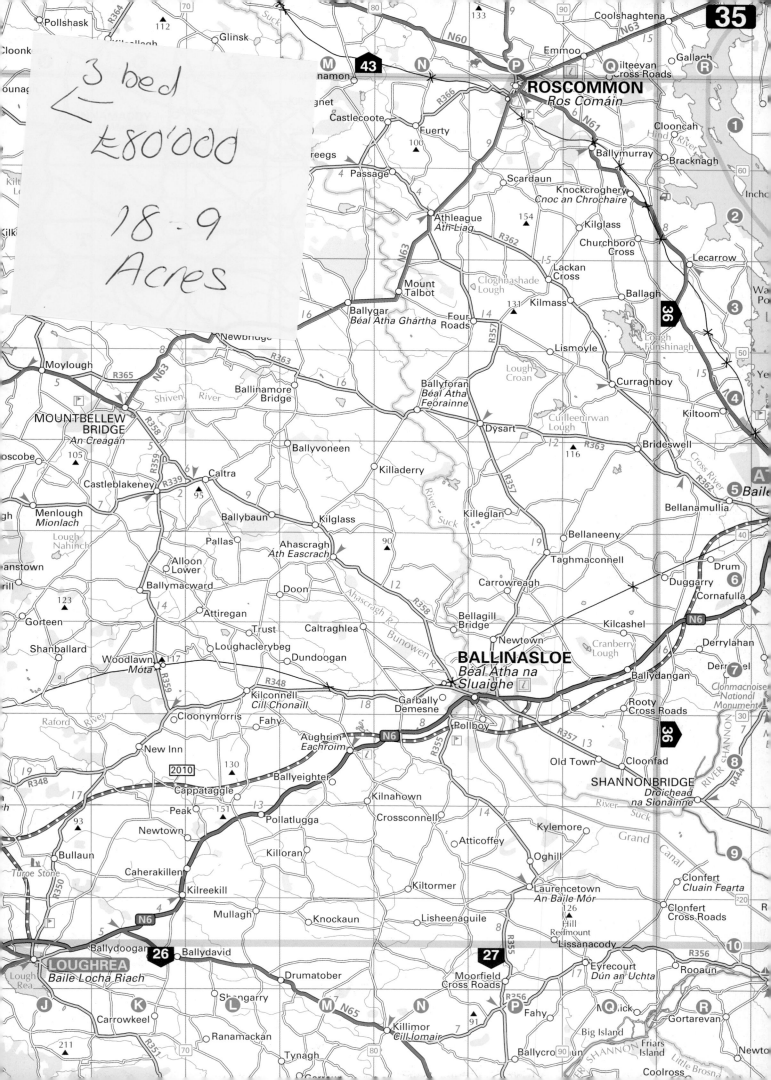

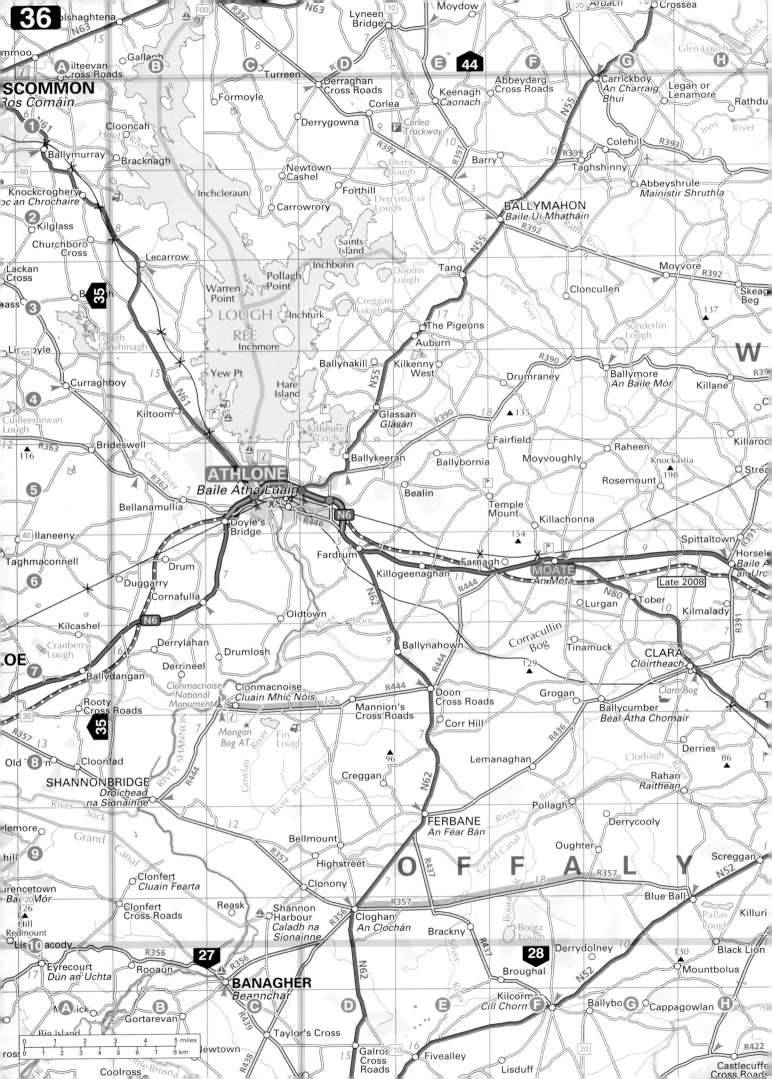

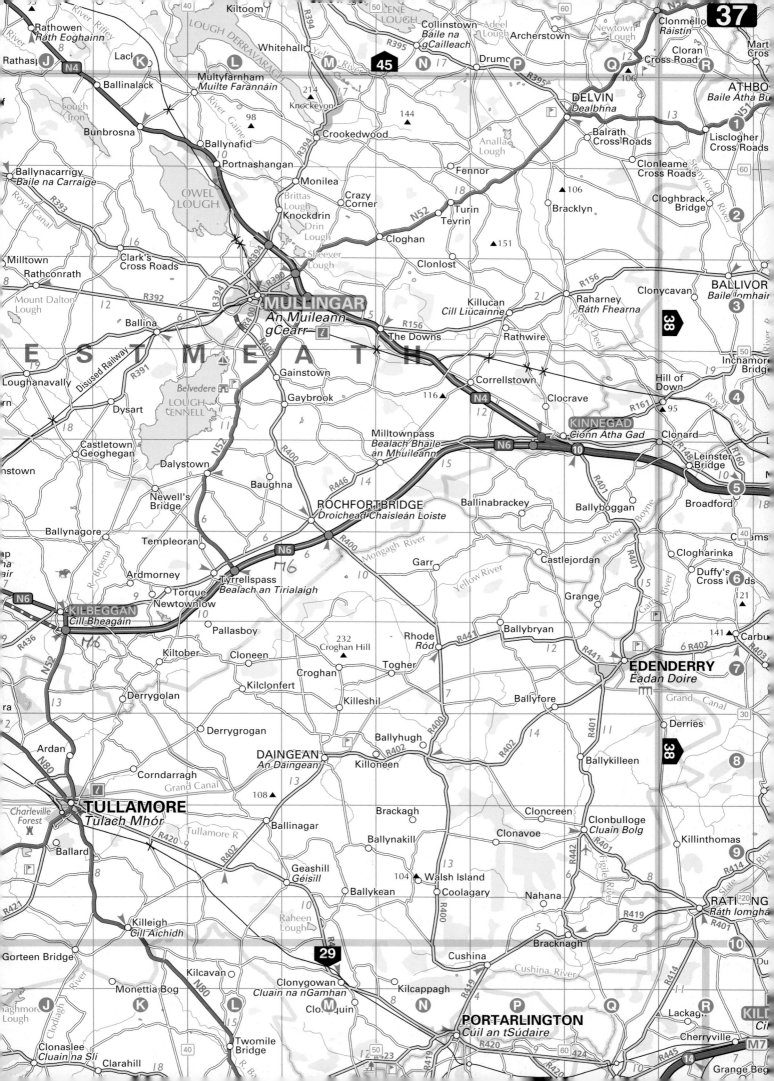

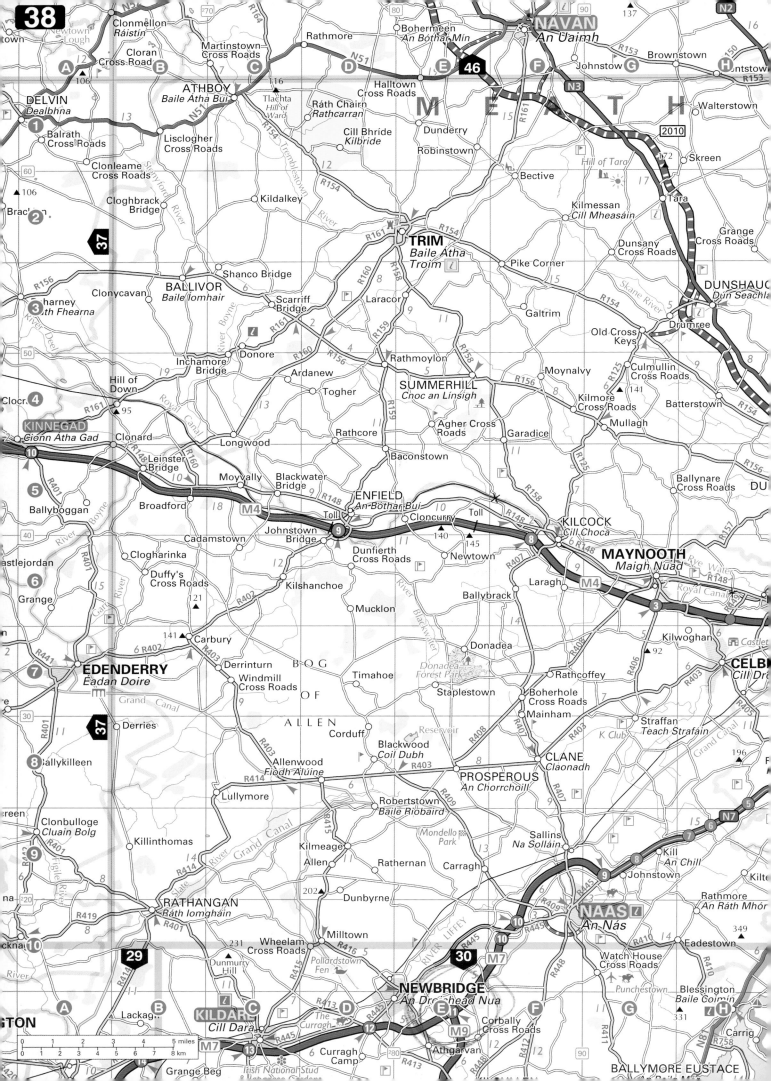

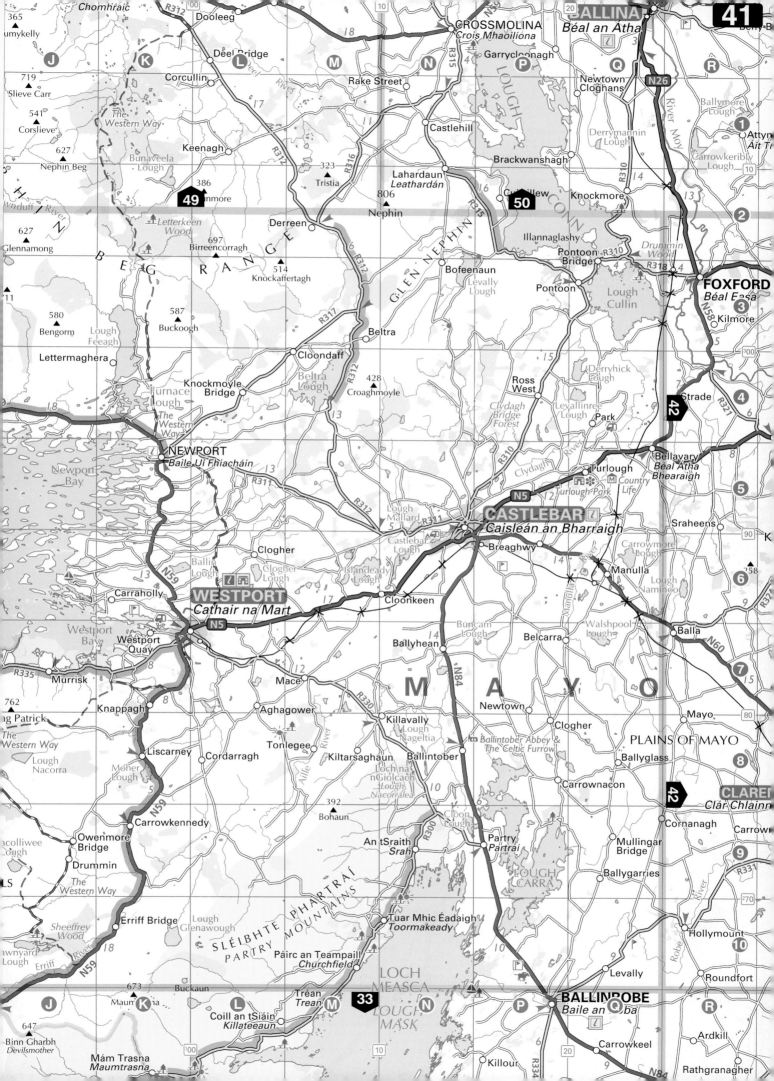

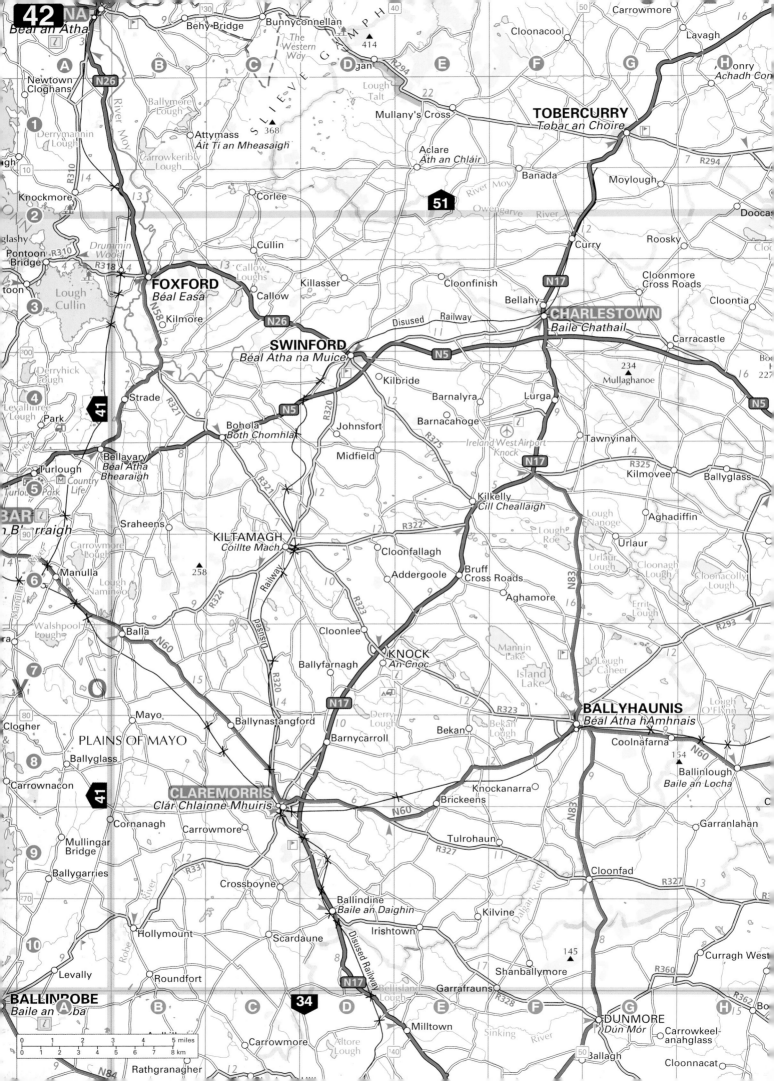

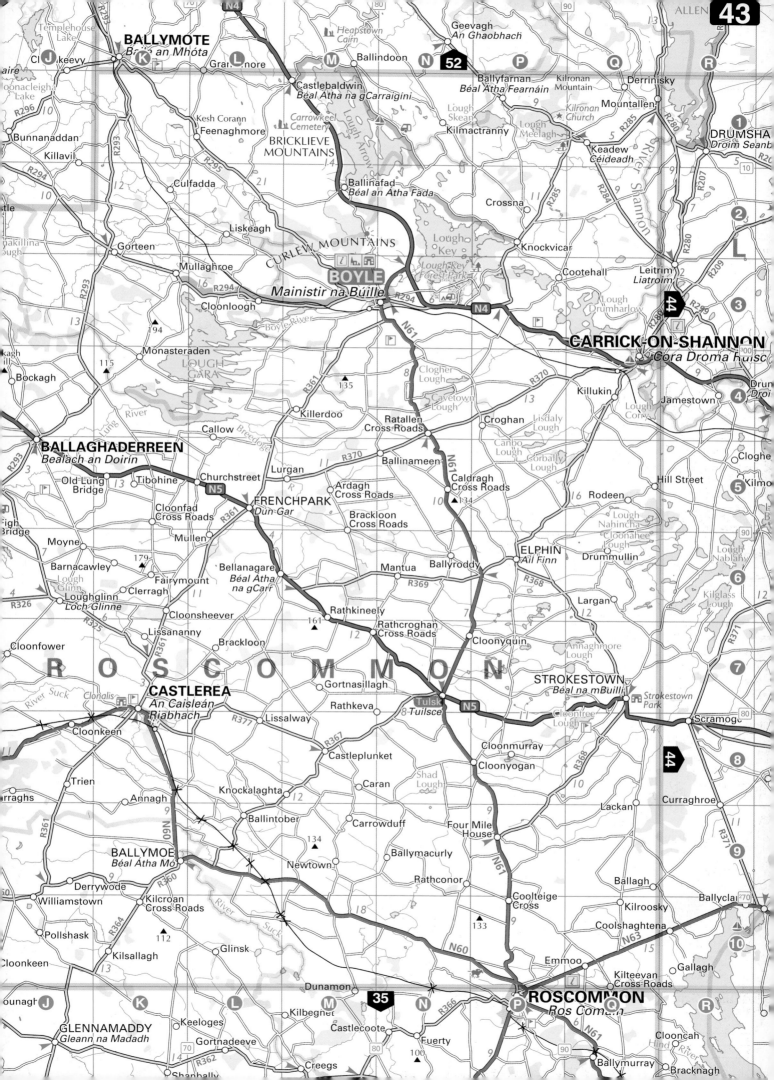

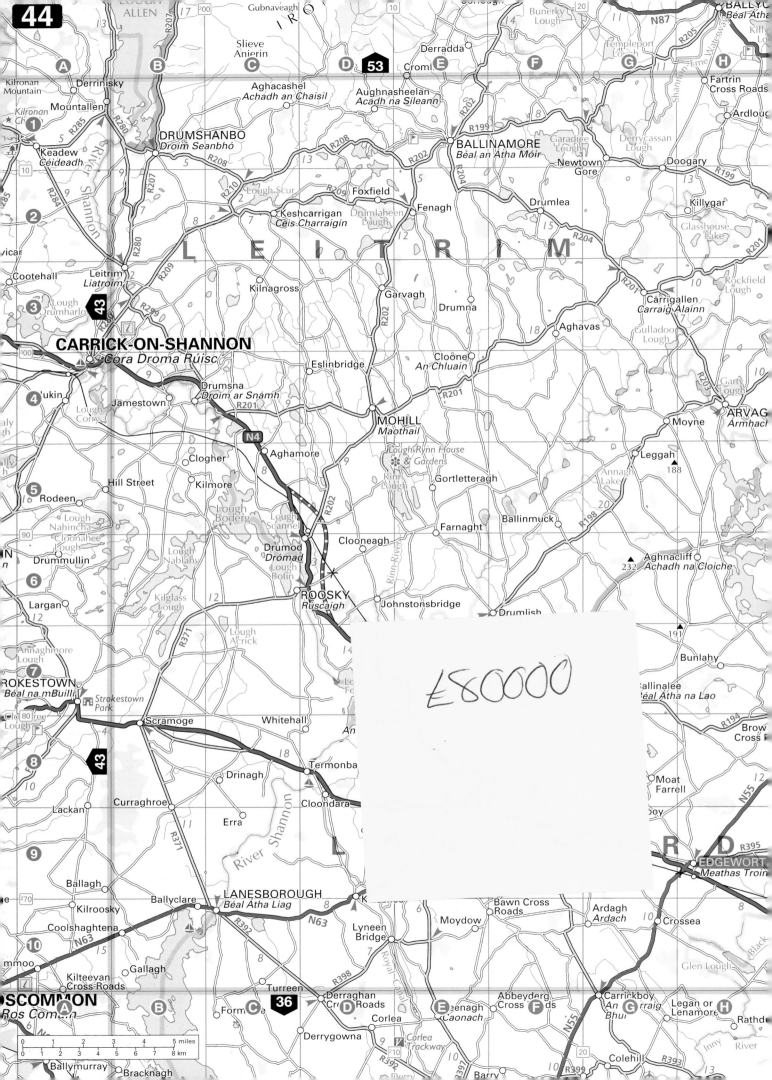

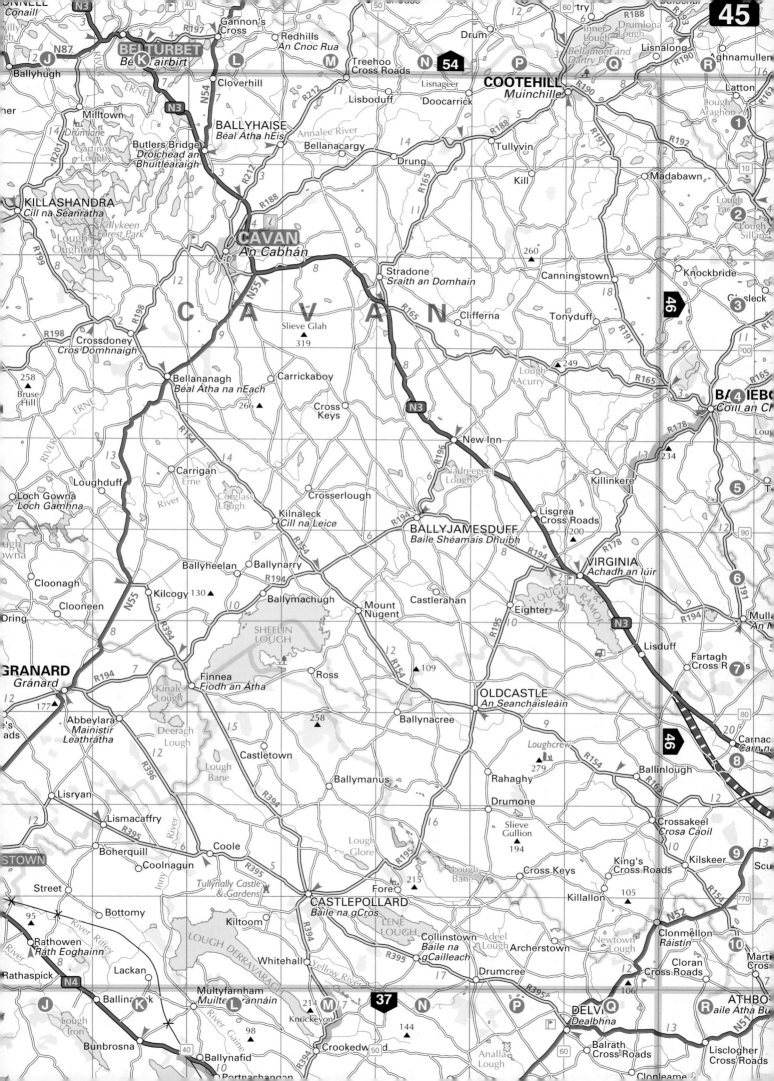

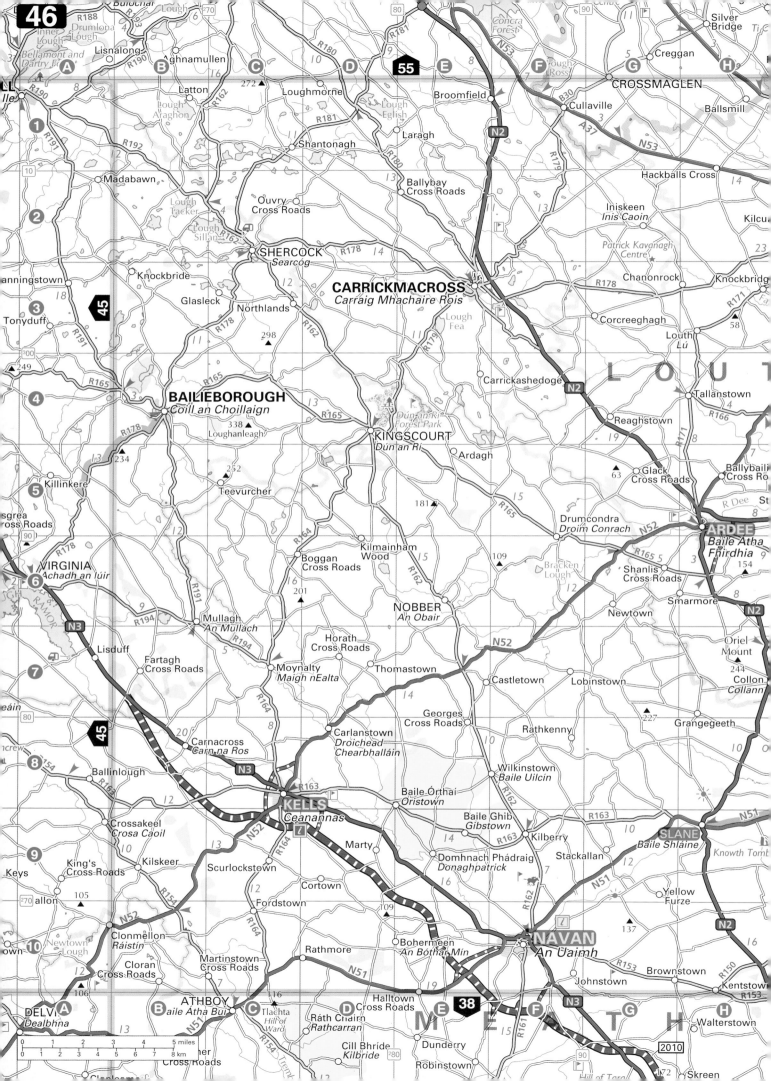

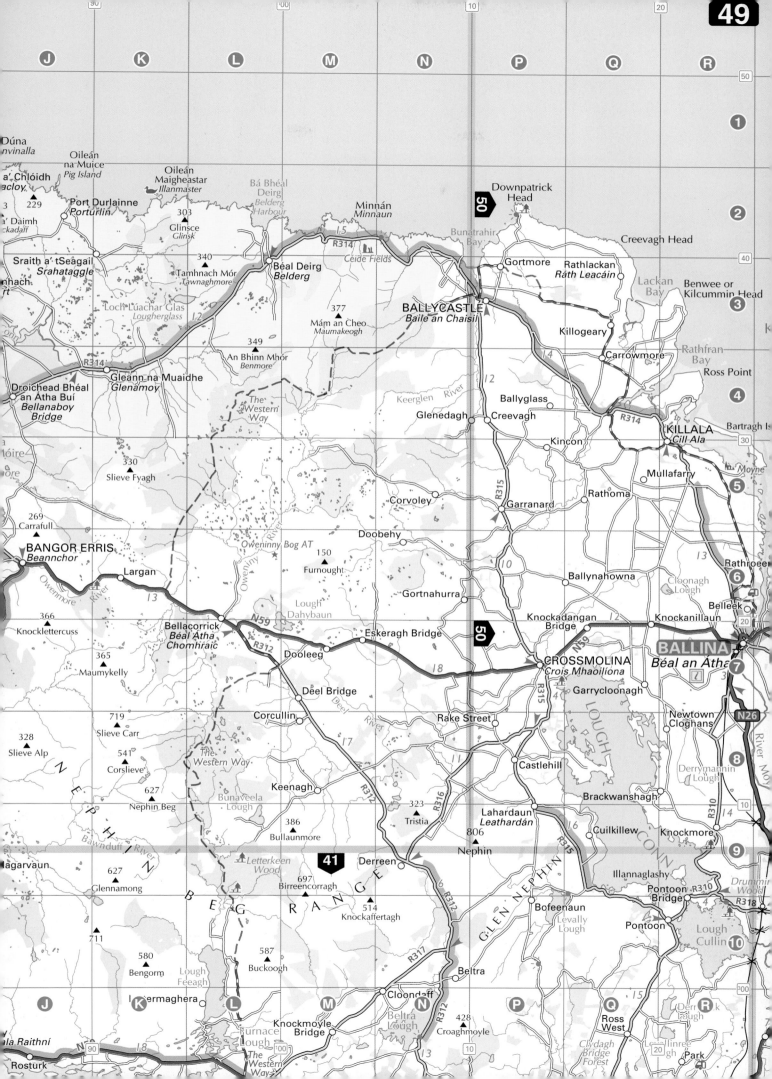

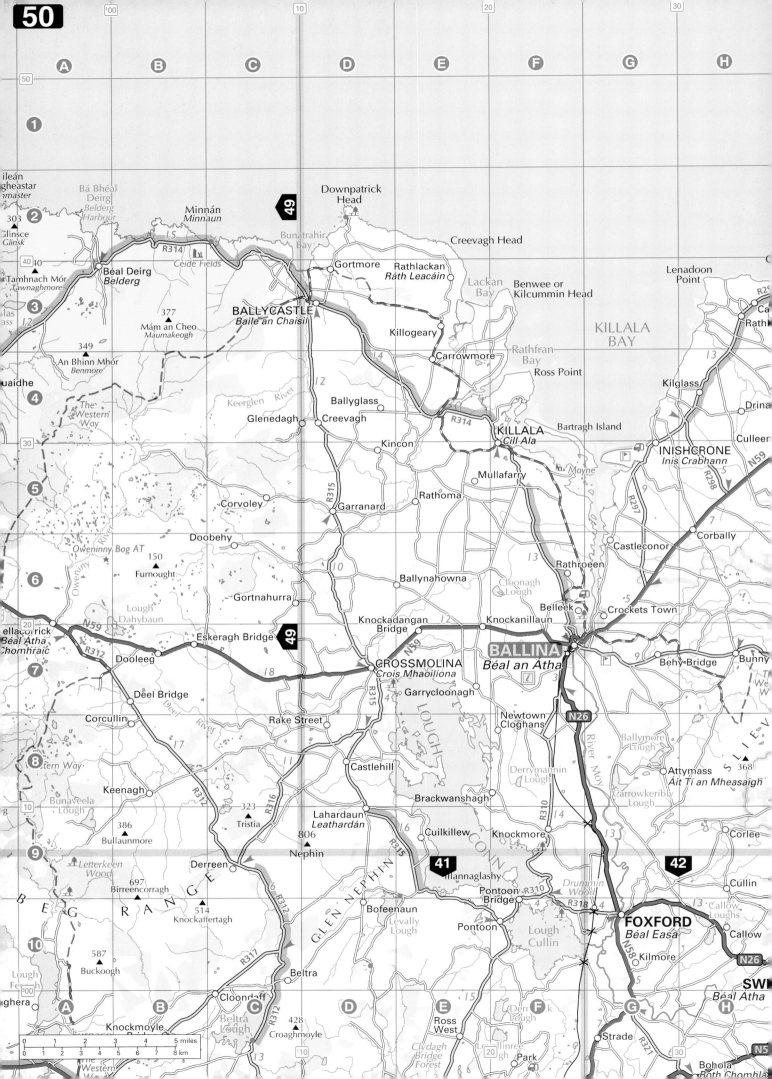

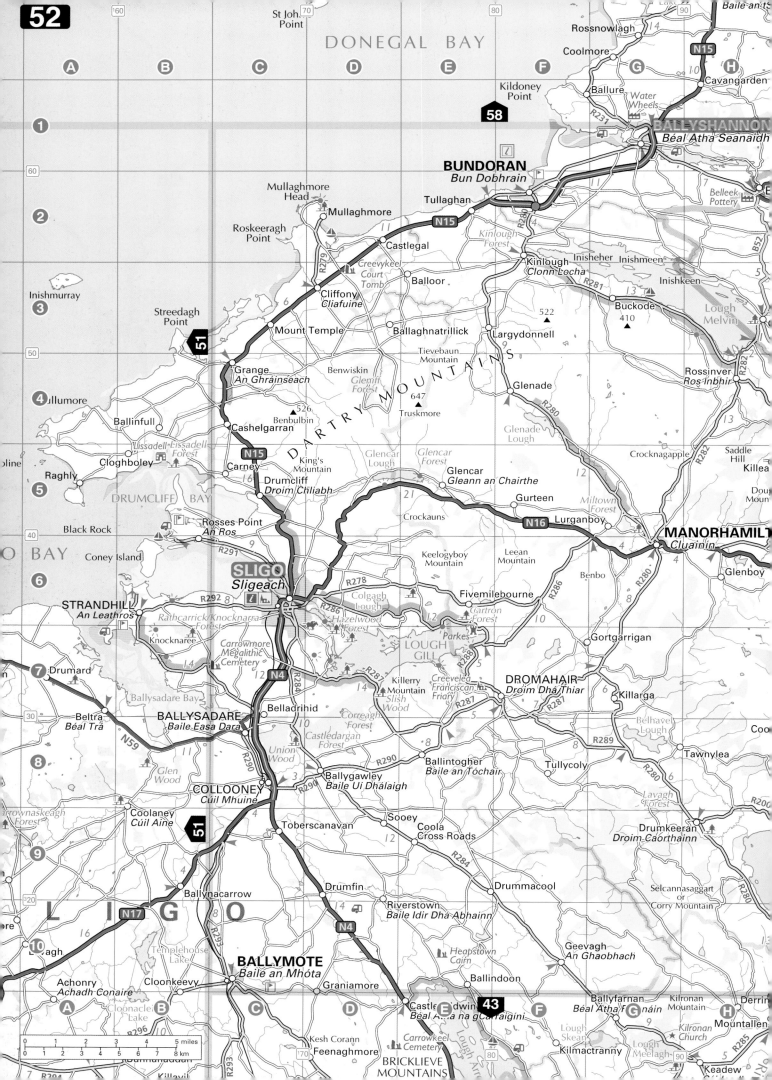

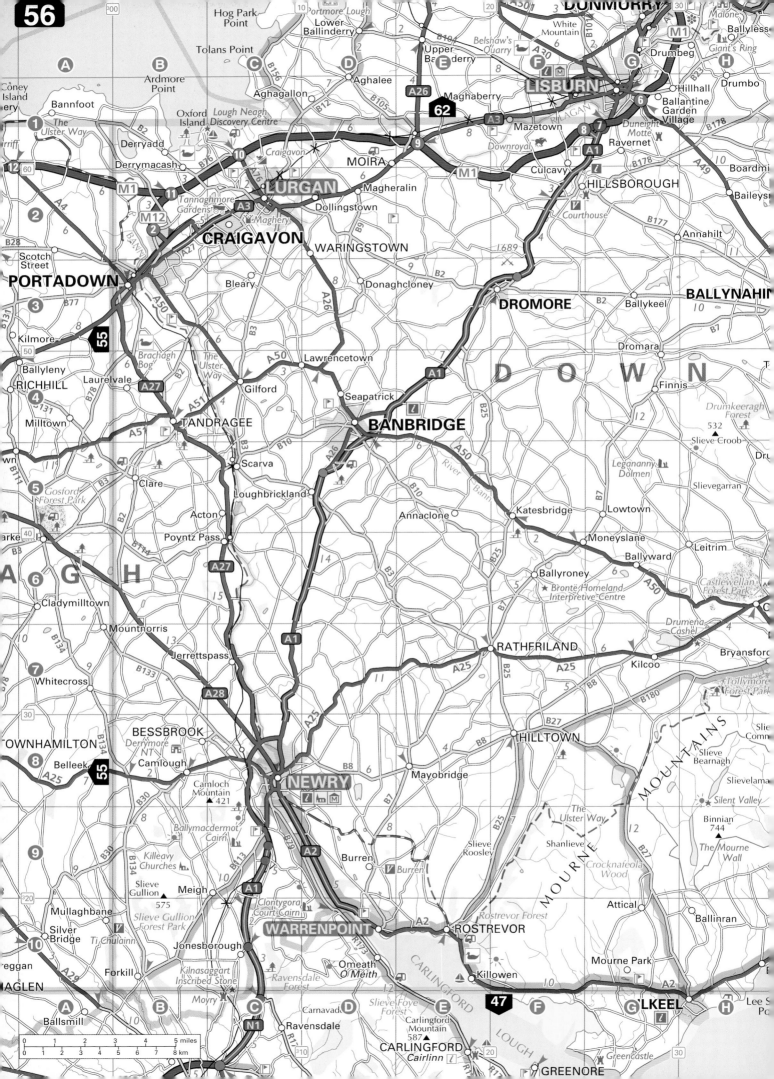

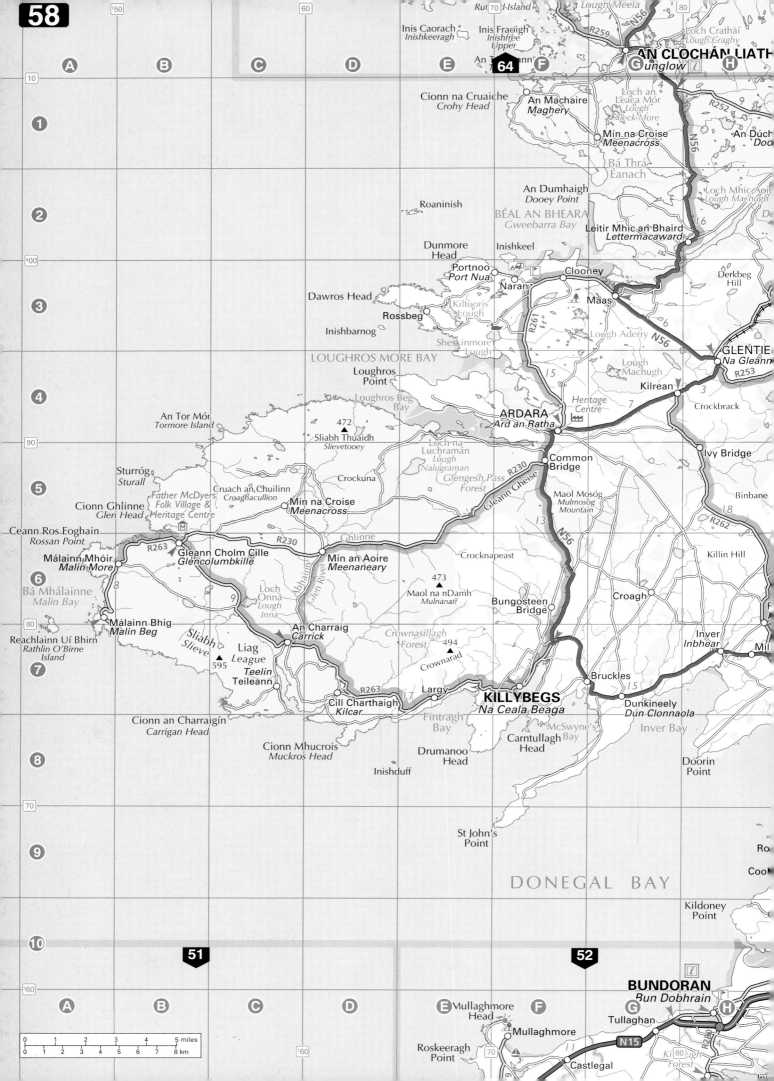

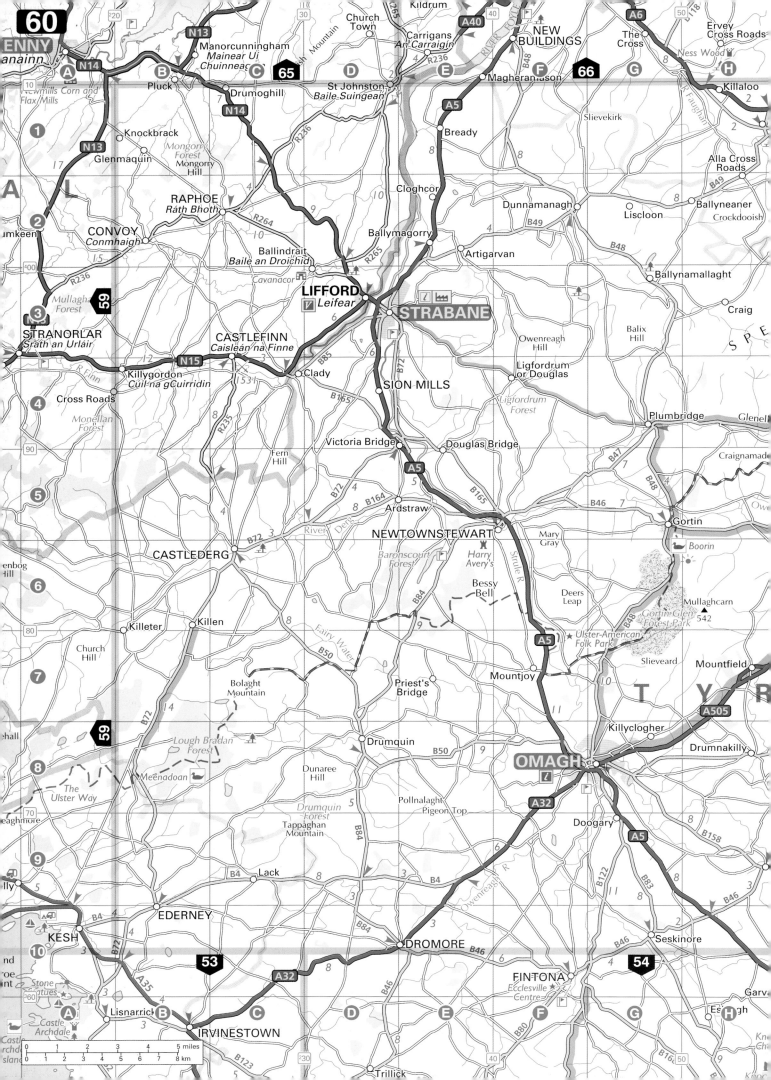

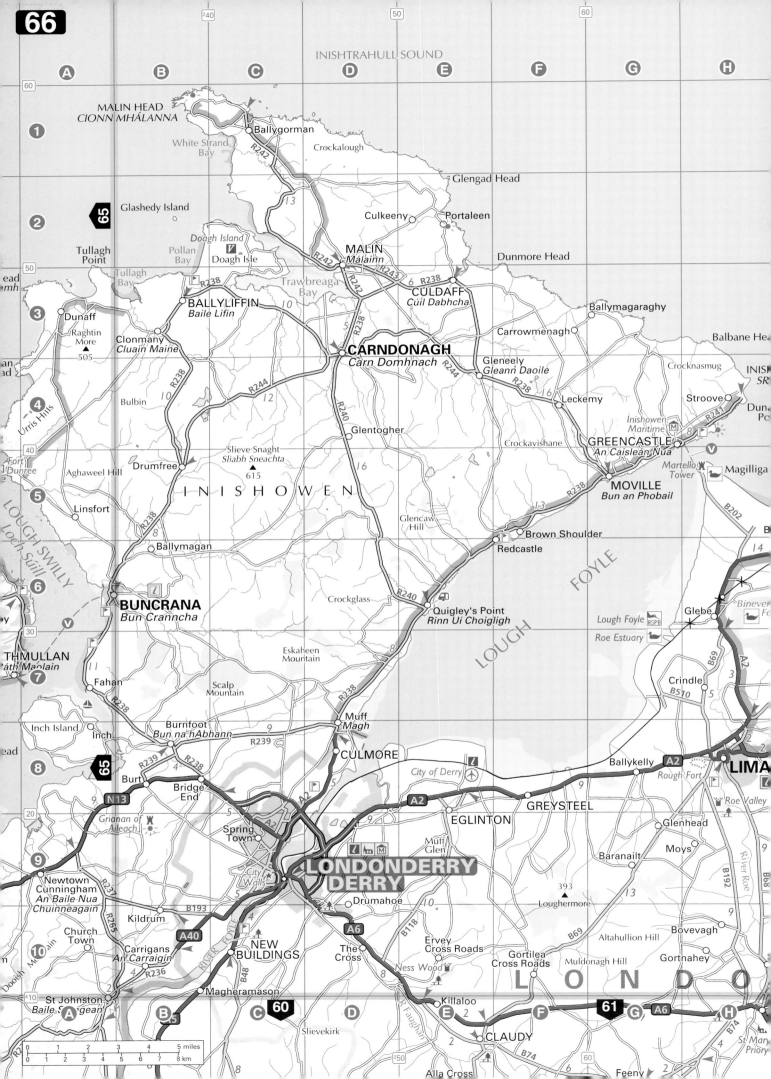

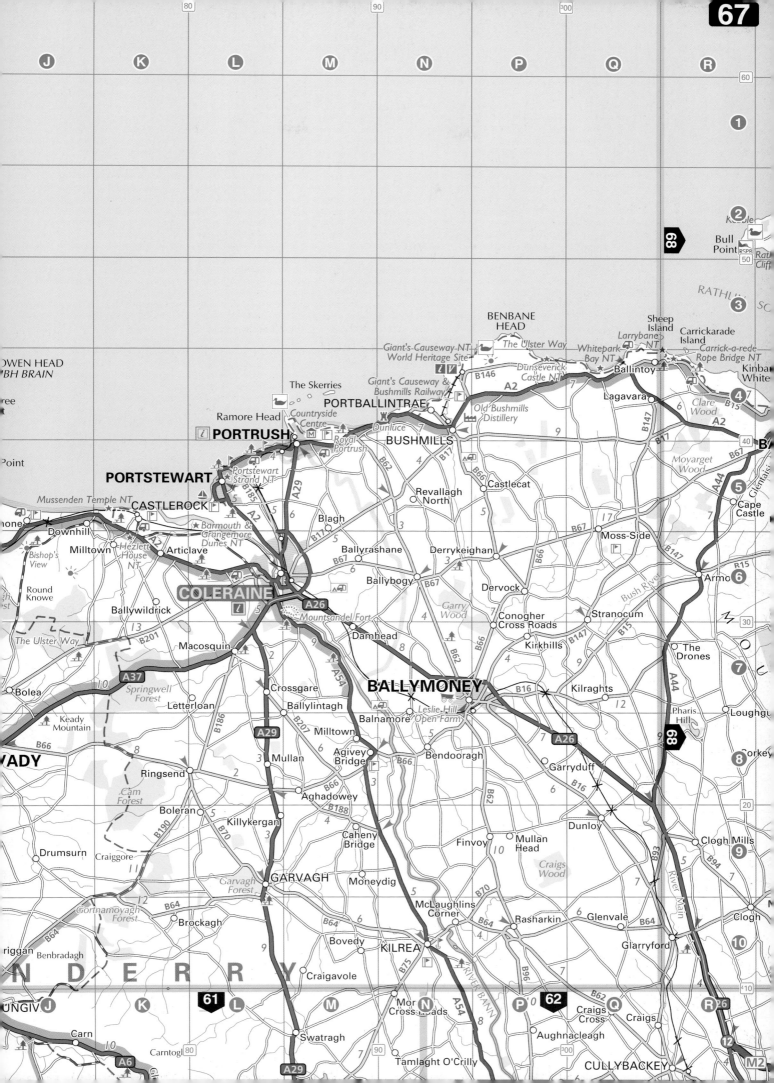

J K L M N P Q R

1

2
Bull Point
50

RATHLIN SC

3

OWEN HEAD
BH BRAIN

BENBANE
HEAD

Sheep
Island
Carrickarade
Island
Larrybane
NT
Carrick-a-rede
Rope Bridge NT

Giant's Causeway NT
World Heritage Site
The Ulster Way
Whitepark
Bay NT
Ballintoy
Kinba
White

The Skerries
Giant's Causeway &
Bushmills Railway
B146
Dunseverick
Castle NT
7
Lagavara
Clare
Wood
A2

4

Ramore Head
PORTBALLINTRAE
Old Bushmills
Distillery
9
B147
B17
40
B

Countryside
Centre
Dunluce
7
A2
Moyarget
Wood
B67

PORTRUSH
BUSHMILLS
4
B62
B17
4
B66
Castlecat
A44

5

Royal
Portrush
Revallagh
North
5
B67
17
Cape
Castle

PORTSTEWART
Portstewart
Strand NT
A29
Blagh
3
Moss-Side
B147

Mussenden Temple NT
CASTLEROCK
B185
5
6
B17
Ballyrashane
Derrykeighan
B66
Armo

6

Downhill
Milltown
Hezlett
House
NT
Articlave
A2
B67
6
Ballybogy
B67
Dervock
5
30

Bishop's
View
Round
Knowe
COLERAINE
Mountsandel Fort
Garry
Wood
7
Conogher
Cross Roads
Stranocum
B15

7

Ballywildrick
A26
5
4
8
B66
Kirkhills
B147
The
Drones

The Ulster Way
B201
13
Damhead
8
B62
A44

Macosquin
2
BALLYMONEY
B16
Kilraghts
Pharis
Hill

Bolea
A37
Springwell
Forest
10
Crossgare
A54
Leslie Hill
Open Farm
12
68

Keady
Mountain
B66
Letterloan
B186
Ballylintagh
Balnamore
5
7
A26
9
Corkey

8

Ringsend
A29
B207
Milltown
Agivey
Bridge
B66
Bendooragh
Garryduff
B16

Cam
Forest
2
Mullan
3
3
B62
6
Dunloy

Drumsurn
Craiggore
Boleran
5
B70
Aghadowey
B188
4
Caheny
Bridge
Finvoy
10
Mullan
Head
B93
Clogh Mills

9

B190
Killykergan
3
Moneydig
B70
Craigs
Wood
7

Garvagh
Forest
GARVAGH
5
McLaughlins
Corner
Rasharkin
6
Glenvale
B64
Clogh

Gortnamoyagh
Forest
B64
Brockagh
B64
Bovedy
6
B70
4
Glarryford
10

Benbradagh
B64
9
Craigavole
KILREA
B75
B96
M2

A6
Carn
10
Swatragh
A29
Mor
Cross Roads
A54
8
Craigs
Cross
Craigs
26

Carntogl 80
Tamlaght O'Crilly
Aughnacleagh
CULLYBACKEY
12

J K 61 L M N P 0 62 Q R

Town plans

Town plans
Page 70........... Belfast
    71........... Cork
    72........... Dublin
    73........... Galway
    73........... Kilkenny
    73........... Killarney
    74........... Limerick
    74........... Londonderry
    75........... Sligo
    75........... Waterford

Port plans
Page III........... Belfast
    III........... Dublin Harbour
    III........... Dún Laoghaire
    III........... Larne
    III........... Ringaskiddy
    III........... Rosslare Europort

Key to town plans
Eochair   Légende   Legende

Bóthar príomha náisiúnta (IRL)	**N4**	**National primary route (IRL)**
Nationalstraße erster Ordnung (IRL)		Route nationale (IRL)
Bóthar príomha (NI)	**A12**	**Primary route (NI)**
Straße erster Ordnung (NI)		Route nationale (NI)
Bóthar tánaisteach náisiúnta (IRL)	**N69**	**National secondary route (IRL)**
Nationalstraße zweiter Ordnung (IRL)		Route départementale (IRL)
Bóthar A (NI)	**A501**	**A road (NI)**
Nationalstraße (NI)		Catégorie A (NI)
Bóthar réigiúnach (IRL)	**R118**	**Regional road (IRL)**
Regionalstraße (IRL)		Route communale (IRL)
Bóthar B (NI)	**B123**	**B road (NI)**
Nebenstraße (NI)		Catégorie B (NI)
Bóithre eile		**Other roads**
Andere Straßen		Autres routes
Crios coisí		**Pedestrian zone**
Fußgängerzone		Zone piétonne
Bealach fithiseach istigh		**Inner orbital route**
Innere Ringstraße		Périphérique interne

Foirgneamh Suimiúil	**COLLEGE**	**Building of interest**
Interessantes Gebäude		Bâtiment d'intérêt historique
Eaglais, séipéal	✝	**Church, chapel**
Kirche, Kapelle		Église, chapelle
Páirc nó spás oscailte		**Park or open space**
Park oder Freifläche		Parc ou espace ouvert
Páirceáil	**P**	**Car parking**
Parkplatz		Parking
Leithris		**Toilets**
Toiletten		Toilettes
Sráid aon-bhealach	←	**One-way street**
Einbahnstraße		Sens unique
Ionad eolais turasóireachta	**i**	**Tourist information**
Fremdenverkehrsamt		Office de tourisme
Gluaisteacht siopaí		**Shopmobility**
Mobilität für Behinderte beim Einkaufen		Magasin ambulant
Siopa AA	**AA**	**AA shop**
AA Geschäft		Magasin de AA

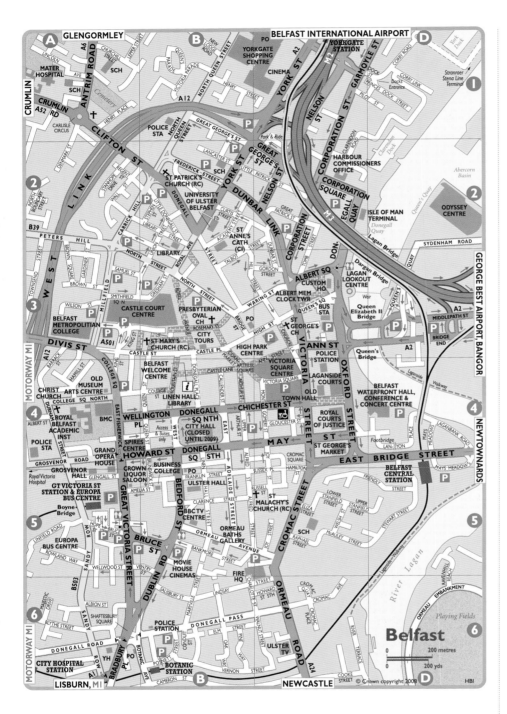

Belfast

Belfast is found on atlas page **63 J8**

B2	Academy Street	A4	Barrack Street	B6	Cameron Street	A1	Clifton Street	C6	Cromac Place	A2	Peters Hill
B5	Adelaide Street	B5	Bedford Street	A1	Carlisle Circus	A4	College Square	C6	Cromac Quay	C1	Pilot Street
C3	Albert Square	A6	Blythe Street	A2	Carrick Hill	A4	College Square North	C4	Cromac Square	B6	Pine Way
A4	Albert Street	A6	Botanic Avenue	B4	Castle Lane	B4	College Street	C5	Cromac Street	B6	Posnett Street
A6	Albion Street	A6	Bradbury Place	B3	Castle Place	B6	Conduit Street	A1	Crumlin Road	D1	Princes Dock Street
B5	Alfred Street	B3	Bridge End	B3	Castle Street	C6	Cooke Street	B2	Curtis Street	B4	Queen Street
A5	Amelia Street	B3	Bridge Street	B6	Charlotte Street	B4	Cornmarket	A2	Denmark Street	B1	Queen's Parade
C3	Ann Street	A3	Brown Square	B4	Chichester Street	C2	Corporation Square	A3	Divis Street	D3	Queen's Quay
A1	Antrim Road	A3	Brown Street	C3	Church Lane	C2	Corporation Street	D1	Dock Street	C3	Queen's Square
B4	Arthur Square	B5	Bruce Street	A1	Churchill Street	D1	Corry Link	B6	Donegall Pass	C5	Raphael Street
B4	Arthur Street	B4	Brunswick Street	B5	Clarence Street	D1	Corry Road	B4	Donegall Place	D6	Ravenhill Reach
B5	Bankmore Street	B4	Callender Street	C2	Clarendon Road	C6	Cromac Avenue	C3	Donegall Quay	A2	Regent Street
								A6	Donegall Road	C6	River Terrace
								B4	Donegall Square East	B3	Rosemary Street
								B4	Donegall Square North	A5	Rowland Way
								B4	Donegall Square South	B3	Royal Avenue
								B4	Donegall Square West	C5	Russell Street
								B2	Donegall Street	B6	Salisbury Street
								B6	Dublin Road	A3	Samuel Street
								B2	Dunbar Link	A6	Sandy Row
								C2	Dunbar Street	A6	Shaftesbury Square
								A4	Durham Street	A3	Smithfield Square North
								C4	East Bridge Street	A2	Stanhope Drive
								A4	East Fisherwick	B2	Stephen Street
								C5	Eliza Street	D5	Stewart Street
								B6	Elm Street	C5	Sussex Place
								B4	Fountain Street	D2	Sydenham Road
								B5	Franklin Street	B3	Talbot Street
								B2	Fredrick Street	C3	Tomb Street
								D5	Friendly Street	A3	Townsend Street
								A3	Gardiner Street	B2	Union Street
								C1	Garmoyle Street	B4	Upper Arthur Street
								A5	Glengall Street	C5	Upper Stanfield Street
								C4	Gloucester Street	B5	Ventry Street
								C3	Gordon Street	B6	Vernon Street
								B1	Great George's Street	B1	Victoria Parade
								C2	Great Patrick Street	C4	Victoria Square
								A5	Great Victoria Street	C3	Victoria Street
								B3	Gresham Street	A2	Wall Street
								A4	Grosvenor Road	C6	Walnut Street
								A4	Hamill Street	C3	Waring Street
								C5	Hamilton Street	A4	Wellington Place
								A1	Henry Place	A5	Wellwood Street
								B1	Henry Street	C5	Welsh Street
								C3	High Street	A3	West Link
								B3	Hill Street	A3	Wilson Street
								A5	Hope Street	B2	York Street
								A4	Howard Street		
								C6	Howard Street South		
								C4	Joy Street		
								A3	King Street		
								D4	Laganbank Road		
								B2	Lancaster Street		
								D4	Lanyon Place		
								A1	Lepper Street		
								B2	Library Street		
								A1	Lincoln Avenue		
								B6	Lindsay Street		
								B4	Linen Hall Street		
								A5	Linfield Road		
								B2	Little Donegall Street		
								C2	Little Patrick Street		
								C5	Lower Stanfield Street		
								A6	Majestic Drive		
								B6	Maryville Street		
								C4	May Street		
								D4	Mays Meadows		
								C5	McAuley Street		
								D3	Middlepath Street		
								A3	Millfield		
								C4	Montgomery Street		
								C2	Nelson Street		
								B1	New Lodge Road		
								A2	North Boundary Street		
								B1	North Queen Street		
								B3	North Street		
								B6	Oak Way		
								B5	Ormeau Avenue		
								D6	Ormeau Embankment		
								C6	Ormeau Road		
								C4	Oxford Street		

Cork

Cork is found on atlas page **6 A5**

B5	Abbey Street
B3	Academy Street
A4	Adelaide Street
D4	Albert Quay
D3	Albert Road
D4	Albert Street
D1	Alexandra Road
D3	Alfred Street
C3	Anderson Quay
D4	Anglesea Street
B1	Assumption Road
B2	Audley Place
A4	Bachelor's Quay
D1	Ballyhooly New Road
A6	Bandon Road
B5	Barrack Street
C4	Beasly Street
C2	Bellevue Park
C2	Bellview Crescent
A5	Bishop Street
B1	Blackpool Bypass
A3	Blarney Street
B5	Bonaventure Place
B3	Camden Place
B3	Camden Quay
D6	Capwell Road
B3	Carrolls Quay
A3	Castle Market Avenue
B4	Castle Street
A2	Cathedral Road
A2	Cathedral Street
A2	Cathedral Walk
A3	Church Street
B3	Coal Quay
B3	Coburg Street
A5	College Road
C6	Congress Road
A5	Connaught Avenue
B4	Cook Street
C4	Copley Street
B3	Corn Market Street
B5	Cove Street
D6	Curragh Road
A5	Dean Street
B6	Deerpark Road
C6	Derrynane Road
B5	Desmond Square
B3	Dominick Street
C5	Douglas Street
C6	Doyle Road
C4	Dunbar Street
A4	Dyke Parade
B3	Eason's Hill
B3	Emmet Place
D6	Evergreen Road
B5	Evergreen Street
A3	Fair Street
C6	Father Mathew Road
B5	Fort Street
C4	Friar Matthew Quay
B5	Friar Street
C6	Friars Road
C6	Friars Walk
D1	Gardiners Hill
D4	Gas Works Road
C4	George's Quay
A2	Gerald Griffin Avenue
A2	Gerald Griffin Street
A5	Gill Abbey Street
D2	Glanmire Road
B1	Glen Avenue
A3	Glen Ryan Road
A6	Gould's Street
B4	Grand Parade
A4	Grattan Street
A1	Great William O'Brien Street
B6	Green Street
A6	Greenmount Avenue
A4	Greenville Place
A4	Hanover Street
A6	Hartlands Road
A4	Henry Street
D5	High Street
D3	Horgan's Quay
B5	Industry Street
D5	Infirmary Road
B3	John Redmond Street
B2	John Street
B2	John Street Upper
B5	Kevin Street South
B3	Kyle Street
A3	Kyrl's Quay
A5	Lancaster Quay
D5	Langford Row
C3	Lapp's Quay
B3	Lavitt's Quay
B2	Leitrim Street
B4	Liberty Street
A6	Lough Road
A1	Lover's Walk
D2	Lower Glanmire Road
D2	Mahony's Avenue
B4	Marlborough Street
A3	Mary Aikenhead Place
C4	Mary Street
C3	Maylor Street
C3	McCurtain Street
C3	Merchants Quay
D2	Military Hill
C1	Military Road
A2	Monastery Road
C4	Morrison's Quay
B5	Mount Carmel Road
C6	Mount Pleasant Avenue
C6	Mount Pleasant Road
B5	Mount Sion Road
A3	Newsom's Quay
C5	Nicholas Road
A5	Noonan Road
A3	North Main Street
A3	North Mall
D6	O'Connell Avenue
A2	O'Connell Street
D5	Old Blackrock Road
A3	Old Market Place
D4	Old Station Road
B4	Oliver Plunkett Street
C3	Oliver Plunkett Street Lower
C3	Parnell Place
B4	Paul Street
C3	Penrose's Quay
B3	Pope's Quay
B1	Pope's Road
B6	Pouladuff Road
B5	Presentation Place
B4	Princess Street
B5	Proby's Quay
C5	Quaker Road
D3	Railway Street
B2	Rathmore Park
C1	Rathmore Road
A2	Redemption Road
B5	Reed Street
B2	Richmond Hill
D4	Rockborough Road
B2	Roman Street
C5	Rutland Street
A5	St Finbars Road
D2	St Luke's Cross
A2	St Mary's Road
B2	St Patrick's Hill
C3	St Patrick's Quay
C6	St Patrick's Road
B4	St Patrick's Street
B3	St Paul's Avenue
C4	Sawmill Street
A1	Seminary Road
A3	Shandon Street
A5	Sharman Crawford Street
A4	Sheares Street
C2	Sidney Park
C4	Smith Street
D4	South City Link Road
B4	South Main Street
C4	South Mall
C4	South Terrace
D5	Southern Road
B4	Sullivan's Quay
D2	Summer Hill
C5	Summer Hill South
B5	Tower Street
B5	Townsend Place
B4	Tuckey Street
C4	Union Quay
B5	Vicar Street
D3	Victoria Road
A4	Wandesford Quay
B4	Washington Street
A4	Washington Street West
B1	Watercourse Road
C2	Wellington Road
C5	White Street
D5	Windmill Road
A2	Wolfe Tone Street
A4	Woods Street
C3	York Street
C2	Youghal Old Road

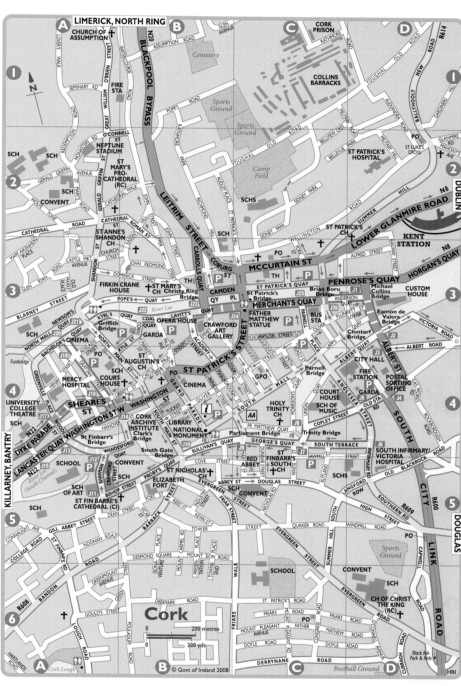

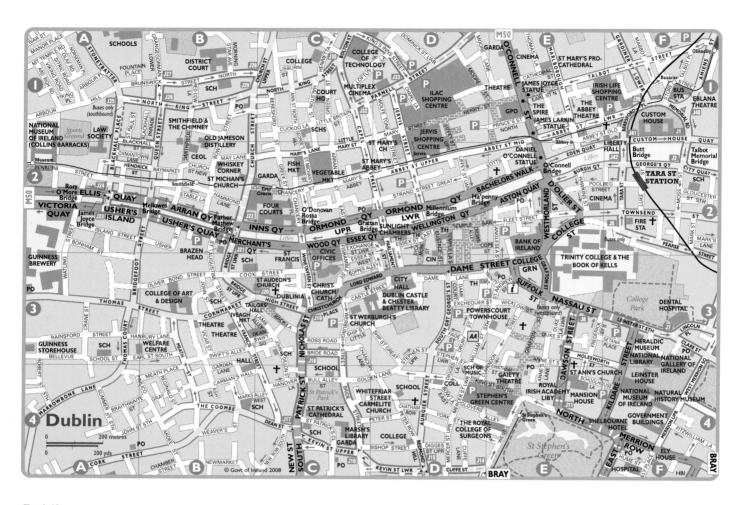

Dublin

Dublin is found on atlas page **39 M7**

E1 Abbey Street Lower	C3 Castle Street	B3 Earl Street South	C3 John Dillon Street	F2 Moss Street
E2 Abbey Street Middle	E1 Cathedral Street	E2 Eden Quay	B3 John Street	A1 Mount Temple Road
E1 Abbey Street Old	B4 Chamber Street	A2 Ellis Quay	A4 John Street South	E3 Nassau Street
D2 Abbey Street Upper	C3 Chancery Lane	F4 Ely Place	D4 Kevin Street Lower	C4 New Row South
F1 Amiens Street	C2 Chancery Place	C2 Essex Quay	C4 Kevin Street Upper	C4 New Street South
E2 Anglesea Street	C2 Chancery Street	D2 Essex Street East	F4 Kildare Street	B4 Newmarket
C1 Ann Street North	D1 Chapel Lane	D2 Essex Street West	D4 King Street South	C3 Nicholas Street
E3 Anne Street South	D4 Chatham Row	D2 Eustace Street	C1 King's Inns Street	A1 Norseman Place
E4 Anne's Lane	E4 Chatham Street	C2 Exchange Street Lower	C3 Lamb Alley	A1 Olaf Road
A1 Arbour Hill	C3 Christchurch Place	D3 Exchequer Street	F3 Leinster Street South	E1 O'Connell Street
A1 Arbour Place	B2 Church Street	D3 Fade Street	D2 Liffey Street Lower	A1 Olaf Road
A1 Ard Right Road	B2 Church Street New	C2 Fishamble Street	D1 Liffey Street Upper	B3 Oliver Bond Street
B4 Ardee Street	C1 Church Street Upper	F4 Fitzwilliam Lane	F3 Lincoln Place	D2 Ormond Quay Lower
B2 Arran Quay	F2 City Quay	E2 Fleet Street	C1 Lisburn Street	C2 Ormond Quay Upper
C2 Arran Street East	F3 Clare Street	A1 Fountain Place	C1 Little Britain Street	A2 Oxmantown Lane
B4 Ash Street	E3 Clarendon Street	B3 Francis Street	C1 Little Mary Street	D2 Parliament Street
E2 Aston Quay	E3 College Green	E3 Frederick Street South	C3 Lord Edward Street	D1 Parnell Street
D4 Aungier street	E3 College Street	B4 Garden Lane	E2 Lotts	C4 Patrick Street
D2 Bachelors Walk	B3 Cook Street	F1 Gardiner Street Lower	F2 Luke Street	F2 Pearse Street
C3 Back Lane	C3 Copper Alley	C1 George's Hill	F1 Mabbot Lane	D4 Peter Row
A3 Bellevue	A4 Cork Street	F2 George's Quay	B4 Manor Place	D4 Peter Street
A2 Benburb Street	A3 Crane Street	F2 Gloucester Street South	F2 Mark Street	B4 Pimlico
F1 Beresford Place	D2 Crown Alley	D4 Glovers Alley	B4 Marks Alley West	E2 Poolbeg Street
C1 Beresford Street	C1 Cuckoo Lane	C4 Golden Lane	F2 Mark's Lane	E1 Prince's Street North
D4 Bishop Street	D4 Cuffe Lane	E3 Grafton Street	A4 Marlborough Street	B2 Queen Street
B1 Blackhall Parade	D4 Cuffe Street	B1 Grangegorman Lower	A4 Marrowbone Lane	A3 Rainsford Street
A2 Blackhall Place	F1 Custom House Quay	B4 Gray Street	D1 Mary Street	B1 Red Cow Lane
B2 Blackhall Street	D3 Dame Court	C2 Greek Street	C2 Mary's Abbey	D4 Redmond Hill
C1 Bolton Street	D3 Dame Lane	C1 Green Street	C2 Mary's Lane	B4 Reginald Street
A2 Bonham Street	D3 Dame Street	C1 Halston Street	B2 May Lane	A4 Robert Street South
A4 Bow Lane East	E4 Dawson Street	B2 Hammond Lane	B4 Meath Place	C3 Ross Road
C3 Bride Road	C4 Dean Street	A3 Hanbury Lane	B3 Meath Street	E3 St Andrew Street
C4 Bride Street	C3 Dean Swift Square	C4 Hanover Lane	F1 Memorial Road	B2 St Augustine Street
B3 Bridge Street Lower	D4 Digges Lane	B2 Haymarket	D4 Mercer Street Lower	C2 St Michan's Street
B3 Bridge Street Upper	D4 Digges Street Upper	A2 Hendrick Street	D4 Mercer Street Upper	A1 St Paul Street
A3 Bridgefoot Street	E2 D'Olier Street	C1 Henrietta Place	B2 Merchant's Quay	F4 St Stephen's Green East
A1 Brunswick Street North	D1 Dominick Street Lower	D1 Henry Street	F4 Merrion Row	E4 St Stephen's Green North
C4 Bull Alley Street	D3 Drury Street	C3 High Street	F4 Merrion Street Upper	E4 St Stephen's Green West
E2 Burgh Quay	E3 Duke Lane Lower	F4 Hume Street	E3 Molesworth Street	A3 School Street
C1 Capel Street	E3 Duke Street	C2 Inns Quay	D1 Moore Lane	E4 Schoolhouse Lane
B4 Carman's Hall	E1 Earl Street North	A2 Island Street	D1 Moore Street	F3 Setana Place
		D1 Jervis Street	B1 Morning Star Avenue	D3 Ship Street Great

C3 Ship Street Little	
A1 Sitric Road	
B2 Smithfield	
D3 South Great George's Street	
B2 Stable Lane	
D3 Stephen Street Lower	
D3 Stephen Street Upper	
A1 Stoneybatter	
F1 Store Street	
D2 Strand Street Great	
E3 Suffolk Street	
A4 Summer Street South	
B3 Swift's Alley	
D2 Sycamore Street	
F1 Talbot Place	
E1 Talbot Street	
F2 Tara Street	
D2 Temple Bar	
D2 Temple Lane South	
B4 The Coombe	
A3 Thomas Court	
E1 Thomas Lane	
A3 Thomas Street	
F2 Townsend Street	
E3 Trinity Street	
B2 Usher Street	
A2 Usher's Island	
B2 Usher's Quay	
B3 Vicar Street	
A2 Victoria Quay	
A1 Viking Place	
A1 Viking Road	
A3 Watling Street	
B4 Weaver's Street	
D2 Wellington Quay	
C3 Werburgh Street	
E2 Westmorland Street	
D3 Wicklow Street	
D3 William Street South	
C3 Winetavern Street	
D1 Wolfe Tone Street	
C2 Wood Quay	
D4 York Street	

© Govt of Ireland 2008

Galway

Galway is found on atlas page **34 C8**

C2	Abbey Gate Street	B3	Munster Avenue
A1	Ash Road	C3	New Dock Street
D2	Bótha Na Mban	B2	New Road
B2	Bóthar Einde	B1	Newcastle Avenue
D2	Bothar Irwin	B2	Newcastle Road
A1	Bóthar Phadraic Ui	C2	Newtown Smith
	Chonnaire	B2	Nun's Island Street
C3	Bridge Street	A1	O'Flaherty Road
B2	Canal Road Lower	A2	Palmyra Avenue
B1	Canal Road Upper	B2	Presentation Road
B3	Claddagh Quay	D2	Prospect Hill
A1	Colmcillie Road	C3	Quay Street
A1	Costello Road	D3	Queen Street
A1	Davis Road	A2	Raleigh Row
C3	Dock Road	C3	St Augustine Street
C3	Dock Street	C2	St Brendan's Avenue
B3	Dominick Street	D1	St Bridget's Place
D1	Dyke Road	C2	St Francis Street
C2	Eglinton Street	B2	St Helen's Street
D2	Eyre Square	A2	St Mary's Park
C2	Eyre Street	A2	St Mary's Road
B3	Father Burke Road	C2	St Vincent's Avenue
A3	Father Griffin Avenue	A3	Sea Road
A3	Father Griffin Road	A1	Shantalla Road
D2	Forster Street	C2	Shop Street
A1	Fursey Road	D2	Station Road
D1	Headford Road	A2	Taylor's Hill Road
B2	Henry Street	A3	The Crescent
C3	High Street	C3	The Long Walk
D3	Lough Atalia Road	B1	University Road
C2	Market Street	D1	Water Lane
A1	McDara Road	C1	Waterside
C3	Merchants Road	A3	Whitestrand Road
C3	Middle Street	C2	William Street
B2	Mill Street	B3	William Street West

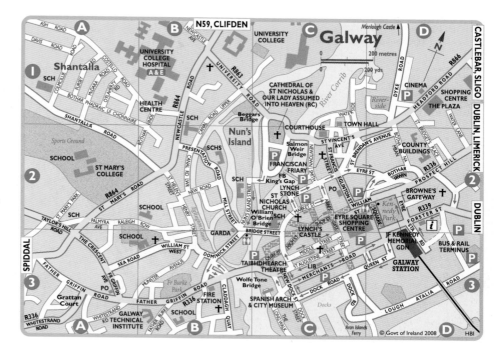

Kilkenny

Kilkenny is found on atlas page **21 N5**

A2	Abbey Street
B1	Ballybought Street
B1	Barrack Street
A2	Bateman's Quay
A2	Canal Square
B3	Castle Road
B1	Castlecomer Road
A3	College Road
A1	Dean Street
B2	Dublin Road
A2	Evan's Lane
B3	Father Hayden Road
A3	Friary Street
A3	Gaol Road
A1	Green Street
A1	Green's Hill
A1	Greensbridge Street
B1	Hebron Road
A2	High Street
A2	Irish Town
A2	James's Street
B2	John Street Lower
B2	John Street Upper
B2	John's Green
A2	John's Quay
A3	Lower New Street
B2	Maudlin Street
A2	Michael Street
A2	New Building Lane
A1	New Road
A3	Ormonde Street
A2	Parliament Street
A2	Parnell Street
A3	Patrick Street
A2	Rose Inn Street
A2	St Kiernan's Street
A3	The Parade
A2	Tilbury Place
A1	Vicar Street
A3	Walkin Street
B1	Wolfe Tone Street

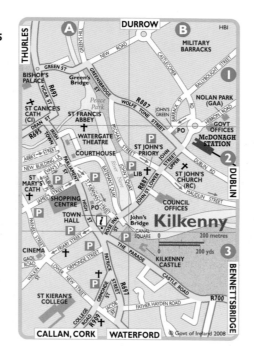

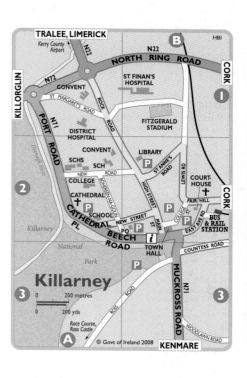

Killarney

Killarney is found on atlas page **10 B6**

A3	Beech Road	B3	Muckross Road
A2	Bohereen-na-Goun	A2	New Road
A2	Cathedral Place	B2	New Street
B2	College Street	A1	North Ring Road
B3	Countess Road	A1	Port Road
B2	East Avenue Road	A1	Rock Road
B2	Fair Hill	A3	Ross Road
B2	High Street	B2	St Anne's Road
B2	Lewis Road	A1	St Margaret's Road
B2	Main Street	B3	Woodlawn Road

Limerick

Limerick is found on atlas page **18 H3**

B3	Anne Street	B2	Honans Quay
B2	Arthurs Quay	A2	Howley's Quay
C1	Athlunkard Street	C2	John Square
B1	Bank Place	C2	John's Street
B2	Bedford Row	D2	Keane Street
A1	Belfield Gardens	D2	Keating Street
C1	Bishop's Street	C1	Lock Quay
D3	Blackboy Road	A2	Lower Cecil Street
C2	Brennans Row	C3	Lower Gerald Griffin
B1	Bridge Street		Street
C2	Broad Street	A3	Lower Mallow Street
B1	Castle Street	B3	Mallow Street
C3	Cathedral Place	C2	Market Street
B3	Catherine Street	C1	Mary Street
B3	Cecil Street	B2	Michael Street
C1	Charlotte's Quay	C2	Milk Street
B1	Clancy's Strand	A3	Mount Kennett Place
D2	Clare Street	C3	Mulgrave Street
A1	Clareview Avenue	C2	Mungret Street
B3	Davis Street	C2	New Road
B2	Denmark Street	A3	Newenham Street
A3	Dock Road	B1	Nicholas Street
B3	Dominick Street	A2	North Circular Road
D2	Downey Street	D2	North Claughaun
B2	Ellen Street		Road
A1	Ennis Road	A2	O'Callaghan's Strand
A1	Farranshone Road	A3	O'Connell Street
D2	Flood Street	A3	O'Curry Street
B2	Francis Street	C2	Old Clare Street
C1	Gaol Lane	C2	Old Francis Street
D3	Garryowen	B3	Parnell Street
C1	George's Quay	B2	Patrick Street
D3	Geraldine Terrace	D2	Pennywell
A3	Glentworth Street	D2	Pennywell Lane
A1	Glenview Gardens	B3	Pery Square
C2	Grattan Street	B3	Pery Street
D3	Greenhill Road	D3	Pike Avenue
A3	Hartstonge Street	B1	Priory Park
A2	Harvey's Quay	B3	Roche's Street
A3	Henry Street	A1	Rockspring Gardens
C2	High Street	C3	Rossa Avenue

C3	Roxborough Avenue	B2	Shannon Street	A3	The Bishop's Quay	C3	Upper William Street
C3	Roxborough Road	D3	Singland Crescent	C1	The Island Road	D3	West Singland Road
B2	Rutland Street	C1	Sir Harry's Mall	A1	Thomond Row	B3	Wickham Street
B1	St Augustine Place	D3	South Claughaun Road	B2	Thomas Street	B2	William Street
D2	St Lelia Street	A3	Steamboat Quay	B3	Upper Gerald Griffin	A3	Windmill Street
B2	Sarsfield Street	A2	Strandville Gardens		Street		
C3	Sexton Street	C3	Summer Street	A3	Upper Henry Street		

Londonderry

Londonderry is found on atlas page **66 C9**

B1	Abbey Street	C1	Foyle Embankment
B3	Abercorn Road	B3	Foyle Road
A3	Anne Street	C2	Foyle Street
C2	Artillery Street	B1	Francis Street
C1	Bank Place	B1	Frederick Street
B3	Barrack Street	B1	Great James Street
A1	Beechwood Avenue	B1	Harvey Street
A2	Beechwood Street	C2	Hawkin Street
D3	Benvarden Avenue	D3	Hayesbank Park
A3	Bishop Street	B1	High Street
A2	Bligh's Lane	B3	Ivy Terrace
A1	Blucher Street	C3	John Street
A3	Bluebell Hill Gardens	D1	King Street
D2	Bond's Hill	D3	Knockdara Park
D1	Bond's Street	A3	Lecky Road
A3	Brandywell Road	D1	Limavady Road
C2	Bridge Street	A2	Limewood Street
B2	Butchers Street	C2	Linenhall Street
A2	Cable Street	B1	Lisfannon Park
C3	Carlisle Road	B1	Little Diamond
A3	Carrigans Lane	B1	Little James Street
C1	Castle Street	B2	London Street
B1	Chamberlain Street	A2	Lone Moor Road
D3	Chapel Road	B2	Long Tower Street
D2	Clooney Terrace	B3	Lower Bennett Street
B3	Cooke Street	B1	Lower Road
B1	Creggan Street	D2	Lower Violet Street
A2	Dove Gardens	B2	Magazine Street
D3	Duke Street	D3	Malvern Terrace
D2	Dungiven Road	D3	Margaret Street
D3	Dunnfield Terrace	C2	Market Street
A1	Eastway	A1	Marlborough Road
B1	Eglinton Place	A1	Marlborough Street
A2	Elmwood Road	A3	Maureen Avenue
A2	Elmwood Street	B3	Miller Street
B3	Ewing Street	A2	Nualamount Drive
B1	Fahan Street	A1	Oakfield Crescent
B2	Fahan Street	A1	Oakfield Road
B3	Ferguson Street	C2	Orchard Street
D3	Fountain Hill	B2	Palace Street
C2	Fountain Street	D1	Pine Street

D2	Primrose Street	A3	Southend Park	C3	Wapping Lane		
C2	Pump Street	D3	Spencer Road	B1	Waterloo Street		
B2	Rossville Street	A2	Stanleys Walk	D2	Waterside Link		
B1	Sackville Street	B2	The Diamond	A1	Westland Avenue		
A3	St Columbas Walk	C1	Union Hall Place	A1	Westland Street		
C2	Shipquay Street	D2	Union Street	A1	Westland Terrace		
D2	Simpson's Brae	B3	Upper Bennett Street	B1	William Street		

Sligo

Sligo is found on atlas page **52 C6**

C2	Abbey Street	C2	O'Connell Street
B2	Adelaide Street	C3	Old Market Street
B1	Ballast Quay	D3	Pearse Road
C1	Barrack Street	B1	Prin Mill Road
C1	Bridge Street	B1	Quay Street
C3	Burton Street	D2	Riverside
C2	Castle Street	C3	St Brigets Place
D3	Chapel Hill	C1	Stephen Street
D2	Chapel Street	C2	Teeling Street
C2	Charles Street	B2	Temple Street
A2	Church Hill	B2	The Lungy
B3	Circular Road	D1	The Mall
C1	Connaughton Road	C2	Thomas Street
C3	Connolly Street	B1	Union Place
D2	Cranmore Mass Lane	B1	Union Street
A1	Finiskiln Road	A2	Upper John Street
C3	Gallows Hill	B1	Wine Street
D2	Gaol Road	B2	Wolfe Tone Street
C2	Grattan Street		
C2	Harmony Hill		
C2	High Street		
C1	Holborn Hill		
C1	Holborn Street		
B1	Hughes Bridge		
A2	Jinks Avenue		
B2	John Street		
C2	Kennedy Parade		
A2	Knappagh Road		
B2	Lord Edward Street		
D2	Lower Abbey Street		
B1	Lower Quay Street		
B1	Lynn's Place		
C3	Mail Coach Road		
C2	Market Street		
C1	Markievicz Road		

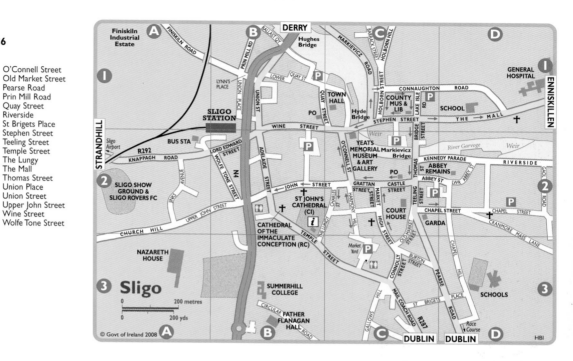

Waterford

Waterford is found on atlas page **14 E6**

D1	Abbey Road	B3	Manor Hill
D3	Adelphi Quay	B3	Manor Street
B1	Anne Street	A1	Mary Street
D1	Ard Mhuire	B3	Mayors Walk
B2	Barker Street	B1	Merchant's Quay
B3	Barrack Street	C3	Michael Street
C2	Barron Strand Street	A2	Military Road
C3	Beau Street	A2	Morgan Street
A3	Bernard Place	A3	Morrissons Avenue
A1	Bilberry Road	A3	Morrissons Road
C1	Bishopsgrove	A3	Mount Sion Avenue
B1	Bridge Street	B3	New Street
C2	Broad Street	B3	Newgate Street
D3	Canada Street	B2	Newports Square
A3	Cannon Street	B3	Newports Terrace
B3	Castle Street	B2	O'Connell Street
A2	Cathal Brugha Street	A2	Ozanam Street
C3	Catherine Street	C3	Parnell Street
B3	Convent Hill	B2	Patrick Street
C2	Custom House Quay	C2	Peter Street
B1	Dock Road	A2	Philip Street
A3	Doyle's Street	A1	Rockfield Park
A3	Emmett Place	D1	Rockshire Court
D1	Fountain Street	D1	Rockshire Road
B2	Francis Street	D3	Rose Lane
A1	Gracedieu Road	D3	Scotch Quay
A1	Grattan Quay	B3	Short Course
C2	Great Georges Street	A3	Slievekeale Road
B2	Green Street	C3	Spring Garden Alley
A3	Griffith Place	B3	Stephen Street
B3	Hennessy's Road	B1	Suir Street
C2	High Street	A2	Summer Hill
C3	John Street	A1	Summerhill Terrace
B3	Johns Lane	B2	The Glen
C3	Johnstown	C3	The Mall
C3	Lady Lane	B2	Thomas Hill
A3	Leamy Avenue	B2	Thomas Street
D3	Lombard Street	A2	Upper Yellow Road
A2	Lower Yellow Road	C3	Waterside
A3	Luke Wadding Street	D3	William Street

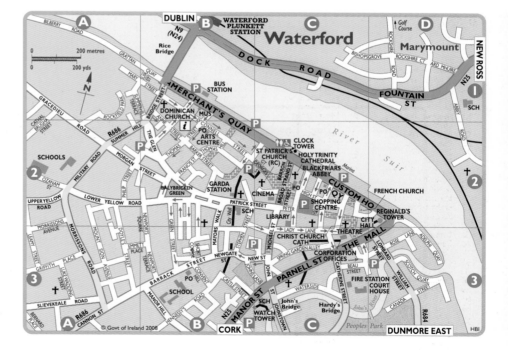

Motorways

The motorway maps on these pages consist of signposting panels, the layout of junctions, road numbers and exit destinations. To reflect the distances shown on the motorway signs, distances are given in miles in Northern Ireland and in kilometres in the Republic of Ireland.

Northern Ireland

M1   Belfast - Dungannon...................79-80
M2, M22   Belfast - Randalstown.................80
M2   Ballymena Bypass......................80

Republic of Ireland

M1   Dublin - Dundalk.........................77
M4   Leixlip - Kinnegad.......................78
M7   Naas - Portlaoise 79
M11   Bray and Shankill Bypass............78
M50   Dublin Ring Road......................78

Key to motorway maps

Restricted Motorway Junctions

Northern Ireland

M1 BELFAST - DUNGANNON

Junction		
3 (pg 62/63)	Westbound	No access. Exit only
	Eastbound	No exit. Access only

M2, M22 BELFAST - RANDALSTOWN

Junction		
2 (pg 63)	Westbound	No restriction.
	Southbound	No exit to M5.

Republic of Ireland

M1 DUBLIN - DUNDALK

Junction		
with R152 (pg 47)	Northbound	No access. Exit only
	Southbound	No exit. Access only
at Donore (pg 47)	Northbound	No restriction.
	Southbound	No exit. Access only
with R132 (pg 47)	Northbound	No exit. Access only
	Southbound	No access. Exit only
with R170 (pg 47)	Northbound	No access. Exit only
	Southbound	No exit. Access only

M7 NAAS & NEWBRIDGE BYPASS

Junc 11 (pg 30)	Westbound	No access. Exit only to M9 (southbound)
	Eastbound	No exit. Access only from M9 (northbound)

M50 DUBLIN RING ROAD

Junc 14 (pg 39)	Northbound	No access. Exit only
	Southbound	No restriction
Junc 17 (pg 39)	Northbound	No restriction.
	Southbound	No exit to N11 (North)

M1 Dublin - Drogheda

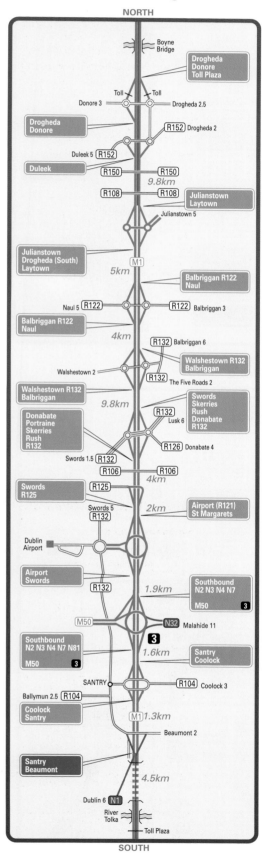

M1 Drogheda - Dundalk

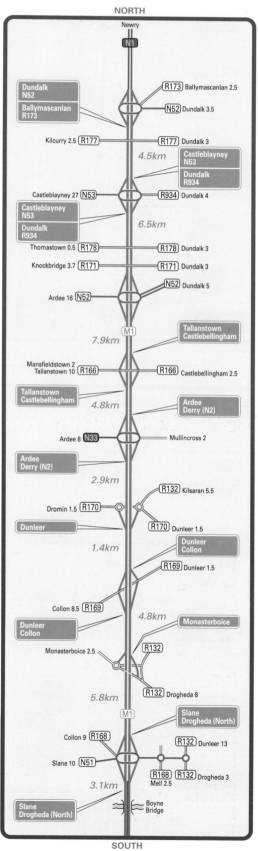

M4 Leixlip - Kinnegad

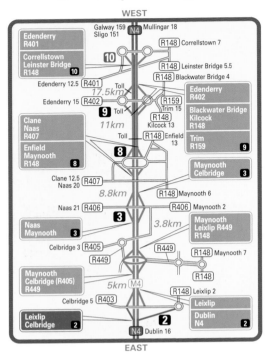

M11 Bray and Shankill Bypass

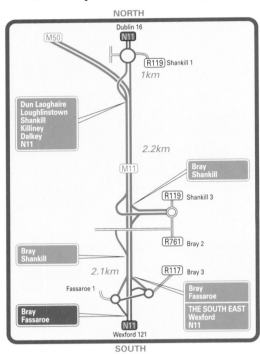

M50 Dublin Ring Road

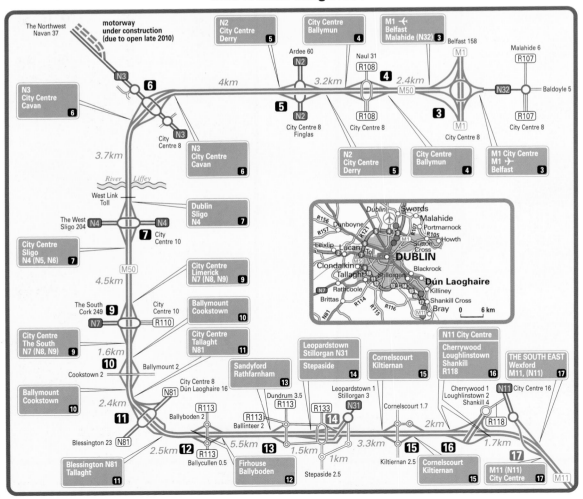

M7 Naas - Portlaoise

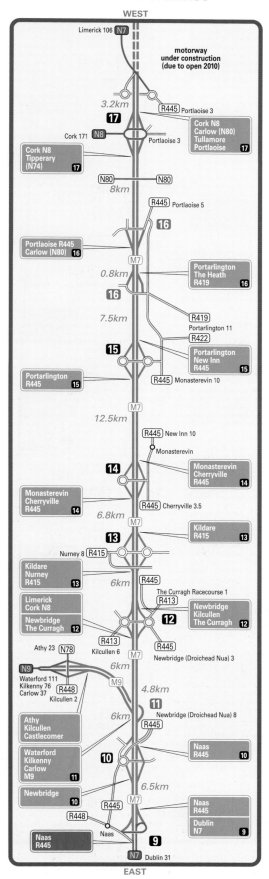

M1 Belfast - Craigavon

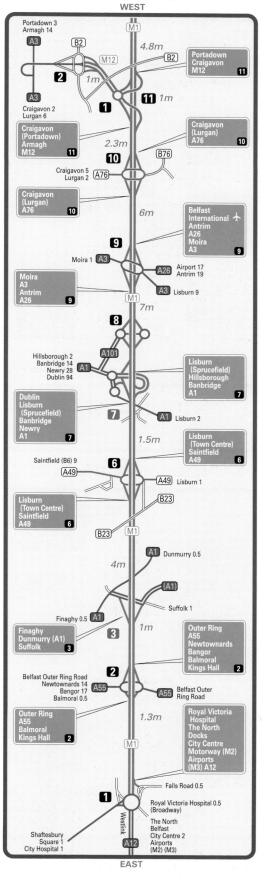

M1 Craigavon - Dungannon

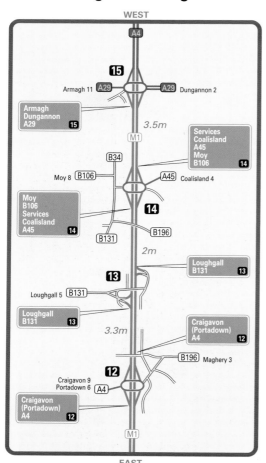

M2 Ballymena Bypass

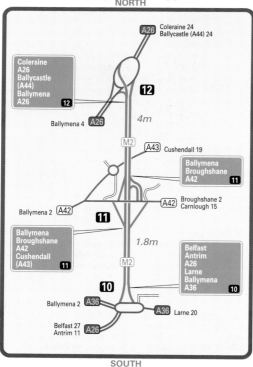

M2, M22 Belfast - Randalstown

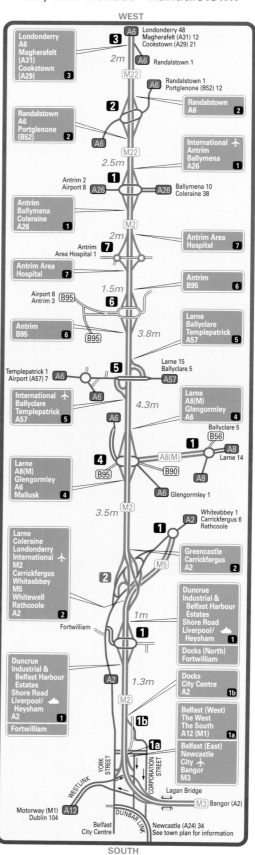

ms

Counties and administrative areas

The index lists places appearing in the main-map section of the atlas in alphabetical order. The reference before each name gives the atlas page number and grid reference of the square in which the place appears. The map shows counties and other internal administration areas in each country, together with a list of the abbreviated county name forms used in the index.

More than 50 top places of interest are indexed in red, airports in blue.

Northern Ireland

Antrim	Antrim
Armagh	Armagh
Belfast	Belfst
Down	Down
Fermanagh	Ferman
Londonderry	Lderry
Tyrone	Tyrone

Republic of Ireland

Carlow	Carlow	**Leitrim**	Leitrm
Cavan	Cavan	**Limerick**	Limrck
Clare	Clare	**Longford**	Longfd
Cork	Cork	**Louth**	Louth
Donegal	Donegl	**Mayo**	Mayo
Dublin	Dublin	**Meath**	Meath
Dublin City (1)	Dublin	**Monaghan**	Monhan
Dún Laoghaire-		**Offaly**	Offaly
Rathdown (2)	Dublin	**Roscommon**	Roscom
Fingal (3)	Dublin	**Sligo**	Sligo
South Dublin (4)	Dublin	**Tipperary North**	Tippry
Galway	Galway	**Tipperary South**	Tippry
Kerry	Kerry	**Waterford**	Watfd
Kildare	Kildre	**Westmeath**	Wmeath
Kilkenny	Kilken	**Wexford**	Wexfd
Laois	Laois	**Wicklow**	Wicklw

| 0 | 10 | 20 | 30 | 40 | 50 miles |
| 0 | 20 | 40 | 60 | 80 km |

82 Abbey - Ballyfad

A

26 H3 Abbey Galway
34 G5 Abbey Galway
36 F1 Abbeyderg Cross Roads Longfd
16 F10 Abbeydorney/Mainistir Ó dTorna Kerry
17 L9 Abbeyfeale/Mainistir na Féile Limrck
45 K8 Abbeylara/Mainistir Leathrátha Longfd
29 K8 Abbeyleix/Mainistir Laoise Laois
36 G2 Abbeyshrule/Mainistir Shruthla Longfd
19 L4 Abington Limrck
48 E3 Achadh/Aghadoon Mayo
40 E4 Achill Sound/Gob an Choire Mayo
51 N8 Achonry/Achadh Conaire Sligo
51 K8 Aclare/Áth an Chláir Sligo
56 C5 Acton Armagh
15 K3 Adamstown Wexfd
18 F5 Adare/Áth Dara Limrck
42 D6 Addergoole Mayo
34 C7 Addergoole/Eadargúil Galway
3 L4 Adrigole/Eadargóil Cork
28 H7 Aghaboe Laois
44 F7 Aghaboy Longfd
11 L9 Aghabullogue Cork
44 C1 Aghacashel/Achadh an Chaisil Leitrm
6 E7 Aghada Cork
42 G5 Aghadiffin Mayo
48 E3 Aghadoon/Achadh Mayo
67 M8 Aghadowey Lderry
4 B8 Aghadown Cork
62 E10 Aghagallon Antrim
41 L7 Aghagower Mayo
62 E10 Aghalee Antrim
44 C5 Aghamore Leitrm
42 F6 Aghamore Mayo
40 E7 Aghany Mayo
31 K7 Aghavannagh Wicklw
44 F3 Aghavas Leitrm
38 E4 Agher Cross Roads Meath
12 E8 Aghern Cork
48 D6 Aghleam/An Eachléim Mayo
44 H6 Aghnacliff/Achadh na Cloiche Longfd
8 F10 Aghnagar Bridge Kerry
5 L2 Aghnamarroge Cross Roads Cork
55 J10 Aghnamullen Monhan
67 M8 Agivey Bridge Lderry
27 M5 Aglish Tippry
13 K8 Aglish Watfd
8 G5 Aglish/An Eaglais Kerry
11 N7 Ahadallane Cross Roads Cork
16 F6 Ahafona Kerry
3 M7 Ahakista Cork
35 M6 Ahascragh/Áth Eascrach Galway
5 L1 Aherla Cork
12 E3 Ahnaseed Bridge Tippry
62 D2 Ahoghill Antrim
64 C9 Ailt an Chorráin/Burtonport Donegl
62 F7 Aldergrove Antrim
60 H2 Alla Cross Roads Lderry
38 D9 Allen Kildre
38 D8 Allenwood/Fiodh Alúine Kildre
2 F5 Allihies/Na hAilichí Cork
55 N4 Allistragh Armagh
35 K6 Alloon Lower Galway
22 F3 Altamont Gardens Carlow
59 N3 Altnapaste Donegl
64 D9 Anagaire/Annagary Donegl
8 H4 Anascaul/Abhainn an Scáil Kerry
2 E1 An Baile Breac/Ballybrack Kerry
8 E4 An Baile Íochtarach/Ballyeightragh Kerry
64 F3 An Baile Thiar/West Town Donegl
64 F3 An Baile Thoir/East Town Donegl
64 E8 An Bun Beag/Bunbeg Donegl
40 E3 An Caiseal/Cashel Mayo
65 M4 An Caiseal/Cashel Glebe Donegl
48 E4 An Carn/Carn Mayo
34 D8 An Carn Mór/Carnmore Galway
33 P7 An Chaothach/Keeagh Galway
58 C7 An Charraig/Carrick Donegl
33 J9 An Cheathrú Rua/Carraroe Galway
33 L2 An Chloc Bhreac/Cloghbrack Galway
40 E5 An Chloich Mhór/Cloghmore Mayo
59 L1 An Cionn Garbh/Kingarrow Donegl
8 G2 An Clochán/Cloghane Kerry
64 D10 An Clochán Liath/Dunglow Donegl
48 D6 An Clochar/Clogher Mayo
59 M3 An Coimín/Commeen Donegl
2 E1 An Coireán/Waterville Kerry
24 D4 An Córa Galway
40 E5 An Corrán/Corraun Mayo
8 E4 An Daingean/Dingle Kerry
40 E4 An Doirín/Derreen Mayo
8 G2 An Drom/Drom Kerry
59 J1 An Dúchoraidh/Doocharry Donegl
40 G5 An Dumhach Bheag/Dooghbeg Mayo
8 G5 An Dún Meánach/Doonmanagh Kerry
48 D6 An Eachléim/Aghleam Mayo
8 G5 An Eaglais/Aglish Kerry
64 G6 An Fál Carrach/Falcarragh Donegl
33 M2 An Fhairche/Clonbur Galway
8 D3 An Fheothanach/Feohanagh Kerry
48 D7 An Fód Dubh/Blacksod Mayo
48 E4 An Geata Mór/Binghamstown Mayo
8 D3 An Ghlaise Bheag/Glashabeg Kerry
19 N10 Anglesborough Limrck
19 P3 Anglesey Bridge Tippry
13 M9 An Goirtín/Gorteen Watfd
33 J6 An Gort Mór/Gortmore Galway
10 E10 An Leaca Bhán/Lackabaun Cork
64 B9 An Leadhb Gharbh/Leabgarrow Donegl
33 M9 An Lochán Beag/Loughaunbeg Galway
54 F8 Anlore Monhan
58 F1 An Machaire/Maghery Donegl
33 K3 An Mám/Maum Galway
40 D3 An Mhaoilinn/Mweelin Mayo
8 D3 An Mhuiríoch/Murreagh Kerry
26 G9 Annacarriga Clare
19 Q5 Annacarty Tippry
56 E5 Annaclone Down
57 L4 Annacloy Down
19 J3 Annacotty Limrck
31 L9 Annacurragh Wicklw
8 H4 Annagap Kerry
64 D9 Annagary/Anagaire Donegl
47 K5 Annagassan Louth
19 K3 Annagh Limrck
43 K8 Annagh Roscom
24 F9 Annagh Cross Roads Clare
34 B6 Annaghdown/Eanach Dhúin Galway
26 D8 Annaghneal Clare
18 F1 Annagore Bridge Clare
56 G2 Annahilt Down
57 J10 Annalong Down
31 M5 Annamoe/Áth na mBó Wicklw
55 L9 Annayalla Monhan
11 J3 Anne's Bridge Cork
14 B9 Annestown Watfd
20 C4 Annfield Tippry
57 J6 Annsborough Down
13 N9 An Rinn/Ringville Watfd
33 N9 An Spidéal/Spiddal Galway
33 K4 An Teach Dóite/Maam Cross Galway
65 L8 An Teampann/Termon Donegl
8 F10 An tImleach Mór/Emlaghmore Kerry
8 G2 An Tír/Teer Kerry
8 E10 An Trian Iarach/Teeranearagh Kerry
62 F5 Antrim Antrim
41 N9 An tSraith/Srah Mayo
48 F5 An tSraith/Srah Mayo
33 L9 An Tulaigh/Tully Galway
12 F5 Araglin Cork
12 E6 Araglin Bridge Cork
24 D2 Aran Islands/Oileáin Árann Galway
45 P10 Archerstown Wmeath
46 E5 Ardagh Meath
17 P7 Ardagh/Ardach Limrck
44 G10 Ardagh/Ardach Longfd
43 M5 Ardagh Cross Roads Roscom
37 J8 Ardan Offaly
38 C4 Ardanew Meath
58 F4 Ardara/Ard an Rátha Donegl
22 F3 Ardattin Carlow
59 K5 Ardbane Donegl
62 B7 Ardboe Tyrone
2 E2 Ard Caorach/Ardkearagh Kerry
39 K1 Ardcath Meath
16 D10 Ardconnell Kerry
27 L7 Ardcrony Tippry
3 K2 Ardea Bridge Kerry
46 H5 Ardee/Baile Átha Fhirdhia Louth
16 D10 Ardfert/Ard Fhearta Kerry
5 J7 Ardfield Cork
13 J3 Ardfinnan/Ard Fhíonáin Tippry
6 E3 Ardglass Cork
57 N6 Ardglass Down
2 H3 Ardgroom/Dhá Dhrom Cork
2 E2 Ardkearagh/Ard Caorach Kerry
57 P2 Ardkeen Down
34 B1 Ardkill Mayo
29 K6 Ardlea Laois
44 H1 Ardlougher Cavan
7 L4 Ardmore/Aird Mhór Watfd
37 K6 Ardmorney Wmeath
8 C3 Ard na Caithne/Smerwick Kerry
18 H2 Ardnacrusha Clare
34 F5 Ardnasodan Galway
19 J10 Ardpatrick Limrck
6 E7 Ardra Cork
3 Q5 Ardrah Cork
4 C4 Ardrah Cork
26 C2 Ardrahan/Ard Raithin Galway
55 P2 Ardress Armagh
30 C5 Ardscull Cross Roads Kildre
60 D5 Ardstraw Tyrone
61 Q7 Ardtrea Tyrone
4 H6 Argideen Bridge Cork
23 N2 Arklow/An tInbhear Mór Wicklw
29 Q8 Arless Laois
55 N4 Armagh Armagh
68 B6 Armoy Antrim
53 P6 Arney Ferman
17 P9 Arranagh Limrck
14 G6 Arthurstown Wexfd
67 K6 Articlave Lderry
60 E2 Artigarvan Tyrone
44 H4 Arvagh/Armhach Cavan
39 K3 Ashbourne/Cill Dhéagláin Meath
17 P10 Ashford Limrck
31 P5 Ashford/Áth na Fuinseoige Wicklw
20 E7 Ashill Tippry
23 J5 Askamore Wexfd
31 K8 Askanagap Wicklw
18 C4 Askeaton/Eas Géitine Limrck
16 G5 Astee Kerry
38 C1 Athboy/Baile Átha Buí Meath
17 L7 Athea/Áth an tSléibhe Limrck
34 G8 Athenry/Baile Átha an Rí Galway
30 E2 Athgarvan Kildre
18 H8 Athlacca Limrck
35 N2 Athleague/Áth Liag Roscom
36 C5 Athlone/Baile Átha Luain Wmeath
36 C5 Athlone Castle Wmeath
20 F4 Athnid Tippry
30 B6 Athy/Baile Átha Í Kildre
29 K9 Attanagh Laois
56 G10 Attical Down
35 N9 Atticoffey Galway
35 L6 Attiregan Galway
50 G8 Attymass/Áit Tí an Mheasaigh Mayo
34 H7 Attymon/Áth Tiomáin Galway
36 E3 Auburn Wmeath
34 D6 Aucloggeen Galway
9 J2 Aughacasla Kerry
54 G3 Augher Tyrone
15 L5 Aughfad Wexfd
9 L4 Aughils Kerry
62 B1 Aughnacleagh Antrim
55 J3 Aughnacloy Tyrone
20 B10 Aughnagawer Cross Roads Tippry
44 D1 Aughnasheelan/Acadh na Síleann Leitrm
25 N5 Aughrim Clare
35 M8 Aughrim/Eachroim Galway
31 L9 Aughrim/Eachroim Wicklw
31 N9 Avoca/Abhóca Wicklw

B

38 D5 Baconstown Meath
22 C4 Bagenalstown/Muine Bheag Carlow
8 D4 Baile an Éanaigh/Ballineanig Kerry
8 D4 Baile an Fheirtéaraigh/Ballyferriter Kerry
8 E3 Baile an Lochaigh/Ballinloghig Kerry
8 E4 Baile an Mhuilinn/Milltown Kerry
8 D3 Baile an Reannaigh/Ballinrannig Kerry
2 C1 Baile an Sceilg/Ballinskelligs Kerry
24 D4 Baile an Teampaill Galway
10 F9 Baile Bhuirne/Ballyvourney Cork
34 D7 Baile Chláir/Claregalway Galway
46 E9 Baile Ghib/Gibstown Meath
3 N10 Baile Iarthach/Ballyieragh Cork
10 G9 Baile Mhic Íre/Ballymakeery Cork
59 K2 Baile na Finne/Fintown Donegl
2 B1 Baile na hAbhann/Ballynahow Kerry
33 K9 Baile na hAbhann/Ballynahown Galway
8 D4 Baile na nAith/Ballynana Kerry
8 D3 Baile na nGall/Ballynagall Kerry
13 N9 Baile na nGall/Ballynagaul Watfd
46 E8 Baile Órthaí/Oristown Meath
8 E2 Baile Reo/Ballyroe Kerry
8 G2 Baile Uí Dhuinn/Ballyquin Kerry
56 H2 Baileysmill Down
46 B4 Bailieborough/Coill an Chollaigh Cavan
39 N1 Balbriggan/Baile Brigín Dublin
51 P1 Balinfull Sligo
42 B7 Balla Mayo
26 C4 Ballaba Galway
5 Q3 Ballady Cork
34 F1 Ballagh Galway
17 P9 Ballagh Limrck
35 Q3 Ballagh Roscom
43 Q9 Ballagh Roscom
20 C7 Ballagh Tippry
15 J3 Ballagh Wexfd
43 J5 Ballaghaderreen/Bealach an Doirín Roscom
17 L9 Ballaghbehy Limrck
20 F8 Ballaghboy Tippry
23 K9 Ballaghkeen Wexfd
28 F6 Ballaghmore Laois
52 D3 Ballaghnatrillick Sligo
62 H10 Ballantine Garden Village Down
37 J9 Ballard Offaly
22 H3 Ballard Cross Roads Wicklw
26 C4 Ballardiggan Galway
15 Q3 Ballare Wexfd
21 K3 Balleen Kilken
29 Q8 Ballickmoyler Laois
22 B10 Ballilogue Kilken
26 H10 Ballina Tippry
37 K3 Ballina Wmeath
50 F7 Ballina/Béal an Átha Mayo
5 P2 Ballinaboy Cork
32 D4 Ballinaboy Galway
37 P5 Ballinabrackey Meath
22 B2 Ballinabranagh Carlow
31 M8 Ballinaclash Wicklw
5 N4 Ballinadee Cork
43 M2 Ballinafad/Béal an Átha Fada Sligo
37 G9 Ballinagar Offaly
53 J9 Ballinagleragh Leitrm
19 L1 Ballinahinch Tippry
29 L8 Ballinakill/Baile na Coille Laois
37 K1 Ballinalack Wmeath
31 P5 Ballinalea Wicklw
44 G7 Ballinalee/Béal Átha na Lao Longfd
53 Q3 Ballinamallard Ferman
21 L5 Ballinamara Cross Roads Kilken
43 N5 Ballinameen Roscom
44 E1 Ballinamore/Béal an Átha Móir Leitrm
35 M4 Ballinamore Bridge Galway
5 K5 Ballinascarty Cork
35 P7 Ballinasloe/Béal Átha na Sluaighe Galway
12 H7 Ballinaspick Watfd
5 Q4 Ballinclashet Cork
15 L3 Ballinclay Wexfd
16 F9 Ballincloher Cross Roads Kerry
11 P10 Ballincollig/Baile an Chollaigh Cork
27 M3 Ballincor Tippry
14 E5 Ballincrea Kilken
6 D3 Ballincurrig Cork
22 F7 Ballindaggan Wexfd
12 C5 Ballindangan Cork
25 N1 Ballinderreen/Baile an Doirín Galway
27 L5 Ballinderry Tippry
42 D10 Ballindine/Baile an Daighin Mayo
52 E10 Ballindoon Sligo
60 D3 Ballindrait/Baile an Droichid Donegl
8 D4 Ballineanig/Baile an Éanaigh Kerry
4 H4 Ballineen/Béal Átha Fhínín Cork
18 D6 Ballingarrane Limrck
27 N5 Ballingarry Tippry
21 J7 Ballingarry/Baile an Gharraí Tippry
18 E7 Ballingary/Baile an Gharraí Limrck
4 E1 Ballingeary/Béal Átha an Ghaorthaidh Cork
31 K9 Ballinglen Wicklw
4 G5 Ballingurteen Cork
5 P2 Ballinhassig Cork
34 E9 Ballinillaun Galway
22 C5 Ballinkillin Carlow
18 F8 Ballinleeny Limrck
8 E3 Ballinloghig/Baile an Lochaig Kerry
45 Q8 Ballinlough Meath
42 H8 Ballinlough/Baile an Locha Roscom
6 C8 Ballinluska Cork
44 F5 Ballinmuck Longfd
5 K6 Ballinoroher Cork
56 H10 Ballinran Down
8 D3 Ballinrannig/Baile an Reannaigh Kerry
27 M9 Ballinree Tippry
6 B7 Ballinreeshig Cork
33 P1 Ballinrobe/Baile an Róba Mayo
25 P7 Ballinruan Clare
2 C1 Ballinskelligs/Baile an Sceilg Kerry
5 N5 Ballinspittle/Béal Átha an Spidéil Cork
41 N8 Ballintober Mayo
43 L9 Ballintober Roscom
52 E8 Ballintogher/Baile an Tóchair Sligo
67 Q4 Ballintoy Antrim
59 K9 Ballintra/Baile an tSratha Donegl
29 P6 Ballintubbert Laois
20 G7 Ballinunty Tippry
20 F7 Ballinure Tippry
13 Q1 Ballinurra Tippry
22 C9 Ballinvarry Kilken
20 C2 Ballinveny Tippry
5 J2 Ballinvoher Cork
5 N5 Ballinvronig Cork
30 D5 Ballitore/Béal Átha an Tuair Kildre
38 B3 Ballivor/Baile Íomhair Meath
22 E3 Ballon/Balana Carlow
57 L1 Balloo Down
52 E3 Balloor Leitrm
46 H1 Ballsmill Armagh
57 N4 Balltculter Down
58 H10 Ballure Donegl
18 E6 Ballvea Limrck
12 D4 Ballyaghaderg Bridge Cork
18 F9 Ballyagran Limrck
18 D7 Ballyallinan Limrck
46 H5 Ballybailie Cross Roads Louth
35 L5 Ballybaun Galway
55 K9 Ballybay/Béal Átha Beithe Monhan
46 E2 Ballybay Cross Roads Monhan
13 K3 Ballybeg Tippry
27 P9 Ballybeg Tippry
39 L8 Ballyboden Dublin
59 P4 Ballybofey/Bealach Féich Donegl
37 Q5 Ballyboggan Meath
39 M3 Ballyboghil/Baile Bachaille Dublin
67 N6 Ballybogy Antrim
36 E5 Ballybornia Wmeath
28 F2 Ballyboy Offaly
3 M9 Ballybrack Cork
38 F6 Ballybrack Kildre
7 J2 Ballybrack Watfd
2 E1 Ballybrack/An Baile Breac Kerry
20 E3 Ballybristy Tippry
29 N3 Ballybrittas Laois
16 E10 Ballybroman Kerry
19 K5 Ballybrood Limrck
28 G8 Ballybrophy/Baile Uí Bhróithe Laois
18 F2 Ballybroughan Clare
37 P6 Ballybryan Offaly
16 F6 Ballybunion/Baile an Bhuinneánaigh Kerry
30 D8 Ballyburn Kildre
19 M1 Ballycahane Tippry
20 D5 Ballycahill Tippry
21 L6 Ballycallan Kilken
23 L6 Ballycanew/Baile Uí Chonnmhaí Wexfd
18 H2 Ballycar Clare
22 H7 Ballycarney Wexfd
63 L4 Ballycarry Antrim
14 D7 Ballycashin Watfd
68 C4 Ballycastle Antrim
50 D3 Ballycastle/Baile an Chaisil Mayo
62 H4 Ballyclare Antrim
44 B10 Ballyclare Roscom
13 L1 Ballyclerahan Tippry
11 M4 Ballyclogh/Baile Cloch Cork
15 N6 Ballycogly Wexfd
29 J8 Ballycolla Laois
3 P6 Ballycommane Cork
27 K8 Ballycommon Tippry
21 N2 Ballycomy Kilken
32 C5 Ballyconneely/Baile Conaola Galway
53 Q10 Ballyconnell/Béal Átha Conaill Cavan
17 P1 Ballycorick Bridge Clare
6 G7 Ballycotton/Baile Choitín Cork
27 L2 Ballycrossaun Galway
48 H8 Ballycroy/Baile Chruaich Mayo
13 M8 Ballycullane Watfd
14 H6 Ballycullane/Baile Uí Choileáin Wexfd
31 N5 Ballycullen Wicklw
36 G7 Ballycumber/Béal Átha Chomair Offaly
7 L2 Ballycurrane Watfd
12 A7 Ballydague Cork
10 G6 Ballydaly Cork
35 Q7 Ballydangan Roscom
6 F7 Ballydavid Cork
26 G1 Ballydavid Galway
3 P7 Ballydehob/Béal an Dá Chab Cork
12 C5 Ballydeloughy Cork
10 F4 Ballydesmond/Baile Deasumhan Cork
2 F6 Ballydonegan Cork
26 G1 Ballydoogan Galway
12 A6 Ballydoyle Cork
14 C7 Ballyduff Watfd
23 J6 Ballyduff Wexfd
16 F8 Ballyduff/An Baile Dubh Kerry
12 G7 Ballyduff/An Baile Dubh Watfd
31 N4 Ballyduff Cross Roads Wicklw
12 G5 Ballyeafy Watfd
62 H4 Ballyeaston Antrim
28 C4 Ballyeighan Offaly
35 M8 Ballyeighter Galway
8 E4 Ballyeightragh/An Baile Íochtarach Kerry
23 M3 Ballyfad Wexfd

42 D7 **Ballyfarnagh** Mayo
43 P1 **Ballyfarnan**/*Baile Átha Fearnáin* Roscom
14 E3 **Ballyfasy** Kilken
6 B8 **Ballyfeard** Cork
8 D4 **Ballyferriter**/*Baile an Fheirtéaraigh* Kerry
23 L6 **Ballyfin** Wexfd
29 J4 **Ballyfin**/*An Baile Fionn* Laois
35 N4 **Ballyforan**/*Béal Átha Feorainne* Roscom
37 P7 **Ballyfore** Offaly
21 N4 **Ballyfoyle** Kilken
28 D5 **Ballygaddy Cross Roads** Offaly
63 K1 **Ballygalley** Antrim
35 M3 **Ballygar**/*Béal Átha Ghártha* Galway
13 R7 **Ballygarran** Watfd
14 B7 **Ballygarran** Watfd
23 N7 **Ballygarrett** Wexfd
41 Q9 **Ballygarries** Mayo
5 Q2 **Ballygarvan** Cork
54 H2 **Ballygawley** Tyrone
52 D8 **Ballygawley**/*Baile Uí Dhálaigh* Sligo
62 F2 **Ballygelly** Antrim
41 Q8 **Ballyglass** Mayo
42 H5 **Ballyglass** Mayo
50 D4 **Ballyglass** Mayo
14 C6 **Ballygorey** Kilken
66 C1 **Ballygorman** Donegl
23 L8 **Ballygortin** Wexfd
63 L10 **Ballygowan** Down
11 L3 **Ballygrady** Cork
20 C8 **Ballygriffin** Tippry
22 B9 **Ballygub** Kilken
18 H9 **Ballygubba** Limrck
14 G6 **Ballyhack** Wexfd
30 E9 **Ballyhacket Cross Roads** Carlow
18 H10 **Ballyhahill** Limrck
17 M5 **Ballyhahill** Limrck
45 L1 **Ballyhaise**/*Béal Átha hÉis* Cavan
63 Q10 **Ballyhalbert** Down
33 Q5 **Ballyhale** Galway
21 N9 **Ballyhale**/*Baile Héil* Kilken
19 Q1 **Ballyhane Cross Roads** Tippry
5 N1 **Ballyhank** Cork
9 Q5 **Ballyhar** Kerry
42 F8 **Ballyhaunis**/*Béal Átha hAmhnais* Mayo
41 N7 **Ballyhean** Mayo
34 D2 **Ballyhear** Galway
45 L6 **Ballyheelan** Cavan
16 D9 **Ballyheige**/*Baile Uí Thaidhg* Kerry
34 B2 **Ballyhenry** Mayo
25 P9 **Ballyhickey** Clare
22 H10 **Ballyhoge** Wexfd
14 E4 **Ballyhomuck** Kilken
11 J4 **Ballyhoolahan** Cork
12 B7 **Ballyhooly**/*Baile Átha hÚlla* Cork
57 N5 **Ballyhornan** Down
54 B10 **Ballyhugh** Cavan
37 N8 **Ballyhugh** Offaly
3 N10 **Ballyieragh**/*Baile Iarthach* Cork
45 N5 **Ballyjamesduff**/*Baile Shéamais Dhuibh* Cavan
37 M9 **Ballykean** Offaly
21 L6 **Ballykeefe Cross Roads** Kilken
56 G3 **Ballykeel** Down
36 D5 **Ballykeeran** Wmeath
66 G8 **Ballykelly** Lderry
37 Q8 **Ballykilleen** Offaly
6 H4 **Ballykilty** Cork
57 K6 **Ballykinler** Down
14 E7 **Ballykinsella** Watfd
31 J3 **Ballyknockan** Wicklw
6 F7 **Ballylanders** Cork
19 M10 **Ballylanders**/*Baile an Londraigh* Limrck
13 R6 **Ballylaneen** Watfd
5 M3 **Ballylangley** Cork
14 B8 **Ballyleen** Watfd
55 Q4 **Ballyleny** Armagh
63 J9 **Ballylesson** Down
3 Q4 **Ballylickey** Cork
66 B3 **Ballyliffin**/*Baile Lifin* Donegl
21 K7 **Ballyline** Kilken
29 M9 **Ballylinnen** Kilken
67 M7 **Ballylintagh** Lderry
16 H6 **Ballylongford**/*Béal Átha Longfoirt* Kerry
19 M8 **Ballylooby** Limrck
12 H3 **Ballylooby** Tippry
23 K10 **Ballylucas** Wexfd
63 L2 **Ballylumford** Antrim
29 P7 **Ballylynan**/*Baile Uí Laigheanáin* Laois
13 L4 **Ballymacarbry**/*Béal Mhac Cairbre* Watfd
14 E9 **Ballymacaw** Watfd
9 Q2 **Ballymacelligott** Kerry
45 L6 **Ballymachugh** Cavan
27 M8 **Ballymackey** Tippry
13 M7 **Ballymacmague** Watfd
6 H5 **Ballymacoda** Cork
26 C3 **Ballymacquiff** Galway
43 N9 **Ballymacurly** Roscom
35 K6 **Ballymacward** Galway
7 J5 **Ballymadog** Cork
66 B6 **Ballymagan** Donegl
66 G3 **Ballymagaraghy** Donegl
60 E2 **Ballymagorry** Tyrone
36 F2 **Ballymahon**/*Baile Uí Mhathain* Longfd
10 G9 **Ballymakeery**/*Baile Mhic Íre* Cork
47 K7 **Ballymakenny** Louth
45 M8 **Ballymanus** Wmeath

56 H10 **Ballymartin** Down
5 P3 **Ballymartin** Down
62 E2 **Ballymena** Antrim
43 K9 **Ballymoe**/*Béal Átha Mó* Galway
67 N7 **Ballymoney** Antrim
23 N4 **Ballymoney Cross Roads** Wexfd
6 D6 **Ballymore** Cork
65 J6 **Ballymore** Donegl
36 G4 **Ballymore**/*An Baile Mór* Wmeath
30 G2 **Ballymore Eustace**/*An Baile Mór* Kildre
14 C8 **Ballymorris** Watfd
52 C10 **Ballymote**/*Baile an Mhóta* Sligo
30 E4 **Ballymount** Kildre
23 J10 **Ballymurn** Wexfd
22 D7 **Ballymurphy** Carlow
17 N9 **Ballymurragh** Limrck
35 Q1 **Ballymurray** Roscom
14 H4 **Ballynabola** Wexfd
34 E10 **Ballynabucky** Galway
2 D6 **Ballynacallagh** Cork
17 P2 **Ballynacally** Clare
4 G4 **Ballynacarriga** Cork
37 J2 **Ballynacarrigy**/*Baile na Carraige* Wmeath
51 P6 **Ballynacarrow** Sligo
27 M10 **Ballynaclogh** Tippry
6 F4 **Ballynacole** Cork
6 E5 **Ballynacorra** Cork
5 Q3 **Ballynacourty** Cork
13 N8 **Ballynacourty** Watfd
45 N7 **Ballynacree** Meath
37 L1 **Ballynafid** Wmeath
8 D3 **Ballynagall**/*Baile na nGall* Kerry
6 C4 **Ballynagaul** Cork
13 N9 **Ballynagaul**/*Baile na nGall* Watfd
6 A2 **Ballynaglogh West** Cork
37 K6 **Ballynagore** Wmeath
11 K8 **Ballynagree** Cork
5 P2 **Ballynagrumoolia** Cork
13 L6 **Ballynaguilkee** Watfd
57 J3 **Ballynahinch** Down
2 B1 **Ballynahow**/*Baile na hAbhann* Kerry
36 F7 **Ballynahown** Wmeath
33 K9 **Ballynahown**/*Baile na hAbhann* Galway
50 E6 **Ballynahowna** Mayo
10 E4 **Ballynahulla** Kerry
37 M9 **Ballynakill** Offaly
36 D4 **Ballynakill** Wmeath
3 J6 **Ballynakilla** Cork
60 G3 **Ballynamallaght** Tyrone
5 P3 **Ballynamaul** Cork
11 P6 **Ballynamona** Cork
15 J5 **Ballynamona** Wexfd
47 N2 **Ballynamoy** Louth
12 B7 **Ballynamuddagh** Cork
13 L5 **Ballynamult** Watfd
8 D4 **Ballynana**/*Baile na nÁith* Kerry
38 G5 **Ballynare Cross Roads** Meath
45 L6 **Ballynarry** Cavan
16 E8 **Ballynaskreena** Kerry
42 C8 **Ballynastangford** Mayo
60 H2 **Ballyneaner** Tyrone
19 J5 **Ballyneety** Limrck
13 Q2 **Ballyneil** Tippry
21 J8 **Ballynennan** Tippry
12 F9 **Ballynoe**/*An Baile Nua* Cork
18 D8 **Ballynoe Bridge** Limrck
63 J4 **Ballynure** Antrim
12 A3 **Ballyorgan** Limrck
23 L6 **Ballyoughter** Wexfd
4 C6 **Ballyourane** Cork
13 P1 **Ballypatrick** Tippry
13 J9 **Ballyphilip** Watfd
12 F4 **Ballyporeen**/*Béal Átha Póirín* Tippry
13 R3 **Ballyquin** Watfd
8 G2 **Ballyquin**/*Baile Uí Dhuinn* Kerry
21 L2 **Ballyragget**/*Béal Átha Ragad* Kilken
67 M6 **Ballyrashane** Lderry
6 G3 **Ballyre** Cork
55 J2 **Ballyreagh** Tyrone
5 P4 **Ballyregan** Cork
29 L7 **Ballyroan**/*Baile Átha an Róine* Laois
43 N6 **Ballyroddy** Roscom
8 E2 **Ballyroe**/*Baile Reo* Kerry
22 H5 **Ballyroebuck** Wexfd
62 A5 **Ballyronan** Lderry
56 F6 **Ballyroney** Down
3 K7 **Ballyroon** Cork
22 C3 **Ballyryan** Carlow
52 C8 **Ballysadare**/*Baile Easa Dara* Sligo
52 G1 **Ballyshannon**/*Béal Átha Seanaiah* Donegl
16 E10 **Ballysheen** Kerry
14 E8 **Ballyshoneen** Watfd
27 J3 **Ballyshrule** Galway
11 N6 **Ballysimon Cross Roads** Cork
20 H6 **Ballysloe** Tippry
20 F2 **Ballysorrell** Tippry
18 D3 **Ballysteen** Limrck
40 D6 **Ballytoohy** Mayo
23 M9 **Ballyvaldon** Wexfd
19 N6 **Ballyvalode** Limrck
11 P8 **Ballyvaloon** Cork
25 K3 **Ballyvaughan**/*Baile Uí Bheacháin* Clare
22 E3 **Ballyveal** Carlow
13 J3 **Ballyveera** Tippry
4 G7 **Ballyvireen Bridge** Cork
12 A4 **Ballyvisteen** Cork
3 K9 **Ballyvoge** Cork

35 M5 **Ballyvoneen** Galway
25 N10 **Ballyvonnavaun** Clare
6 B9 **Ballyvorane** Cork
10 F9 **Ballyvourney**/*Baile Bhuirne* Cork
68 D4 **Ballyvoy** Antrim
13 P7 **Ballyvoyle Cross Roads** Watfd
63 Q9 **Ballywalter** Down
56 G6 **Ballyward** Down
12 A5 **Ballywater** Cork
67 K6 **Ballywildrick** Lderry
5 N4 **Ballywilliam** Cork
22 D10 **Ballywilliam** Wexfd
67 N7 **Balnamore** Antrim
39 J1 **Balrath** Meath
37 Q1 **Balrath Cross Roads** Wmeath
39 N1 **Balrothery** Dublin
39 M1 **Balscaddan** Dublin
4 B9 **Baltimore**/*Dún na Séad* Cork
30 F7 **Baltinglass**/*Bealach Conglais* Wicklw
16 E9 **Baltovin** Kerry
47 L8 **Baltray**/*Baile Trá* Louth
51 L9 **Banada** Sligo
27 P1 **Banagher**/*Beannchar* Offaly
56 D4 **Banbridge** Down
5 L3 **Bandon**/*Droichead na Bandan* Cork
16 G9 **Banemore** Kerry
63 N6 **Bangor** Down
49 J6 **Bangor Erris**/*Beannchor* Mayo
16 D10 **Banna** Kerry
11 L4 **Bannagh Cross Roads** Cork
62 B10 **Bannfoot** Armagh
25 L10 **Bansha** Clare
20 B10 **Bansha**/*An Bháinseach* Tippry
11 K5 **Banteer**/*Bántir* Cork
3 P5 **Bantry**/*Beanntraí* Cork
3 P5 **Bantry Gardens** Cork
66 G9 **Baranailt** Lderry
25 N8 **Barefield** Clare
4 C9 **Barloge** Cork
19 M6 **Barna** Limrck
27 P7 **Barna** Offaly
33 Q9 **Barna**/*Bearna* Galway
42 E4 **Barnacahoge** Mayo
43 K6 **Barnacawley** Roscom
34 G4 **Barnaderg** Galway
3 P6 **Barnaghgeehy** Cork
4 D4 **Barnagowlane** Cork
20 F3 **Barnalisheen** Tippry
42 E4 **Barnalyra** Mayo
10 C10 **Barnastooka** Kerry
48 G4 **Barnatra**/*Barr na Trá* Mayo
59 M6 **Barnesmore** Donegl
42 D8 **Barnycarroll** Mayo
3 N3 **Barony Bridge** Cork
11 L1 **Barrack Cross Roads** Cork
10 D6 **Barraduff** Kerry
26 G3 **Barratoor** Galway
4 D4 **Barrboy** Cork
21 N9 **Barrettstown** Kilken
17 P4 **Barrigone** Limrck
19 K4 **Barringtonsbridge** Limrck
48 G4 **Barr na Trá**/*Barnatra* Mayo
9 L1 **Barrow** Kerry
36 F1 **Barry** Longfd
12 D9 **Bartlemy** Cork
15 M8 **Bastardstown** Wexfd
17 K10 **Bateman's Bridge** Kerry
38 H4 **Batterstown** Meath
62 G3 **Battery Bridge** Antrim
37 L5 **Baughna** Wmeath
4 H2 **Baulbrack** Cork
21 P9 **Baunskeha** Kilken
25 J8 **Bauntlieve** Clare
10 H4 **Bawnaneel** Cork
4 C5 **Bawnboy** Cork
53 P10 **Bawnboy**/*An Bábhún Buí* Cavan
11 K3 **Bawn Cross Roads** Cork
44 F10 **Bawn Cross Roads** Longfd
13 L3 **Bawnfune** Watfd
4 D9 **Bawnlahan** Cork
34 F2 **Beagh** Galway
16 F5 **Beal** Kerry
25 L3 **Bealaclugga** Clare
33 J7 **Bealadangan**/*Béal an Daingin* Galway
16 G2 **Bealaha** Clare
9 L8 **Bealalaw Bridge** Kerry
59 L2 **Béal an Átha Móir**/*Bellanamore* Donegl
33 J7 **Béal na Daingin**/*Bealadangan* Galway
48 F4 **Béal an Mhuirthead**/*Belmullet* Mayo
4 E1 **Béal Átha an Ghaorthaidh**/*Ballingeary* Cork
49 L3 **Béal Deirg**/*Belderg* Mayo
36 E5 **Bealin** Wmeath
5 K2 **Bealnablath** Cork
11 L9 **Bealnamorive** Cork
33 Q9 **Bearna**/*Barna* Galway
9 P6 **Beaufort** Kerry
38 F2 **Bective** Meath
12 B9 **Behernagh** Cork
50 G7 **Behy Bridge** Mayo
42 E8 **Bekan** Mayo
41 P7 **Belcarra** Mayo
34 D4 **Belclare** Galway
53 L6 **Belcoo** Ferman
49 L3 **Belderg**/*Béal Deirg* Mayo
63 J8 **Belfast** Belfst
62 E7 **Belfast International** Antrim
5 Q4 **Belgooly** Cork

49 L6 **Bellacorrick**/*Béal Átha Chomhraic* Mayo
52 C7 **Belladrihid** Sligo
40 G2 **Bellagarvaun** Mayo
62 B3 **Bellaghy** Lderry
35 N7 **Bellagill Bridge** Galway
42 F3 **Bellahy** Sligo
49 J4 **Bellanaboy Bridge**/*Droichead Bhéal an Átha Buí* Mayo
43 L6 **Bellanagare**/*Béal Átha na gCarr* Roscom
53 P6 **Bellanaleck** Ferman
59 L2 **Bellanamore**/*Béal an Átha Móir* Donegl
36 B5 **Bellanamullia** Roscom
45 K4 **Bellananagh**/*Béal Átha na nEach* Cavan
45 M1 **Bellancargy** Cavan
35 Q6 **Bellaneeny** Roscom
54 H6 **Bellanode** Monhan
41 Q5 **Bellavary**/*Béal Átha Bhearaigh* Mayo
55 Q8 **Belleek** Armagh
52 H2 **Belleek** Ferman
56 P6 **Belleek** Mayo
52 H2 **Belleek Pottery** Ferman
47 K10 **Bellewstown** Meath
36 D9 **Bellmount** Offaly
48 F4 **Belmullet**/*Béal an Mhuirthead* Mayo
63 L4 **Beltoy** Antrim
41 M3 **Beltra** Mayo
51 N4 **Beltra**/*Béal Trá* Sligo
54 C10 **Belturbet**/*Béal Tairbirt* Cavan
6 C5 **Belvelly** Cork
55 M3 **Benburb** Tyrone
67 N8 **Bendooragh** Antrim
30 D9 **Bennekerry** Carlow
21 P7 **Bennettsbridge**/*Droichead Binéid* Kilken
67 J5 **Benone** Lderry
60 H9 **Beragh** Tyrone
11 M8 **Bernard Cross Roads** Cork
11 N9 **Berrings** Cork
56 B8 **Bessbrook** Armagh
47 M9 **Bettystown**/*Baile an Bhiataigh* Meath
59 N6 **Big Bridge** Tyrone
62 G3 **Big Collin** Antrim
21 Q2 **Bilboa** Laois
48 E4 **Binghamstown**/*An Geata Mór* Mayo
19 L1 **Birdhill** Tippry
28 C3 **Birr**/*Biorra* Offaly
28 C4 **Birr Castle Demesne** Offaly
57 N5 **Bishops Court** Down
14 D5 **Bishopshall** Kilken
12 F6 **Black** Watfd
39 J4 **Black Bull** Meath
20 E10 **Blackcastle** Tippry
15 L3 **Blackhall** Wexfd
53 L6 **Blacklion** Cavan
36 H10 **Black Lion** Offaly
6 B5 **Blackrock** Cork
39 N8 **Blackrock** Dublin
47 K3 **Blackrock**/*Na Creagacha Dubha* Louth
48 D7 **Blacksod**/*An Fód Dubh* Mayo
9 L7 **Blackstones Bridge** Kerry
23 L10 **Blackwater**/*An Abhainn Dubh* Wexfd
3 K1 **Blackwater Bridge** Kerry
38 C5 **Blackwater Bridge** Kildre
55 M3 **Blackwatertown** Armagh
38 D8 **Blackwood**/*Coil Dubh* Kildre
67 M5 **Blagh** Lderry
39 K6 **Blanchardstown** Dublin
17 L7 **Blane Bridge** Limrck
11 Q9 **Blarney**/*An Bhlarna* Cork
11 Q9 **Blarney Castle** Cork
56 C3 **Bleary** Down
9 N2 **Blennerville** Kerry
30 H2 **Blessington**/*Baile Coimín* Wicklw
36 H10 **Blue Ball** Offaly
10 H3 **Blueford** Cork
6 B8 **Boardee** Cork
57 J2 **Boardmills** Down
43 J4 **Bockagh** Roscom
26 E8 **Bodyke** Clare
41 N3 **Bofeenaun** Mayo
21 J5 **Boggan** Kilken
46 C6 **Boggan Cross Roads** Meath
28 E9 **Boggaun** Tippry
39 M1 **Bog of The Ring** Dublin
4 F1 **Bohane's Cross Roads** Cork
9 L8 **Boheeshil** Kerry
19 K4 **Boher** Limrck
28 E5 **Boheraphuca** Offaly
13 K7 **Boheravaghera Cross Roads** Watfd
11 P3 **Boherboy Cross Roads** Cork
10 H4 **Boherbue** Cork
19 J4 **Bohereen** Limrck
38 F7 **Boherlahan Cross Roads** Kildre
20 D7 **Boherlahan** Tippry
46 E10 **Bohermeen**/*An Bóthar Mín* Meath
12 G2 **Bohernarnane** Tippry
45 N9 **Boherquill** Wmeath
19 L6 **Boherroe** Limrck
42 C4 **Bohola**/*Both Chomhla* Mayo
67 J7 **Bolea** Lderry
67 L6 **Boleran** Lderry
29 P7 **Boley** Laois
22 H3 **Boley** Wicklw
30 C3 **Boleybeg Cross Roads** Kildre

30 C4 **Boley Cross Roads** Kildre
23 K7 **Boleyvogue** Wexfd
40 E5 **Bolinglanna**/*Buaile an Ghleanna* Mayo
17 J8 **Bolton's Cross Roads** Kerry
7 J3 **Boola** Watfd
12 G2 **Boolakennedy** Tippry
22 C6 **Borris**/*An Bhuiríos* Carlow
28 F7 **Borris in Ossory**/*Buirios Mór Osraí* Laois
27 M6 **Borrisokane**/*Buiríos Uí Chéin* Tippry
20 C3 **Borrisoleigh**/*Buiríos Ó Luigheach* Tippry
25 N5 **Boston** Clare
19 K8 **Bottomstown** Limrck
45 K10 **Bottomy** Wmeath
20 D4 **Bouladuff** Tippry
67 M10 **Bovedy** Lderry
66 H10 **Bovevagh** Lderry
43 N3 **Boyle**/*Mainistir na Búille* Roscom
34 H1 **Boyounagh** Galway
37 N9 **Brackagh** Offaly
12 E3 **Brackbaun Bridge** Limrck
3 J1 **Brackloon** Kerry
43 L7 **Brackloon** Roscom
43 M6 **Brackloon Cross Roads** Roscom
37 P2 **Bracklyn** Wmeath
37 Q10 **Bracknagh** Offaly
36 B1 **Bracknagh** Roscom
36 E10 **Brackny** Offaly
50 F8 **Brackwanshagh** Mayo
3 N6 **Brahalish** Cork
8 G2 **Brandon**/*Cé Bhréanainn* Kerry
8 F2 **Brandon Mountain**/*Cnoc Bréanainn* Kerry
54 H7 **Brandrum** Monhan
30 F3 **Brannockstown** Kildre
39 P10 **Bray**/*Bré* Wicklw
60 E1 **Bready** Tyrone
5 J4 **Breaghna** Cork
16 E4 **Breaghva** Clare
41 P6 **Breaghwy** Mayo
22 G10 **Bree** Wexfd
6 H2 **Breeda** Cork
42 E8 **Brickeens** Mayo
12 D8 **Bridebridge** Cork
35 Q5 **Brideswell** Roscom
66 B8 **Bridge End** Donegl
23 J2 **Bridgeland** Wicklw
59 K8 **Bridgetown** Donegl
19 J1 **Bridgetown**/*Baile an Droichid* Clare
15 M7 **Bridgetown**/*Baile an Droichid* Wexfd
61 Q8 **Brigh** Tyrone
64 E6 **Brinlack**/*Bun na Leaca* Donegl
13 P6 **Briska** Watfd
39 J9 **Brittas** Dublin
12 E9 **Britway** Cork
38 B5 **Broadford** Kildre
18 C10 **Broadford** Limrck
26 E10 **Broadford**/*Áth Leathan* Clare
15 Q7 **Broadway** Wexfd
67 K10 **Brockagh** Lderry
18 D9 **Broken Bridge** Limrck
54 C9 **Brookeborough** Ferman
19 P8 **Brookville Bridge** Tippry
46 E1 **Broomfield** Monhan
10 E1 **Brosna** Kerry
28 C6 **Brosna** Offaly
28 E1 **Broughal** Offaly
11 Q3 **Brough Cross Roads** Cork
62 F1 **Broughshane** Antrim
45 J8 **Browne's Cross Roads** Longfd
7 J2 **Brown's Cross Roads** Watfd
66 F5 **Brown Shoulder** Donegl
46 G10 **Brownstown** Meath
14 E9 **Brownstown** Watfd
30 D3 **Brownstown Cross Roads** Kildre
20 E4 **Brownstown Cross Roads** Tippry
20 G3 **Bruckana** Kilken
58 F7 **Bruckles** Donegl
19 J7 **Bruff**/*An Brú* Limrck
42 E6 **Bruff Cross Roads** Mayo
18 H8 **Bruree**/*Brú Rí* Limrck
56 H7 **Bryansford** Down
40 E5 **Buaile an Ghleanna**/*Bolinglanna* Mayo
62 G1 **Buckna** Antrim
52 G3 **Buckode** Leitrim
14 B7 **Buck's Cross Roads** Watfd
19 J9 **Bulgaden** Limrck
35 J9 **Bullaun** Galway
40 D3 **Bunacurry**/*Bun an Churraigh* Mayo
40 D3 **Bun an Churraigh**/*Bunacurry* Mayo
3 N2 **Bunane** Kerry
3 K2 **Bunaw** Kerry
64 E8 **Bunbeg**/*An Bun Beag* Donegl
37 K1 **Bunbrosna** Wmeath
22 G5 **Bunclody**/*Bun Clóidí* Wexfd
65 Q6 **Buncrana**/*Bun Cranncha* Donegl
52 F2 **Bundoran**/*Bun Dobhrain* Donegl
9 K7 **Bunglasha** Kerry
58 F6 **Bungosteen Bridge** Donegl
44 H7 **Bunlahy** Longfd
4 A9 **Bunmahon**/*Bun Machan* Watfd
33 Q3 **Bunnafollistran** Mayo

32 G5 Bun na hAbhann/Bunnahown Galway
48 G5 Bun na hAbhann/Bunnahowen Mayo
48 G5 Bunnahowen/Bun na hAbhna Mayo
32 G5 Bunnahown/Bun na hAbhann Galway
64 E6 Bun na Leaca/Brinlack Donegl
51 P8 Bunnanaddan Sligo
50 H7 Bunnyconnellan Mayo
18 F2 Bunratty Clare
18 F2 Bunratty Castle and Folk Park Clare
21 M7 Burnchurch Kilken
12 F3 Burncourt Tippry
66 B8 Burnfoot/Bun na hAbhann Donegl
11 P6 Burnfort Cork
17 N2 Burren Clare
56 D9 Burren Down
25 L2 Burren/Boirinn Clare
17 M2 Burrenfadda Clare
66 B8 Burt Donegl
64 C9 Burtonport/Ailt an Chorráin Donegl
30 C6 Burtown Cross Roads Kildre
67 N4 Bushmills Antrim
45 L1 Butlers Bridge/Droichead an Bhuitléaraigh Cavan
5 L7 Butlerstown Cork
11 N3 Buttevant/Cill na Mallach Cork
11 N7 Bweeng Cork

C

55 K1 Cabragh Tyrone
38 C6 Cadamstown Kildre
28 F3 Cadamstown Offaly
62 D4 Caddy Antrim
67 M9 Caheny Bridge Lderry
26 E6 Caher Clare
3 K7 Caher Cork
9 K4 Caheracruttera Kerry
34 D9 Caheradrine Clare
4 C6 Caheragh Cork
35 L9 Caherakillen Galway
2 E1 Caherbarnagh Kerry
19 K5 Caherconlish/Cathair Chinn Lis Limrck
2 F3 Caherdaniel/Cathair Dónall Kerry
17 P1 Caherea Clare
17 L10 Caher Hill Limrck
34 E7 Caherlea Galway
34 C3 Caherlistrane Galway
2 F6 Cahermore Cork
25 P3 Cahermore Galway
4 C3 Cahermuckee Cork
17 K1 Cahermurphy Clare
24 G9 Caherogan Clare
34 F5 Caherphuca Clare
25 J7 Cahersherkin Clare
8 F9 Cahersiveen/Cathair Saidhbhín Kerry
13 J2 Cahir/An Chathair Tippry
13 J2 Cahir Castle Tippry
22 G8 Caim Wexfd
43 N5 Caldragh Cross Roads Roscom
55 L4 Caledon Tyrone
21 L8 Callan/Callainn Kilken
42 C3 Callow Mayo
43 L4 Callow Roscom
35 L5 Caltra Galway
35 M7 Caltraghlea Galway
30 E4 Calverstown Kildre
33 K6 Camas/Camus Galway
56 B8 Camlough Armagh
23 K6 Camolin/Cam Eolaing Wexfd
9 K3 Camp Kerry
14 G5 Campile/Ceann Poill Wexfd
28 G6 Camross/Camros Laois
33 K6 Camus/Camas Galway
45 Q3 Canningstown Cavan
4 E2 Caolmhagh/Kealvaugh Cork
68 B5 Cape Castle Antrim
4 C2 Cappaboy Beg Cork
12 C7 Cappagh Cork
18 D5 Cappagh Limrck
61 L9 Cappagh Tyrone
25 M3 Cappaghmore Galway
19 P5 Cappagh White /An Cheapach Tippry
28 F2 Cappagowlan Offaly
28 F9 Cappalinnan Laois
19 M4 Cappamore/An Cheapach Mhór Limrck
35 L8 Cappataggle Galway
4 H2 Cappeen Cork
13 K7 Cappoquin/Ceapach Choinn Watfd
9 K6 Caragh Bridge Kerry
43 M8 Caran Roscom
38 B7 Carbury Kildre
10 D4 Carker Kerry
61 N9 Carland Tyrone
46 D8 Carlanstown/Droichead Chearbhalláin Meath
47 M1 Carlingford/Cairlinn Louth
30 C9 Carlow/Ceatharlach Carlow
61 M1 Carn Lderry
36 H4 Carn Wmeath
48 E4 Carn/An Carn Mayo
32 F7 Carna/Carna Galway
62 H1 Carnalbanagh Sheddings Antrim
61 J2 Carnanreagh Lderry

46 B8 Carnaross/Carn na Ros Meath
63 K1 Carncastle Antrim
66 D3 Carndonagh/Carn Domhnach Donegl
23 J4 Carnew/Carn an Bhua Wicklw
52 C5 Carney Sligo
27 L6 Carney Tippry
68 F9 Carnlough Antrim
63 J6 Carnmoney Antrim
34 D8 Carnmore/An Carn Mór Galway
34 E6 Carnoneen Galway
55 J3 Carnteel Tyrone
42 G3 Carracastle Mayo
38 E9 Carragh Kildre
43 J8 Carragh Roscom
41 K6 Carraholly Mayo
65 L5 Carraig Airt/Carrickart Donegl
25 L5 Carran Clare
21 P6 Carran Kilken
33 J9 Carraroe/An Cheathrú Rua Galway
9 N8 Carrauntoohil Kerry
15 K6 Carrick Wexfd
58 C7 Carrick/An Charraí Donegl
45 L4 Carrickaboy Cavan
68 B4 Carrick-a-Rede Rope Bridge NT Antrim
65 L5 Carrickart/Carraig Airt Donegl
46 E4 Carrickashedoge Monhan
36 G1 Carrickboy/An Charraig Bhuí Longfd
63 L5 Carrickfergus Antrim
46 E3 Carrickmacross/Carraig Mhachaire Rois Monhan
39 N9 Carrickmines Dublin
61 K8 Carrickmore or Termon Rock Tyrone
43 Q4 Carrick-on-Shannon/Cora Droma Rúisc Leitrm
13 R2 Carrick-on-Suir/Carraig na Siúire Tippry
54 H4 Carrickroe Monhan
27 P4 Carrig Tippry
30 H2 Carrig Wicklw
9 J2 Carrigaday Kerry
11 L10 Carrigadrohid Cork
11 K8 Carrigagulla Cork
16 E4 Carrigaholt/Carrig an Chabhaltaigh Clare
27 M4 Carrigahorig Tippry
6 B7 Carrigaline/Carraig Uí Leighin Cork
44 G3 Carrigallen/Carraig Álainn Leitrm
45 K5 Carrigan Cavan
10 H8 Carriganimmy Cork
12 F3 Carriganroe Tippry
66 B10 Carrigans/An Carraigín Donegl
27 K9 Carrigatogher Tippry
4 E6 Carrigbaun Cross Roads Cork
31 N3 Carriggeeny Cork
17 N7 Carrigkerry Limrck
17 R8 Carrignavar Cork
6 D5 Carrigtohill/Carrig Thuathail Cork
14 B7 Carroll's Cross Roads Watfd
20 B7 Carrow Tippry
63 P8 Carrowdore Down
24 G6 Carrowduff Clare
43 M9 Carrowduff Roscom
51 M6 Carroweden Sligo
26 G2 Carrowkeel Galway
33 Q1 Carrowkeel Mayo
65 N6 Carrowkeel/An Cheathrú Chaol Donegl
34 G1 Carrowkeelanahglass Galway
41 K9 Carrowkennedy Mayo
66 F3 Carrowmenagh Donegl
34 D10 Carrowmore Galway
34 C1 Carrowmore Mayo
42 C9 Carrowmore Mayo
50 E4 Carrowmore Mayo
51 M7 Carrowmore Sligo
33 Q5 Carrowmoreknock Galway
52 C7 Carrowmore Megalithic Cemetery Sligo
41 P8 Carrownacon Mayo
50 H3 Carrowpadeen Sligo
35 P6 Carrowreagh Roscom
36 C2 Carrowrory Longfd
48 H2 Carrowteige/Ceathrú Thaidhg Mayo
53 Q6 Carry Bridge Ferman
63 K9 Carryduff Down
26 E1 Cartron Galway
22 D6 Cashel Carlow
29 L6 Cashel Laois
32 G5 Cashel/An Caiseal Galway
40 E3 Cashel/An Caiseal Mayo
20 D8 Cashel/Caiseal Tippry
52 C4 Cashelgarran Sligo
65 M4 Cashel Glebe/An Caiseal Donegl
34 E8 Cashla Galway
32 D1 Cashleen Galway
33 K8 Casla/Costelloe Galway
14 H4 Cassagh Wexfd
43 M1 Castlebaldwin/Béal Átha na gCarraigíní Sligo
41 N5 Castlebar/Caislean an Bharraigh Mayo
47 K4 Castlebellingham/Baile an Ghearlánaigh Louth
12 B7 Castleblagh Cork
35 K5 Castleblakeney Galway

55 M10 Castleblaney/Baile na Lorgan Monhan
15 P3 Castlebridge/Droichead an Chaisleáin Wexfd
67 P5 Castlecat Antrim
61 N10 Castlecaulfield Tyrone
21 N2 Castlecomer/Caisleán an Chomair Kilken
19 K2 Castleconnell/Caisleán Uí Chonnaill Limrck
50 G6 Castleconor Sligo
35 N1 Castlecoote Roscom
11 M3 Castlecor Cork
2 F2 Castle Cove Kerry
28 G2 Castlecuffe Cross Roads Laois
22 A4 Castledawson Lderry
60 C6 Castlederg Tyrone
30 D7 Castledermot/Díseart Diarmada Kildre
22 G7 Castledockerell Wexfd
60 C3 Castlefinn/Caisleán na Finne Donegl
4 H7 Castlefreke Cork
52 D2 Castlegal Sligo
9 J2 Castlegregory/Caisleán Ghriaire Kerry
40 G2 Castlehill Mayo
50 D8 Castlehill Mayo
10 C3 Castleisland/Oileán Ciarraí Kerry
37 P6 Castlejordan Meath
39 K6 Castleknock Dublin
20 E2 Castleleiny Tippry
23 K9 Castlellis Wexfd
12 D8 Castlelyons/Caisleán Ó Liatháin Cork
9 N4 Castlemaine/Caisleán na Mainge Kerry
6 G5 Castlemartyr/Baile na Martra Cork
43 M8 Castleplunket Roscom
45 M9 Castlepollard/Baile na gCros Wmeath
34 C6 Castlequarter/Ceathrú an Chaisleáin Galway
45 N6 Castlerahan Cavan
43 K7 Castlerea/An Caisleán Riabhach Roscom
67 K5 Castlerock Lderry
55 K7 Castleshane Monhan
25 L5 Castletown Clare
4 H3 Castletown Cork
18 E8 Castletown Limrck
46 E7 Castletown Meath
23 N4 Castletown Wexfd
45 L8 Castletown Wmeath
28 H6 Castletown/Baile an Chaisleáin Laois
2 H5 Castletown Bearhaven/Baile Chaisleáin Bhéarra Cork
37 J5 Castletown Geoghegan Wmeath
38 H7 Castletown House Kildre
12 A6 Castletownroche/Baile Chaisleán an Róistigh Cork
4 E8 Castletownshend/Baile an Chaisleáin Cork
21 Q4 Castlewarren Kilken
56 H6 Castlewellan Down
2 F3 Cathair Dónall/Caherdaniel Kerry
16 E8 Causeway/An Tóchar Kerry
45 L2 Cavan/An Cabhán Cavan
55 J8 Cavanagarvan Monhan
59 K10 Cavangarden Donegl
4 D5 Ceancullig Cork
8 D4 Ceann Trá/Ventry Kerry
34 C6 Ceathrú an Chaisleáin/Castlequarter Galway
48 H2 Ceathrú Thaidhg/Carrowteige Mayo
8 G2 Cé Bhréanainn/Brandon Kerry
11 M4 Cecilstown Cork
49 M2 Ceide Fields Mayo
38 H7 Celbridge/Cill Droichid Kildre
46 H3 Chanonrock Louth
57 N6 Chapeltown Down
8 D9 Chapeltown Kerry
22 H10 Chapel Village Wexfd
55 N2 Charlemont Armagh
42 F3 Charlestown/Baile Chathail Mayo
18 G10 Charleville/An Ráth Cork
14 F6 Cheekpoint Watfd
30 B2 Cherryville Kildre
62 C3 Chesney's Corner Antrim
6 D7 Church Bay Cork
35 Q2 Churchboro Cross Roscom
4 C8 Church Cross Cork
41 M10 Churchfield/Páirc an Teampaill Mayo
9 M1 Church Hill Kerry
65 K9 Church Hill/Mín an Lábáin Donegl
43 L5 Churchstreet Roscom
6 F7 Churchtown Cork
65 Q10 Church Town Donegl
14 D7 Churchtown Watfd
15 Q7 Churchtown Wexfd
11 N2 Churchtown/Baile an Teampaill Cork
38 D1 Cill Bhríde/Kilbride Meath
33 J6 Cill Bhriocáin/Kilbrickan Galway
58 D7 Cill Charthaigh/Kilcar Donegl
32 G7 Cill Chiaráin/Kilkieran Galway
7 M3 Cill Cholmáin/Kilcolman Watfd

8 E3 Cill Chuáin/Kilquane Kerry
24 C3 Cill Éinne/Killeany Galway
8 H10 Cillín Liath/Killeenleagh Kerry
24 B2 Cill Mhuirbhigh/Kilmurvy Galway
10 H10 Cill na Martra/Killnamartery Cork
8 E10 Cill Ó Luaigh/Killoluaig Kerry
24 C3 Cill Rónáin/Kilronan Galway
8 D4 Cill Ura/Kildurrihy Kerry
2 C1 Cill Urlaí/Killurly Kerry
33 K7 Cinn Mhara/Kinvarra Galway
64 C9 Cionn Caslach/Kincaslough Donegl
66 E8 City of Derry Lderry
54 D3 Clabby Ferman
32 B2 Claddaghduff Galway
62 B2 Clady Lderry
60 C4 Clady Tyrone
55 Q6 Cladymilltown Armagh
40 F3 Claggan Mayo
10 F3 Clamper Bridge Cork
58 F8 Clane/Claonadh Kildre
36 H7 Clara/Clóirtheach Offaly
29 J2 Clarahill Laois
56 B5 Clare Armagh
25 M10 Clarecastle/Droichead an Chláir Clare
28 D4 Clareen Offaly
18 C1 Clareen Bridge Clare
34 D7 Claregalway/Baile Chláir Galway
42 C9 Claremorris/Clár Chlainne Mhuiris Mayo
18 G4 Clarina Limrck
34 E9 Clarinbridge/Droichead an Chláirín Galway
37 K2 Clark's Cross Roads Wmeath
27 N8 Clash Tippry
19 M7 Clashdrumsmith Tippry
7 K3 Clashmore/Clais Mhór Watfd
17 M8 Clash North Limrck
14 B5 Clashroe Watfd
17 M8 Clash South Limrck
60 H1 Claudy Lderry
24 C2 Cleggan/An Cloigeann Galway
18 D2 Clenagh Clare
15 M6 Cleristown Wexfd
43 K6 Clerragh Roscom
32 D3 Clifden/An Clochán Galway
45 N3 Clifferna Cavan
52 D3 Cliffony/Cliafuine Sligo
24 F6 Cliffs of Moher Clare
37 P4 Clocrave Wmeath
61 K9 Clogfin Tyrone
14 C5 Clogga Kilken
23 P3 Clogga Wicklw
68 B10 Clogh Antrim
28 H8 Clogh Laois
23 L5 Clogh Wexfd
29 N9 Clogh/An Chloch Kilken
37 N2 Cloghan Wmeath
59 M3 Cloghan/An Clochan Donegl
36 D10 Cloghan/An Clochán Offaly
3 J10 Cloghane Cork
8 G2 Cloghane/An Clochán Kerry
34 C1 Cloghans Hill Mayo
38 B6 Clogharinka Kildre
21 P3 Clogharinka Kilken
17 K1 Cloghaun Clare
34 D6 Cloghaun Galway
26 E8 Cloghaun Bridge Clare
51 P2 Cloghboley Sligo
17 J10 Cloghboola Kerry
33 L2 Cloghbrack/An Chloc Bhreac Galway
38 B2 Cloghbrack Bridge Meath
60 E2 Cloghcor Tyrone
13 L4 Clogheen Watfd
12 H4 Clogheen/An Chloichin Tippry
41 L6 Clogher Mayo
41 P8 Clogher Mayo
44 B5 Clogher Roscom
54 F3 Clogher Tyrone
48 D6 Clogher/An Clochar Mayo
18 H1 Cloghera Clare
47 M7 Clogherhead/Ceann Chlochair Louth
68 B9 Clogh Mills Antrim
40 E5 Cloghmore/An Chloich Mhór Mayo
21 P3 Cloghpook Kilken
39 M5 Cloghran Dublin
11 P10 Cloghroe Cork
10 F2 Cloghvoula Cork
18 D6 Clogh West Limrck
57 P2 Cloghy Down
22 G6 Clohamon/Cloch Ámainn Wexfd
14 D3 Clohernagh Watfd
23 M5 Clologe Wexfd
28 D8 Clonakenny Tippry
5 J6 Clonakilty/Cloich na Coillte Cork
39 K1 Clonalvy Wmeath
7 J5 Clonard Cork
38 B4 Clonard Meath
15 N4 Clonard Wexfd
37 P9 Clonaslee/Cluain na Slí Laois
37 P9 Clonavoe Offaly
34 H2 Clonbern Galway
37 Q9 Clonbulloge/Cluain Bolg Offaly

33 M2 Clonbur/An Fhairche Galway
37 P9 Cloncreen Offaly
36 F3 Cloncullen Wmeath
28 F6 Cloncully Laois
38 E5 Clancurry Kildre
39 K7 Clondalkin Dublin
10 H9 Clondrohid Cork
12 E7 Clondulane Cork
13 Q4 Clonea Watfd
39 J5 Clonee Meath
37 L7 Cloneen Offaly
20 H9 Cloneen Tippry
22 G4 Clonegall/Cluain na nGall Carlow
59 P9 Clonelly Ferman
54 F8 Clones/Cluain Eois Monhan
23 M7 Clonevin Cross Roads Wexfd
36 B9 Clonfert/Cluain Fearta Galway
36 B10 Clonfert Cross Roads Galway
15 J5 Clongeen Wexfd
28 H6 Clonincurragh Laois
10 D8 Clonkeen Kerry
29 K5 Clonkeen Laois
35 J6 Clonkeenkerrill Galway
37 Q1 Clonleame Cross Roads Wmeath
37 N2 Clonlost Wmeath
36 C7 Clonmacnoise/Cluain Mhic Nóis Offaly
21 K4 Clonmantagh Kilken
66 B3 Clonmany/Cluain Maine Donegl
20 G2 Clonmeen Laois
13 M2 Clonmel/Cluain Meala Tippry
45 Q10 Clonmellon Wmeath
30 H9 Clonmore Carlow
47 L6 Clonmore Louth
28 E9 Clonmore Tippry
6 F3 Clonmult Cork
36 D9 Clonony Offaly
20 C6 Clonoulty Tippry
22 F10 Clonroche/Cluain an Róistigh Wexfd
34 L3 Clonroe Cross Roads Wexfd
39 K6 Clonsilla Dublin
39 N6 Clontarf Dublin
55 L8 Clontibret Monhan
21 L3 Clontubbrid Kilken
38 B3 Clonycavan Meath
29 L1 Clonygowan/Cluain na nGamhan Offaly
29 L2 Clonyquin Offaly
34 C7 Cloonacauneen/Cluain Mhic Cáinín Galway
51 L7 Cloonacool Sligo
45 J6 Cloonagh Longfd
34 C6 Cloonboo/Cluain Bú Galway
36 B1 Clooncah Roscom
41 M4 Cloondaff Mayo
44 D8 Cloondara Longfd
44 E4 Cloone/An Chluain Leitrm
44 D6 Clooneagh Leitrm
45 J6 Clooneen Longfd
58 F3 Clooney Roscom
35 Q8 Cloonfad Roscom
42 G9 Cloonfad Roscom
43 K5 Cloonfad Cross Roads Roscom
42 D6 Cloonfallagh Mayo
25 L9 Cloonfeagh Clare
42 E3 Cloonfinish Mayo
43 J7 Cloonfower Roscom
50 J6 Cloonkeelaun Sligo
42 H10 Cloonkeen Galway
41 N6 Cloonkeen Mayo
43 J8 Cloonkeen Roscom
51 P7 Cloonkeevy Sligo
19 J2 Cloonlara/Cluain Lára Clare
42 D7 Cloonlee Mayo
19 N5 Cloonlusk Limrck
42 G3 Cloonmore Cross Roads Mayo
43 P8 Cloonmurray Roscom
34 H1 Cloonnacat Galway
8 G2 Cloonsharragh/Cluain Searrach Kerry
43 K6 Cloonsheever Roscom
42 H3 Cloontia Mayo
26 F7 Cloonusker Clare
35 K8 Cloonymorris Galway
43 P8 Cloonyogan Roscom
43 N7 Cloonyquin Roscom
46 B10 Cloran Cross Roads Wmeath
57 K5 Clough Down
5 L1 Cloughduv Cork
27 N7 Cloughjordan/Cloch Shiurdáin Tippry
18 D8 Clouncagh Limrck
45 L1 Cloverhill Cavan
6 F6 Cloyne/Cluain Cork
34 C6 Cluain Bú/Cloonboo Galway
34 C7 Cluain Mhic Cáinín/Cloonacauneen Galway
8 G2 Cluain Searrach/Cloonsharragh Kerry
4 G5 Clubhouse Cross Roads Cork
17 L10 Clydagh Bridge Kerry
8 E4 Cnoc an Bhróigín/Knockavrogeen Kerry
48 G3 Cnocán na Líne/Knocknalina Mayo
48 G3 Cnoc na Lobhar/Knocknalower Mayo
9 J9 Cnocrua/Knockroe Kerry
11 M10 Coachford/Áth an Choiste Cork
61 Q7 Coagh Tyrone

20 H6 **Coalbrook** Tippry
61 P9 **Coalisland** Tyrone
21 P2 **Coan** Kilken
6 C6 **Cobh/An Cóbh** Cork
33 L1 **Coill an tSiáin/Killateeaun** Mayo
32 H7 **Coill Sáile/Kylesalia** Galway
34 C8 **Coill Uachtar/Kilroghter** Galway
30 E5 **Colbinstown** Wicklw
36 G1 **Colehill** Longfd
67 L6 **Coleraine** Lderry
15 N4 **Colestown** Wexfd
13 M7 **Colligan Bridge** Watfd
45 N10 **Collinstown/Baile na gCailleach** Wmeath
46 H7 **Collon/Collann** Louth
52 C8 **Collooney/Cúil Mhuine** Sligo
3 J3 **Collorus** Kerry
20 F10 **Colman** Tippry
34 H6 **Colmanstown** Galway
47 L9 **Colp** Meath
63 M9 **Comber** Down
19 Q1 **Commaun More** Tippry
59 M3 **Commeen/An Coimín** Donegl
58 F5 **Common Bridge** Donegl
5 K2 **Commons** Cork
21 J6 **Commons** Tippry
33 N2 **Cong/Conga** Mayo
63 N7 **Conlig** Down
12 F8 **Conna** Cork
25 K9 **Connolly/Fíoch Rua** Clare
4 F7 **Connonagh** Cork
62 F3 **Conner** Antrim
67 P7 **Conogher Cross Roads** Cork
60 B2 **Convoy/Conmhaigh** Donegl
61 P7 **Cookstown** Tyrone
12 H6 **Cool** Watfd
52 E9 **Coola Cross Roads** Sligo
37 N9 **Coolagary** Offaly
51 P5 **Coolaney/Cúil Áine** Sligo
13 K7 **Coolanheen** Watfd
23 J3 **Coolattin** Wicklw
21 P2 **Coolbaun** Kilken
27 K6 **Coolbaun** Tippry
20 G8 **Coolbaun Cross Roads** Tippry
65 M9 **Coolboy** Donegl
12 D3 **Coolboy** Limrck
23 J3 **Coolboy** Wicklw
28 D5 **Coolderry** Offaly
45 L9 **Coole** Wmeath
12 B8 **Coolea** Cork
10 F9 **Coolea/Cúil Aodha** Cork
12 E7 **Coole Abbey** Cork
21 P5 **Coolgrange** Kilken
23 M3 **Coolgreany/Cúil Ghréine** Wexfd
6 B3 **Coolgreen** Cork
12 B7 **Coolinny** Cork
E4 **Coolkellure** Cork
53 J8 **Coollegreane** Leitrm
17 M3 **Coolmeen** Clare
59 J9 **Coolmore** Donegl
42 G8 **Coolnafarna** Mayo
45 K9 **Coolnagun** Wmeath
39 M6 **Coolock** Dublin
28 G6 **Coolrain** Laois
23 M8 **Coolroe** Wexfd
27 N2 **Coolross** Tippry
6 B7 **Coolsallagh** Cork
44 B10 **Coolshaghtena** Roscom
43 P10 **Coolteige Cross** Roscom
8 G8 **Coomduff** Kerry
3 P3 **Coomhola Bridge** Cork
4 D4 **Coomleagh** Cork
18 G3 **Coonagh** Limrck
54 E5 **Cooneen** Ferman
43 L3 **Coonloogh** Sligo
17 J2 **Cooraclare/Cuar an Chláir** Clare
21 Q4 **Coorleagh** Kilken
3 P7 **Coosane** Cork
43 P3 **Cootehall** Roscom
45 Q1 **Cootehill/Muinchille** Cavan
11 N4 **Copsetown Cross Roads** Cork
34 C6 **Cor an Dola/Corrandula** Galway
16 F2 **Corbally** Clare
50 H5 **Corbally** Sligo
30 E2 **Corbally Cross Roads** Kildre
44 G9 **Corboy** Longfd
48 E3 **Corclogh/Corrchloch** Mayo
46 G3 **Corcreeghagh** Louth
49 M8 **Corcullin** Mayo
10 D3 **Cordal** Kerry
41 L8 **Cordarragh** Mayo
38 D8 **Corduff** Kildre
5 Q1 **Cork** Cork
6 A5 **Cork/Corcaigh** Cork
68 B8 **Corkey** Antrim
36 D1 **Corlea** Longfd
26 F5 **Corlea Bridge** Clare
50 H9 **Corlee** Mayo
53 N10 **Cornafulla** Roscom
36 B6 **Cornafulla** Roscom
33 L3 **Cornamona/Corr na Móna** Galway
41 Q9 **Cornanagh** Mayo
37 K8 **Corndarragh** Offaly
26 F6 **Corrakyle** Clare
55 P6 **Corran Cross Roads** Armagh
34 C6 **Corrandulla/Cor an Dola** Galway
40 E5 **Corraun/An Corrán** Mayo
48 E3 **Corrchloch/Corclogh** Mayo
62 F1 **Correen** Antrim
37 P4 **Correllstown** Wmeath

36 E8 **Corr Hill** Offaly
22 C5 **Corries Cross** Carlow
33 L3 **Corr na Móna/Cornamona** Galway
34 E5 **Corrofin** Galway
25 L7 **Corrofin/Cora Finne** Clare
53 J9 **Corry** Leitrm
21 L5 **Corstown Cross Roads** Kilken
46 D9 **Cortown** Meath
49 N5 **Corvoley** Mayo
33 K8 **Costelloe/Casla** Galway
8 H4 **Coumduff** Kerry
12 F6 **Countygate** Watfd
15 J3 **Courthoyle** Wexfd
5 M6 **Courtmacsherry/Cúirt Mhic Shéafraidh** Cork
18 C6 **Courtmatrix** Limrck
23 M5 **Courtown/Baile na Cúirte** Wexfd
4 D3 **Cousane** Cork
23 K4 **Craan** Wexfd
23 K5 **Cranford** Wexfd
24 H3 **Craggagh** Clare
26 D8 **Cragroe** Clare
60 H3 **Craig** Tyrone
67 M10 **Craigavole** Lderry
56 C2 **Craigavon** Armagh
62 C1 **Craigs** Antrim
62 C1 **Craigs Cross** Antrim
61 J4 **Cranagh** Tyrone
23 J8 **Crane** Wexfd
65 M6 **Cranford** Donegl
17 M2 **Cranny** Clare
61 P5 **Cranny** Lderry
18 F2 **Cratloe** Clare
34 G9 **Craughwell/Creachmhaoil** Galway
63 M6 **Crawfordsburn** Down
37 M2 **Crazy Corner** Wmeath
4 C8 **Creagh** Cork
55 M8 **Creaghanroe** Monhan
11 M8 **Crean's Cross Roads** Cork
18 G5 **Crecora** Limrck
17 J1 **Creegh** Clare
35 M1 **Creegs** Galway
65 K6 **Creeslough/An Craoslach** Donegl
50 D4 **Creevagh** Mayo
18 C5 **Creeves** Limrck
25 J3 **Cregg** Clare
4 G8 **Cregg** Cork
55 P10 **Creggan** Armagh
36 D8 **Creggan** Offaly
61 K7 **Creggan** Tyrone
40 G9 **Cregganbaun** Mayo
29 N9 **Crettyard** Laois
66 H7 **Crindle** Lderry
28 C4 **Crinkill** Offaly
58 G6 **Croagh** Donegl
18 E6 **Croagh** Limrck
40 B2 **Croaghaun** Mayo
50 G6 **Crockets Town** Mayo
37 M7 **Croghan** Offaly
43 P4 **Croghan** Roscom
64 E8 **Croithlí/Crolly** Donegl
64 E8 **Crolly/Croithlí** Donegl
9 L5 **Cromane** Kerry
53 M10 **Cromlin** Leitrm
29 J6 **Cromoge Cross Roads** Laois
16 F8 **Crompaun Bridge** Kerry
37 M1 **Crookedwood** Wmeath
3 L9 **Crookhaven/An Cruachán** Cork
K1 **Crookstown** Cork
30 E5 **Crookstown** Kildre
18 G6 **Croom/Cromadh** Limrck
16 D4 **Cross** Clare
7 K2 **Cross** Watfd
33 P2 **Cross/An Chrois** Mayo
15 N3 **Crossabeg** Wexfd
45 Q9 **Crossakeel/Crosa Caoil** Meath
5 N2 **Cross Barry** Cork
29 N3 **Crossboyne** Mayo
35 N9 **Crossconnell** Galway
45 K3 **Crossdoney/Cros Domhnaigh** Cavan
44 G10 **Crossea** Longfd
45 M5 **Crosserlough** Cavan
57 L3 **Crossgar** Down
67 L7 **Crossgare** Lderry
6 C7 **Crosshaven/Bun an Tábhairne** Cork
45 M4 **Cross Keys** Cavan
29 Q3 **Crosskeys** Kildre
45 P9 **Cross Keys** Meath
55 P10 **Crossmaglen** Armagh
5 L4 **Cross Mahon** Cork
50 D7 **Crossmolina/Crois Mhaoilíona** Mayo
43 P2 **Crossna** Roscom
25 N2 **Crossooha** Galway
24 H3 **Crosspatrick** Kilken
23 K3 **Crosspatrick** Wicklw
59 Q4 **Cross Roads** Donegl
6 G4 **Crowbally** Cork
62 F7 **Crumlin** Antrim
2 H4 **Crumpane** Cork
25 N7 **Crusheen/Croisín** Clare
29 M4 **Crutt** Kilken
28 H8 **Cuffsborough Cross Roads** Laois
10 F9 **Cúil Aodha/Coolea** Cork
50 E9 **Cúil Killew** Mayo
56 F1 **Culcavy** Down
66 E3 **Culdaff/Cúil Dabhcha** Donegl
43 K2 **Culfadda** Sligo
66 E2 **Culkeeny** Donegl
21 K2 **Cullahill/An Chúlchoill** Laois
19 M10 **Cullane** Limrck
48 F1 **Cullaville** Armagh
51 J5 **Culleens** Sligo
10 G5 **Cullen** Cork
19 N7 **Cullen** Tippry

12 B4 **Cullenagh** Cork
15 K7 **Cullenstown** Wexfd
42 C2 **Cullin** Mayo
4 B6 **Cullomane Cross Roads** Cork
62 D1 **Cullybackey** Antrim
55 P9 **Cullyhanna** Armagh
66 D8 **Culmore** Lderry
38 G4 **Culmullin Cross Roads** Meath
61 Q2 **Culnady** Lderry
12 F7 **Currabeha** Cork
15 P3 **Curracloe** Wexfd
5 J2 **Curraclogh** Cork
7 L4 **Curragh** Watfd
39 J2 **Curragha** Meath
4 F5 **Curraghalicky** Cork
35 Q4 **Curraghboy** Roscom
30 D2 **Curragh Camp** Kildre
23 K2 **Curraghlawn** Wicklw
21 Q10 **Curraghmore** Kilken
27 J10 **Curraghmore** Tippry
44 B8 **Curraghroe** Roscom
42 H10 **Curragh West** Galway
12 G8 **Curraglass** Cork
28 D8 **Curragunneen** Tippry
61 Q3 **Curran** Lderry
9 Q3 **Currans** Kerry
19 Q2 **Curreeny** Tippry
10 B4 **Currow** Kerry
42 F2 **Curry** Sligo
68 E7 **Cushendall** Antrim
68 F6 **Cushendun** Antrim
29 N1 **Cushina** Offaly

D

37 M8 **Daingean/An Daingean** Offaly
39 P8 **Dalkey/Deilginis** Dublin
13 N6 **Dalligan Bridge** Watfd
37 L5 **Dalystown** Wmeath
39 L2 **Damastown** Dublin
67 M7 **Damhead** Lderry
21 N7 **Danesfort** Kilken
6 G3 **Dangan** Cork
20 C9 **Dangandargan** Tippry
22 H9 **Darby's Gap** Wexfd
55 N7 **Darkley** Armagh
54 H10 **Dartry** Monhan
22 H3 **Davidstown** Wexfd
49 M7 **Deel Bridge** Mayo
31 P2 **Delgany/Deilgne** Wicklw
40 G10 **Delphi** Mayo
37 Q1 **Delvin/Dealbhna** Wmeath
10 H5 **Dernagree** Cork
53 M10 **Derradda** Leitrm
25 L10 **Derragh** Clare
36 D1 **Derraghan Cross Roads** Longfd
24 F7 **Derreen** Clare
8 F10 **Derreen** Kerry
41 M2 **Derreen** Mayo
40 E4 **Derreen/An Doirín** Mayo
3 M4 **Derreenacarrin** Cork
4 B7 **Derreenard** Cork
2 G2 **Derreenauliff** Kerry
3 K5 **Derreeny** Cork
36 H8 **Derries** Offaly
38 B8 **Derries** Offaly
36 B7 **Derrineel** Roscom
43 Q1 **Derrinisky** Roscom
38 C7 **Derrinturn** Kildre
66 C9 **Derry** Lderry
56 B1 **Derryadd** Armagh
64 E7 **Derrybeg/Doirí Beaga** Donegl
57 L2 **Derryboy** Down
26 E4 **Derrybrien** Galway
66 C9 **Derry City Walls** Lderry
4 E6 **Derryclogh** Cork
28 H4 **Derrycon** Cork
36 G9 **Derrycooly** Offaly
28 F1 **Derrydolney** Offaly
20 G3 **Derryfadda** Tippry
10 F10 **Derryfineen/Doire Fhinín** Cork
29 L3 **Derrygile** Laois
37 K7 **Derrygolan** Wmeath
54 M3 **Derrygonnelly** Ferman
36 D1 **Derrygowna** Longfd
13 K2 **Derrygrath** Tippry
37 L8 **Derrygrogan** Offaly
67 P6 **Derrykeighan** Antrim
36 B7 **Derrylahan** Roscom
53 Q8 **Derrylin** Ferman
56 B1 **Derrymacash** Armagh
9 L2 **Derrymore** Kerry
4 E3 **Derrynacaheragh** Cork
32 H6 **Derryrush/Doire Iorrais** Galway
32 H3 **Derryvoreada/Doire Bhó Riada** Galway
43 J9 **Derrywode** Galway
67 P6 **Dervock** Antrim
6 D2 **Desert** Cork
61 Q4 **Desertmartin** Lderry
53 P4 **Devenish** Ferman
8 E4 **Dingle/An Daingean** Kerry
16 H5 **Doagh** Antrim
65 N4 **Doagh Beg/Dumhaigh Bhig** Donegl
32 H3 **Doire Bhó Riada/Derryvoreada** Galway
10 F10 **Doire Fhinín/Derryfineen** Cork
32 H6 **Doire Iorrais/Derryrush** Galway
64 E7 **Doirí Beaga/Derrybeg** Donegl
27 L10 **Dolla** Tippry
56 D2 **Dollardstown** Down
39 N6 **Dollymount** Dublin
46 E9 **Domhnach Phádraig/Donaghpatrick** Meath

39 N4 **Donabate/Domhnach Bat** Dublin
47 L9 **Donacarney** Meath
38 E7 **Donadea** Kildre
54 C8 **Donagh** Ferman
63 P7 **Donaghadee** Down
56 D3 **Donaghcloney** Down
28 G8 **Donaghmore** Laois
39 K3 **Donaghmore** Meath
61 N9 **Donaghmore** Tyrone
46 E9 **Donaghpatrick/Domhnach Phádraig** Meath
22 E10 **Donard** Wexfd
30 G5 **Donard/Dún Ard** Wicklw
20 B8 **Donaskeagh** Tippry
64 D8 **Donegal** Donegl
59 K7 **Donegal/Dún na nGall** Donegl
59 K7 **Donegal Castle** Donegl
11 P3 **Doneraile/Dún ar Aill** Cork
19 Q6 **Donohill** Tippry
38 C3 **Donore** Meath
47 J9 **Donore** Meath
11 M8 **Donoughmore** Cork
40 C3 **Dooagh/Dumha Acha** Mayo
49 N6 **Doobehy** Mayo
45 N1 **Doocarrick** Cavan
51 N9 **Doocastle** Sligo
59 J1 **Doocharry/An Dúchoraidh** Donegl
40 D4 **Dooega/Dumha Éige** Mayo
44 G2 **Doogary** Cavan
60 G9 **Doogary** Mayo
40 G5 **Dooghbeg/An Dumhach Bheag** Mayo
48 E9 **Doogort/Dumha Goirt** Mayo
55 L9 **Doohamlat** Monhan
54 G9 **Doohat** Monhan
48 F7 **Doohooma/Dumha Thuama** Mayo
49 M7 **Dooleeg** Mayo
24 G5 **Doolin/Dúlainn** Clare
35 M6 **Doon** Galway
12 G5 **Doon** Tippry
19 N4 **Doon/Dún** Limrck
48 G8 **Doona** Mayo
16 F4 **Doonaha** Clare
16 H1 **Doonbeg** Clare
36 E7 **Doon Cross Roads** Offaly
8 G5 **Doonmanagh/An Dún Meánach** Kerry
32 F5 **Doonreaghan** Galway
14 C6 **Doornane** Kilken
48 F7 **Dooyork/Dumha Dhearc** Mayo
3 K9 **Dough** Meath
34 C8 **Doughiska** Galway
6 B6 **Douglas/Dúglas** Cork
60 E5 **Douglas Bridge** Tyrone
20 D4 **Dovea** Tippry
14 B4 **Dowling** Kilken
67 J5 **Downhill** Lderry
65 L5 **Downies/Na Dúnaibh** Donegl
12 D6 **Downing** Cork
57 L5 **Downpatrick** Down
53 J8 **Dowra/An Damhshraith** Cavan
47 J9 **Dowth** Meath
36 G5 **Doyle's Bridge** Roscom
20 H8 **Drangan/Drongán** Tippry
61 N4 **Draperstown** Lderry
61 K2 **Dreen** Lderry
16 C8 **Dreenagh** Kerry
9 M1 **Drehidasillagh** Kerry
4 E6 **Driminidy** Cork
28 H5 **Drimmo** Laois
4 D5 **Drimoleague/Drom Dhá Liag** Cork
4 F6 **Drinagh** Cork
32 C4 **Drinagh** Galway
44 C8 **Drinagh** Roscom
15 P5 **Drinagh** Wexfd
50 H4 **Drinaghan** Sligo
44 H6 **Dring** Longfd
11 M10 **Dripsey** Cork
3 N7 **Drishane Bridge** Cork
47 K9 **Drogheda/Droichead Átha** Louth
49 J4 **Droichead Bhéal an Átha Buí/Bellanaboy Bridge** Mayo
9 K8 **Droichead Drom an Long Foirt/Dromlonhurt Bridge** Kerry
9 J9 **Droichead Lios an tSonnaigh/Lissatinnig Bridge** Kerry
20 D3 **Drom** Tippry
8 G2 **Drom/An Drom** Kerry
11 J5 **Dromagh** Cork
52 F7 **Dromahair/Droim Dhá Thiar** Leitrm
9 K8 **Dromalonhurt Bridge/Droichead Drom an Long Foirt** Kerry
56 G4 **Dromara** Down
8 G10 **Dromaragh/Drom Oireach** Kerry
11 Q8 **Dromboy South** Cork
18 D10 **Dromcolliher/Drom Collachair** Limrck
16 E10 **Dromcunnig** Kerry
11 Q8 **Dromgarriff** Cork
19 J8 **Dromin** Limrck
47 J6 **Dromin** Louth
11 M1 **Dromina/Drom Aidhne** Cork
27 K7 **Dromineer** Tippry
44 K4 **Dromiskin** Louth
11 N6 **Drommahane** Cork
3 L7 **Dromnea** Cork

8 G10 **Drom Oireach/Dromaragh** Kerry
4 C5 **Dromore** Cork
56 F3 **Dromore** Down
60 E10 **Dromore** Tyrone
13 K8 **Dromore** Watfd
51 K4 **Dromore West** Sligo
11 J9 **Dromree Cross Roads** Cork
17 M10 **Dromtrasna** Limrck
36 B6 **Drum** Monhan
66 D9 **Drum** Roscom
55 N10 **Drumakill** Monhan
26 D6 **Drumandoora** Clare
57 J4 **Drumaness** Down
25 K9 **Drumanure** Clare
51 N4 **Drumard** Sligo
57 J5 **Drumaroad** Down
27 J1 **Drumatober** Galway
20 C5 **Drumbane** Tippry
19 M1 **Drumbaun** Tippry
63 J9 **Drumbeg** Down
63 J10 **Drumbo** Down
47 K5 **Drumcar** Louth
26 D8 **Drumcharley** Clare
25 M8 **Drumcliff** Clare
52 C5 **Drumcliff/Droim Chliabh** Sligo
46 F6 **Drumcondra/Droim Conrach** Meath
45 P10 **Drumcree** Wmeath
22 D5 **Drumfea** Carlow
52 D9 **Drumfin** Sligo
66 B5 **Drumfree** Donegl
34 C6 **Drumgriftin** Galway
59 L6 **Druminnin** Donegl
26 G3 **Drumkeary** Galway
59 Q2 **Drumkeen** Donegl
52 H9 **Drumkeeran/Droim Caorthainn** Leitrm
44 F2 **Drumlea** Leitrm
44 F6 **Drumlish/Droim Lis** Longfd
36 C7 **Drumlosh** Roscom
52 E9 **Drummacool** Sligo
24 G10 **Drummin** Clare
41 J9 **Drummin** Mayo
43 Q6 **Drummullin** Roscom
44 E3 **Drumna** Leitrm
60 H8 **Drumnakilly** Tyrone
44 D6 **Drumod/Drómad** Leitrm
60 C1 **Drumoghill** Donegl
45 P9 **Drumone** Meath
60 D8 **Drumquin** Tyrone
36 F4 **Drumraney** Wmeath
38 G3 **Drumree** Meath
13 J7 **Drumroe** Watfd
44 B1 **Drumshanbo/Droim Seanbhó** Leitrm
33 N2 **Drumsheel** Mayo
44 B4 **Drumsna/Droim ar Snámh** Leitrm
67 J9 **Drumsurn** Lderry
45 N1 **Drung** Cavan
17 K8 **Duagh/Dubháth** Kerry
20 E8 **Dually** Tippry
39 M5 **Dublin** Dublin
39 M7 **Dublin/Baile Átha Cliath** Dublin
38 B6 **Duffy's Cross Roads** Kildre
36 B6 **Duggarry** Roscom
47 J10 **Duleek/Damhliag** Meath
48 F7 **Dumha Dhearc/Dooyork** Mayo
40 D4 **Dumha Éige/Dooega** Mayo
65 N4 **Dumhaigh Bhig/Doagh Beg** Donegl
48 F7 **Dumha Thuama/Doohooma** Mayo
62 G6 **Dunadry** Antrim
65 Q3 **Dunaff** Donegl
35 M1 **Dunamon** Roscom
47 L5 **Dunany** Louth
21 J6 **Dunbell** Kilken
39 J5 **Dunboyne** Meath
38 D9 **Dunbyrne** Kildre
14 G7 **Duncannon/Dún Canann** Wexfd
8 C4 **Dún Chaoin/Dunquin** Kerry
15 L7 **Duncormick** Wexfd
47 K2 **Dundalk/Dún Dealgan** Louth
5 N4 **Dunderrow** Cork
38 E1 **Dunderry** Meath
55 J4 **Dundian** Monhan
63 L8 **Dundonald** Down
35 M7 **Dundoogan** Galway
62 G2 **Dundrod** Antrim
57 K6 **Dundrum** Down
39 M8 **Dundrum** Dublin
20 B7 **Dundrum/Dún Droma** Tippry
65 J5 **Dunfanaghy/Dún Fionnachaidh** Donegl
38 D6 **Dunfierth Cross Roads** Kildre
55 L1 **Dungannon** Tyrone
14 F4 **Dunganstown** Wexfd
21 Q7 **Dungarvan** Kilken
13 N8 **Dungarvan/Dún Garbhán** Watfd
61 L1 **Dungiven** Lderry
64 D10 **Dunglow/An Clochán Liath** Donegl
6 F4 **Dungourney** Cork
14 C8 **Dunhill** Watfd
26 H3 **Duniry** Galway
28 C8 **Dunkerrin** Offaly
58 G7 **Dunkineely/Dún Cionnaola** Donegl
14 D5 **Dunkitt** Kilken
39 N8 **Dún Laoghaire** Dublin
30 F4 **Dunlavin/Dún Luáin** Wicklw
47 K6 **Dunleer/Dún Léire** Louth

64 G9 **Dunlewy**/*Dún Lúiche* Donegl
67 Q9 **Dunloy** Antrim
67 N4 **Dunluce Castle** Antrim
64 G9 **Dún Lúiche**/*Dunlewy* Donegl
3 L8 **Dunmanus** Cork
4 F4 **Dunmanway**/*Dún Mánmhaí* Cork
12 H9 **Dunmoon** Watfd
34 G1 **Dunmore**/*Dún Mór* Galway
14 F8 **Dunmore East**/*Dún Mór* Watfd
62 H9 **Dunmurry** Antrim
21 M9 **Dunnamaggan** Kilken
60 F2 **Dunnamanagh** Tyrone
61 L6 **Dunmore** Tyrone
21 M5 **Dunningstown** Kilken
8 C4 **Dunquin**/*Dún Chaoin* Kerry
38 G2 **Dunsany Cross Roads** Meath
38 H3 **Dunshaughlin**/*Dún Seachlainn* Meath
29 K9 **Durrow**/*Darú* Laois
3 N6 **Durrus**/*Dúras* Cork
35 P4 **Dysart** Roscom
37 K4 **Dysart** Wmeath

E

34 C7 **Eadargúil**/*Addergoole* Galway
38 H10 **Eadestown** Kildre
34 B6 **Eanach Dhúin**/*Annaghdown* Galway
20 H6 **Earlshill** Tippry
51 J3 **Easky**/*Iascaigh* Sligo
53 J6 **East Barrs** Leitrm
64 F3 **East Town**/*An Baile Thoir* Donegl
63 L5 **Eden** Antrim
37 Q7 **Edenderry**/*Eadan Doire* Offaly
60 B10 **Ederney** Ferman
44 H9 **Edgeworthstown**/*Meathas Troim* Longfd
66 E8 **Eglinton** Lderry
55 L2 **Eglish** Tyrone
45 P6 **Eighter** Cavan
43 P6 **Elphin**/*Ail Finn* Roscom
19 K8 **Elton** Limrck
26 D1 **Emlagh Cross Roads** Galway
8 F10 **Emlaghmore**/*An tImleach Mór* Kerry
19 M8 **Emly**/*Imleach* Tippry
43 Q10 **Emmoo** Roscom
29 M3 **Emo**/*Íoma* Laois
55 J5 **Emyvale**/*Scairb na gCaorach* Monhan
38 D5 **Enfield**/*An Bóthar Buí* Meath
25 M9 **Ennis**/*Inis* Clare
22 H9 **Enniscorthy**/*Inis Córthaidh* Wexfd
5 J4 **Enniskean**/*Inis Céin* Cork
31 N1 **Enniskerry**/*Áth na Sceire* Wicklw
53 P5 **Enniskillen** Ferman
24 H7 **Ennistymon**/*Inis Díomáin* Clare
24 C2 **Eochaill** Galway
24 B2 **Eoghanacht**/*Onaght* Galway
44 C9 **Erra** Roscom
41 K10 **Erriff Bridge** Mayo
28 F9 **Errill** Laois
66 E10 **Ervey Cross Roads** Lderry
54 F6 **Eshnadarragh** Ferman
34 G8 **Esker** Galway
49 M7 **Eskeragh Bridge** Mayo
44 F7 **Esker South** Longfd
9 L10 **Eskine** Kerry
54 F2 **Eskragh** Tyrone
44 D4 **Eslinbridge** Leitrm
2 G4 **Eyeries**/*Na hAorai* Cork
27 M1 **Eyrecourt**/*Dún an Uchta* Galway

F

9 P5 **Faha** Kerry
10 C2 **Fahaduff** Kerry
13 Q6 **Faha Glen** Watfd
9 J1 **Fahamore** Kerry
65 Q7 **Fahan** Donegl
8 C5 **Fahan**/*Fán* Kerry
19 M10 **Fahanasoodry** Limrck
27 L2 **Fahy** Galway
35 L8 **Fahy** Galway
36 F5 **Fairfield** Wmeath
25 N8 **Fair Green** Clare
43 K6 **Fairymount** Roscom
64 G6 **Falcarragh**/*An Fál Carrach* Donegl
8 C5 **Fán**/*Fahan* Kerry
24 H3 **Fanore More** Clare
12 A4 **Farahy** Cork
36 D6 **Fardrum** Wmeath
9 P2 **Farmer's Bridge** Kerry
36 F6 **Farnagh** Wmeath
44 E5 **Farnaght** Leitrm
4 E3 **Farnanes** Cork
5 L1 **Farnanes** Cork
14 E4 **Farnoge** Kilken
5 L1 **Farran** Cork
29 J8 **Farran Cross Roads** Laois
9 Q4 **Farranfore**/*An Fearann Fuar* Kerry
46 B7 **Fartagh Cross Roads** Cavan
44 H1 **Fartrin Cross Roads** Cavan

26 E7 **Feakle**/*An Fhiacail* Clare
24 B2 **Fearann an Choirce** Galway
18 H6 **Fedamore**/*Feadamair* Limrck
16 D4 **Feeard** Clare
25 J3 **Feenagh** Clare
18 E9 **Feenagh** Limrck
43 L1 **Feenaghmore** Sligo
61 K1 **Feeny** Lderry
44 E2 **Fenagh** Leitrm
9 L1 **Fenit**/*An Fhianait* Kerry
22 D4 **Fennagh** Carlow
14 C8 **Fennor** Watfd
37 N1 **Fennor** Wmeath
18 C9 **Feohanagh** Limrck
8 D3 **Feohanagh**/*An Fheothanach* Kerry
3 L1 **Feoramore** Kerry
36 E9 **Ferbane**/*An Féar Bán* Offaly
12 D7 **Fermoy**/*Mainistir Fhear Maí* Cork
23 J7 **Ferns**/*Fearna* Wexfd
23 P2 **Ferrybank** Wicklw
18 F4 **Ferry Bridge** Limrck
20 G10 **Fethard**/*Fiodh Ard* Tippry
14 H8 **Fethard**/*Fiodh Ard* Wexfd
13 Q5 **Fews** Watfd
19 M2 **Fiddane** Tippry
14 B4 **Fiddown**/*Fiodh Dúin* Kilken
9 Q4 **Fieries** Kerry
42 H6 **Figh Bridge** Roscom
13 Q2 **Figlash** Tippry
25 L2 **Finavarra** Clare
45 L7 **Finnea**/*Fiodh an Átha* Wmeath
56 G4 **Finnis** Down
33 L2 **Finny**/*Fionnaithe* Mayo
54 D1 **Fintona** Tyrone
59 K2 **Fintown**/*Baile na Finne* Donegl
16 H8 **Finuge**/*Fionnúig* Kerry
67 P9 **Finvoy** Antrim
33 L2 **Fionnaithe**/*Finny* Mayo
2 E6 **Firkeel** Cork
24 G5 **Fisherstreet** Clare
28 D2 **Fivealley** Offaly
62 H4 **Five Corners** Antrim
52 E6 **Fivemilebourne** Leitrm
5 Q2 **Fivemilebridge** Cork
54 D4 **Fivemiletown** Tyrone
26 E6 **Flagmount** Clare
21 Q5 **Flagmount** Kilken
9 J4 **Flemingstown** Kerry
53 N7 **Florence Court NT** Ferman
8 G8 **Foilmore Bridge** Kerry
3 P8 **Foilnamuck** Cork
19 J9 **Foley's Cross Roads** Limrck
30 C4 **Fontstown** Kildre
46 C10 **Fordstown** Meath
45 N9 **Fore** Wmeath
56 B10 **Forkill** Armagh
25 J3 **Formoyle** Clare
25 J9 **Formoyle** Clare
36 C1 **Formoyle** Longfd
40 F8 **Formoyle** Mayo
11 N8 **Fornaght** Cork
36 D2 **Forthill** Longfd
18 G9 **Fort Middle** Limrck
6 C5 **Fota Wildlife Park** Cork
15 K5 **Foulkesmill** Wexfd
20 F8 **Foulkstown** Tippry
25 M9 **Fountain Cross** Clare
43 P9 **Four Mile House** Roscom
35 P3 **Four Roads** Roscom
44 D2 **Foxfield** Leitrm
42 B3 **Foxford**/*Béal Easa* Mayo
17 P4 **Foynes**/*Faing* Limrck
11 K2 **Freemount**/*Cillin an Chrónáin* Cork
43 L5 **Frenchpark**/*Dún Gar* Roscom
21 L4 **Freshford**/*Achadh Úr* Kilken
30 F5 **Freynestown** Wicklw
18 H5 **Friarstown** Limrck
58 H6 **Frosses**/*Na Frosa* Donegl
35 N1 **Fuerty** Roscom
25 M3 **Funshin More** Galway
33 P9 **Furbo**/*Na Forbacha* Galway
3 N4 **Furkeal** Cork
13 P5 **Furraleigh** Watfd
17 M1 **Furroor** Clare
9 M4 **Fybagh** Kerry

G

17 J6 **Gabbett's Bridge** Kerry
37 L4 **Gainstown** Wmeath
15 L3 **Galbally** Wexfd
19 M9 **Galbally**/*An Gallbhaile* Limrck
20 E6 **Galbertstown** Tippry
16 H7 **Galey Cross Roads** Kerry
62 D2 **Galgorm** Antrim
44 B10 **Gallagh** Roscom
20 H2 **Galmoy** Kilken
28 C2 **Galros Cross Roads** Offaly
38 F3 **Galtrim** Meath
32 E2 **Galtymore Mountain** Limrck/Tippry
34 D8 **Galway**/*Gaillimh* Galway
34 C8 **Galway**/*Gaillimh* Galway
19 N3 **Gannavane** Limrck
54 D10 **Gannon's Cross** Cavan
64 E8 **Gaoth Dobhair**/*Gweedore* Donegl
48 G6 **Gaoth Sáile**/*Gweesalia* Mayo
38 F4 **Garadice** Meath

35 N7 **Garbally Demesne** Galway
13 J2 **Garnavilla** Tippry
37 N6 **Garr** Offaly
42 F10 **Garrafrauns** Galway
50 D5 **Garranard** Mayo
11 P1 **Garrane Cross Roads** Cork
5 J2 **Garranereagh** Cork
42 H9 **Garranlahan** Roscom
16 G3 **Garraun** Clare
27 J2 **Garraun** Galway
9 P3 **Garraun** Watfd
30 F8 **Garrettstown** Carlow
52 H3 **Garrison** Ferman
39 K2 **Garristown**/*Baile Gháire* Dublin
12 F9 **Garrycaheragh** Cork
50 E7 **Garrycloonagh** Mayo
15 J6 **Garrycullen** Wexfd
67 P8 **Garryduff** Antrim
18 G9 **Garryfine** Limrck
22 D5 **Garryhill** Carlow
27 J8 **Garrykennedy** Tippry
6 H5 **Garrymore** Cork
27 N9 **Garrynafana** Tippry
6 G6 **Garryvoe** Cork
67 L9 **Garvagh** Lderry
44 D3 **Garvaghy** Leitrm
54 G2 **Garvaghy** Tyrone
19 L9 **Garyspillane** Limrck
21 K3 **Gattabaun** Kilken
34 M4 **Gaybrook** Wmeath
37 M9 **Geashill**/*Géisill* Offaly
52 F10 **Geevagh**/*An Ghaobhach* Sligo
63 K7 **George Best Airport** Belfst
46 E8 **Georges Cross Roads** Meath
14 A8 **Georgestown** Watfd
3 M6 **Gerahies** Cork
67 N4 **Giant's Causeway NT** Antrim
46 E9 **Gibstown**/*Baile Ghib* Meath
56 C4 **Gilford** Down
46 G5 **Glack Cross Roads** Louth
3 N8 **Glan** Clare
3 L7 **Glanalin** Cork
9 K7 **Glanbehy Bridge** Kerry
4 G2 **Glan Cross Roads** Cork
4 C5 **Glandart** Cork
4 F7 **Glandore**/*Cuan Dor* Cork
53 L8 **Glangevlin** Cavan
3 M6 **Glanlough** Cork
6 B5 **Glanmire**/*Gleann Maghair* Cork
16 G9 **Glanoe** Kerry
3 K7 **Glanroon** Cork
11 M6 **Glantane** Cork
12 C6 **Glanworth**/*Gleannúir* Cork
68 B10 **Glarryford** Antrim
8 D3 **Glashabeg**/*An Ghlaise Bheag* Kerry
11 R7 **Glashaboy East** Cork
11 Q7 **Glashaboy North** Cork
28 G9 **Glasha Cross Roads** Laois
17 J10 **Glashananoon** Limrck
17 L6 **Glashapullagh** Limrck
46 C3 **Glasleck** Cavan
55 K5 **Glaslough**/*Glasloch* Monhan
36 D4 **Glassan**/*Glasán* Wmeath
57 P1 **Glastry** Down
58 B6 **Gleann Cholm Cille**/*Glencolumbkille* Donegl
65 J10 **Gleann Domhain**/*Glendowan* Donegl
49 K4 **Gleann na Muaidhe**/*Glenamoy* Mayo
33 K5 **Gleann Trasna**/*Glentrasna* Galway
66 H6 **Glebe** Lderry
65 L6 **Glen** Donegl
61 P2 **Glen** Lderry
6 G2 **Glenacroghery** Cork
52 F4 **Glenade** Leitrm
27 N8 **Glenahilty** Tippry
49 K4 **Glenamoy**/*Gleann na Muaidhe* Mayo
68 E8 **Glenariff or Waterfoot** Antrim
68 G10 **Glenarm** Antrim
62 F8 **Glenavy** Antrim
9 K6 **Glenbeigh**/*Gleann Beithe* Kerry
52 H6 **Glenboy** Leitrm
23 J9 **Glenbrien** Wexfd
19 L9 **Glenbrohane** Limrck
9 L8 **Glencar** Kerry
52 E5 **Glencar**/*Gleann an Chairthe* Leitrm
58 B6 **Glencolumbkille**/*Gleann Cholm Cille* Donegl
33 Q3 **Glencorrib** Mayo
39 L10 **Glencree** Wicklw
39 M9 **Glencullen** Dublin
31 N3 **Glendarragh** Wicklw
16 C9 **Glenderry** Kerry
6 E3 **Glendine Bridge** Cork
65 J10 **Glendowan**/*Gleann Domhain* Donegl
26 D7 **Glendree** Clare
12 E4 **Glenduff** Cork
68 E6 **Glendun Viaduct** Antrim
31 N6 **Glenealy** Wicklw
50 D4 **Glenedagh** Mayo
66 E4 **Gleneely**/*Gleann Daoile* Donegl
53 K6 **Glenfarne** Leitrm
10 D7 **Glenflesk** Cork
31 N3 **Glengarriff**/*An Gleann Garbh* Cork
63 J6 **Glengormley** Antrim
12 G8 **Glengoura** Cork
66 G9 **Glenhead** Lderry
61 K5 **Glenhull** Tyrone

40 G9 **Glenkeen Bridge** Mayo
60 B1 **Glenmaquin** Donegl
17 L1 **Glenmore** Clare
14 F4 **Glenmore**/*An Gleann Mhór* Kilken
13 K1 **Glennagat** Tippry
10 G2 **Glennaknockane** Cork
35 J1 **Glennamaddy**/*Gleann na Madadh* Galway
10 G3 **Glennamucklagh East** Cork
13 R4 **Glennaphuca Cross Roads** Watfd
63 K3 **Glenoe** Antrim
20 B6 **Glenough Lower** Tippry
20 B6 **Glenough Upper** Tippry
12 B3 **Glenroe** Limrck
6 F2 **Glentane** Cork
58 H4 **Glenties**/*Na Gleannta* Donegl
66 D4 **Glentogher** Donegl
33 K5 **Glentrasna**/*Gleann Trasna* Galway
67 Q10 **Glenvale** Antrim
65 P6 **Glenvar** Donegl
65 J8 **Glenveagh Castle** Donegl
12 B9 **Glenville**/*Gleann an Phréacháin* Cork
15 L5 **Glin**/*An Gleann* Limrck
32 F6 **Glinsce**/*Glinsk* Galway
43 L10 **Glinsk** Galway
32 F6 **Glinsk**/*Glinsce* Galway
6 C5 **Glounthaune** Cork
63 L3 **Glynn** Antrim
22 C9 **Glynn** Carlow
15 M3 **Glynn** Wexfd
10 E5 **Gneeveguilla** Kerry
40 E4 **Gob an Choire**/*Achill Sound* Mayo
20 C9 **Golden**/*An Gabhailín* Tippry
39 N9 **Golden Ball** Dublin
3 L9 **Goleen**/*An Góilín* Cork
20 C7 **Goold's Cross** Tippry
22 B6 **Goresbridge**/*An Droichead Nua* Kilken
23 M5 **Gorey**/*Guaire* Wexfd
13 J3 **Gormanstown** Tippry
47 M10 **Gormanstown**/*Baile Mhic Gormáin* Meath
26 C4 **Gort**/*An Gort* Galway
61 L7 **Gortaclady** Tyrone
3 J1 **Gortagowan** Kerry
64 G6 **Gortahork**/*Gort an Choirce* Donegl
20 C3 **Gortalough** Tippry
64 G6 **Gort an Choirce**/*Gortahork* Donegl
27 N2 **Gortarevan** Offaly
7 J4 **Gortaroo** Cork
53 M6 **Gortatole** Ferman
61 M7 **Gorteagh** Tyrone
35 J6 **Gorteen** Galway
29 N9 **Gorteen** Kilken
18 E9 **Gorteen** Limrck
43 K2 **Gorteen** Sligo
13 M9 **Gorteen**/*An Goirtín* Watfd
28 H1 **Gorteen Bridge** Offaly
14 E6 **Gorteens** Kilken
27 J5 **Gorteeny** Galway
2 G4 **Gortgarriff** Cork
52 F7 **Gortgarrigan** Leitrm
10 C3 **Gortglass** Kerry
66 F10 **Gortilea Cross Roads** Lderry
60 G5 **Gortin** Tyrone
44 E5 **Gortletteragh** Leitrm
4 D2 **Gortloughra Bridge** Cork
50 D3 **Gortmore** Mayo
33 J6 **Gortmore**/*An Gort Mór* Galway
35 L1 **Gortnadeeve** Galway
21 K5 **Gortnagap Cross Roads** Kilken
24 B3 **Gort na gCapall** Galway
17 N3 **Gortnahaha** Clare
66 H10 **Gortnahey** Lderry
20 H5 **Gortnahoo** Tippry
4 F2 **Gortnahoughtee** Cork
49 N6 **Gortnahurra** Mayo
9 Q1 **Gortnaleaha** Kerry
26 C7 **Gortnamearacaun** Clare
43 M7 **Gortnasillagh** Roscom
9 L7 **Gortrelig** Kerry
25 N3 **Gortskeagh** Galway
3 L6 **Gouladoo** Cork
2 G6 **Gour Bridge** Cork
32 E1 **Gowlaun** Galway
22 D8 **Gowlin** Carlow
21 Q6 **Gowran**/*Gabhrán* Kilken
62 D2 **Gracehill** Antrim
13 P5 **Graigavearush** Watfd
19 J10 **Graigue Cross Roads** Limrck
22 C8 **Graiguenamanagh**/*Gráig na Manach* Kilken
31 J4 **Granabeg** Wicklw
45 J7 **Granard**/*Gránard* Longfd
30 E8 **Graney** Kildre
37 Q6 **Grange** Kildre
14 B5 **Grange** Kilken
21 M6 **Grange** Kilken
42 E10 **Grange** Louth
13 K2 **Grange** Tippry
7 L3 **Grange** Watfd
15 M7 **Grange** Wexfd
52 C4 **Grange**/*An Ghráinseach* Sligo
30 B2 **Grange Beg** Kildre
28 G8 **Grange Beg** Laois
47 K6 **Grangebellew** Louth
18 C7 **Grange Bridge** Limrck
30 E6 **Grange Con** Wicklw
33 H2 **Grange Cross Roads** Meath
22 E2 **Grangeford** Carlow
46 H7 **Grangegeeth** Meath
52 D10 **Graniamore** Sligo

26 C2 **Grannagh** Galway
55 L1 **Granville** Tyrone
31 L7 **Greenan** Wicklw
54 H8 **Greenans Cross Roads** Monhan
39 L1 **Greenanstown** Meath
61 J6 **Greencastle** Tyrone
66 G4 **Greencastle**/*An Caisleán Nua* Donegl
28 G8 **Green Cross Roads** Laois
63 K5 **Greenisland** Antrim
47 N1 **Greenore**/*An Grianfort* Louth
11 P8 **Grenagh** Cork
63 P9 **Greyabbey** Down
17 L1 **Greygrove** Clare
66 F8 **Greysteel** Lderry
55 L2 **Greystone** Tyrone
31 P2 **Greystones**/*Na Clocha Liatha* Wicklw
19 L10 **Griston** Limrck
36 F7 **Grogan** Offaly
63 N6 **Groomsport** Down
53 K7 **Gubaveeny** Cavan
14 B6 **Guilcagh Cross Roads** Watfd
61 Q3 **Gulladuff** Lderry
10 E5 **Gullaun** Kerry
52 F5 **Gurteen** Leitrm
14 H5 **Gusserane** Wexfd
64 E8 **Gweedore**/*Gaoth Dobhair* Donegl
48 G6 **Gweesalia**/*Gaoth Sáile* Mayo
6 E7 **Gyleen** Cork

H

46 H1 **Hackballs Cross** Louth
30 H8 **Hacketstown**/*Baile Haicéid* Carlow
5 P2 **Halfway** Cork
14 F7 **Halfway House** Watfd
46 E10 **Halltown Cross Roads** Meath
55 P5 **Hamiltonsbawn** Armagh
62 H8 **Hannahstown** Antrim
14 C3 **Harristown** Kilken
34 B4 **Headford**/*Áth Cinn* Galway
10 D7 **Headfort** Kerry
15 M6 **Heavenstown Cross Roads** Wexfd
16 D8 **Heirhill** Kerry
63 M6 **Helen's Bay** Down
19 K6 **Herbertstown**/*Baile Hiobaird* Limrck
36 D9 **Highstreet** Offaly
6 D2 **Hightown** Cork
62 H10 **Hillhall** Down
38 B4 **Hill of Down** Meath
56 F2 **Hillsborough** Down
43 Q5 **Hill Street** Roscom
56 F8 **Hilltown** Down
15 K5 **Hilltown** Wexfd
15 N6 **Hilltown** Wexfd
18 C4 **Hogan's Bridge** Limrck
19 Q4 **Hollyford** Tippry
23 L4 **Hollyfort** Wexfd
26 D3 **Hollymount** Galway
42 B10 **Hollymount** Mayo
30 G3 **Hollywood**/*Cillin Chaoimhín* Wicklw
19 J7 **Holycross** Limrck
20 D6 **Holycross**/*Mainistir na Croiche* Tippry
53 L6 **Holywell** Ferman
63 L7 **Holywood** Down
14 G9 **Hook Lighthouse** Watfd
46 D7 **Horath Cross Roads** Meath
15 P6 **Horetown** Wexfd
20 F6 **Horse & Jockey**/*An Marcach* Tippry
36 H6 **Horseleap**/*Baile Átha an Urchair* Wmeath
19 L7 **Hospital**/*An tOspidéal* Limrck
39 P6 **Howth**/*Binn Éadair* Dublin
21 N10 **Hugginstown** Kilken
18 E2 **Hurlers Cross** Clare

I

9 K5 **Illaunstookagh** Kerry
25 K8 **Inagh**/*Eidhneach* Clare
6 E7 **Inch** Cork
6 H3 **Inch** Cork
65 Q8 **Inch** Donegl
19 Q3 **Inch** Tippry
23 M3 **Inch** Wexfd
9 K4 **Inch**/*Inse* Kerry
19 M9 **Inchabaun** Limrck
38 C4 **Inchamore Bridge** Meath
21 L3 **Inchbeg** Kilken
29 N5 **Inch Cross Roads** Laois
10 D10 **Inche Bridge** Kerry
4 F3 **Inchicahan Cross Roads** Cork
4 F1 **Inchigeelagh**/*Inse Geimhleach* Cork
12 B6 **Inchinapallas** Cork
12 G3 **Inchnamuck** Tippry
33 L9 **Indreabhán**/*Inveran* Galway
5 M3 **Inishannon**/*Inis Eonáin* Cork
50 A5 **Iniscrone**/*Inis Crabhann* Sligo
62 A2 **Inishrush** Lderry
46 G2 **Iniskeen**/*Inis Caoin* Monhan
21 Q9 **Inistioge**/*Inis Tíog* Kilken
58 H7 **Inver**/*Inbhear* Donegl

Inveran - Lackagh 87

33 L9 Inveran/Indreabhán Galway
42 F4 Ireland West Airport Knock Mayo
30 C2 Irish National Stud Kildre
42 E10 Irishtown Mayo
53 P2 Irvinestown Ferman
58 H5 Ivy Bridge Donegl

J

31 P8 Jack White's Cross Roads Wicklw
29 N3 Jamestown Laois
44 B4 Jamestown Leitrm
21 M3 Jenkinstown Kilken
47 L2 Jenkinstown Louth
56 C7 Jerrettspass Armagh
14 G5 John F. Kennedy Ancestral Home Wexfd
42 D4 Johnsfort Mayo
44 D6 Johnstonsbridge Longfd
6 B6 Johnstown Cork
38 G9 Johnstown Kildre
46 F10 Johnstown Meath
15 L6 Johnstown Wexfd
23 M2 Johnstown Wicklw
31 P9 Johnstown Wicklw
20 H3 Johnstown/Baile Sheáin Kilken
38 D6 Johnstown Bridge Kildre
15 N5 Johnstown Castle Wexfd
21 P4 Johnswell Kilken
56 C10 Jonesborough Armagh
47 L9 Julianstown Meath

K

11 K4 Kanturk/Ceann Toirc Cork
9 P7 Kate Kearney's Cottage Kerry
56 F5 Katesbridge Down
43 Q1 Keadew/Céideadh Roscom
55 M7 Keady Armagh
9 L10 Kealariddig Kerry
2 H5 Kealincha Bridge Cork
4 B3 Kealkill Cork
4 E2 Kealvaugh/Caolmhagh Cork
33 P7 Keeagh/An Chaothach Galway
40 C3 Keel/An Caol Mayo
8 G9 Keelnagore Kerry
35 K1 Keeloges Galway
49 M8 Keenagh Mayo
36 E1 Keenagh/Caonach Longfd
13 K8 Keereen Watfd
22 D2 Kellistown Cross Roads Carlow
62 E3 Kells Antrim
8 H7 Kells Kerry
21 M8 Kells/Ceanannas Kilken
46 C8 Kells/Ceanannas Meath
21 Q2 Kelly's Bridge Kilken
30 G7 Kelshabeg Wicklw
9 Q10 Kenmare/Neidín Kerry
28 C3 Kennedy's Cross Roads Offaly
46 H10 Kentstown Meath
15 N5 Kerloge Wexfd
9 Q4 Kerry Kerry
17 P6 Kerryikyle Limrck
9 N2 Kerry the Kingdom Kerry
59 Q10 Kesh Ferman
44 C2 Keshcarrigan/Ceis Charraigín Leitrm
7 M3 Kiely's Cross Roads Watfd
36 H4 Kilane Wmeath
23 M3 Kilanerin Wexfd
16 C5 Kilbaha/Cill Bheathach Clare
22 D2 Kilballyhue Carlow
26 F10 Kilbane Clare
4 G1 Kilbarry Cork
14 D7 Kilbarry Watfd
26 C4 Kilbeacanty Galway
14 B8 Kilbeg Watfd
37 J6 Kilbeggan/Cill Bheagáin Wmeath
35 M1 Kilbegnet Roscom
12 E3 Kilbeheny Limrck
34 E2 Kilbenan Cross Roads Galway
29 Q5 Kilberry Kildre
46 F9 Kilberry Meath
13 P3 Kilbrack Watfd
18 E5 Kilbreedy Limrck
18 H9 Kilbreedy Limrck
20 C8 Kilbreedy Tippry
33 J6 Kilbrickan/Cill Bhriocáin Galway
20 E3 Kilbrickane Tippry
29 J7 Kilbricken Laois
42 D4 Kilbride Mayo
31 J1 Kilbride Wicklw
31 P7 Kilbride Wicklw
38 D1 Kilbride/Cill Bhríde Meath
39 K4 Kilbride Cross Roads Meath
12 C8 Kilbrien Cork
13 M6 Kilbrien Watfd
11 L3 Kilbrin Cork
5 M5 Kilbrittain/Cill Briotáin Cork
34 D9 Kilcaimin Galway
29 M1 Kilcappagh Offaly
58 D7 Kilcar/Cill Charthaigh Donegl
14 E7 Kilcaragh Cross Roads Watfd
31 J8 Kilcarney Wicklw
31 J8 Kilcarney Cross Roads Wicklw
17 J3 Kilcarroll Clare
13 P1 Kilcash Tippry
35 Q7 Kilcashel Roscom
29 K1 Kilcavan Laois
26 E2 Kilchreest/Cill Chríost Galway
26 E7 Kilclaran Clare
57 N4 Kilclief Down
16 D5 Kilcloher Clare
37 L7 Kilclonfert Offaly
38 F6 Kilcock/Cill Choca Kildre
4 B8 Kilcoe Cork
45 K6 Kilcogy Cavan
14 E7 Kilcohan Watfd
34 E10 Kilcolgan/Cill Cholgáin Galway
5 K4 Kilcolman Cork
17 P6 Kilcolman Limrck
7 M3 Kilcolman/Cill Cholmáin Watfd
27 P6 Kilcomin Offaly
12 H2 Kilcommon Tippry
19 Q2 Kilcommon Tippry
34 G9 Kilconierin Galway
34 D2 Kilconly Galway
35 L7 Kilconnell/Cill Chonaill Galway
11 Q3 Kilconnor Cork
56 G7 Kilcoo Down
53 J4 Kilcoo Cross Roads Ferman
31 P3 Kilcoole/Cill Chomhghuill Wicklw
12 E9 Kilcor Cork
25 N5 Kilcorkan Clare
28 E2 Kilcormac/Cill Chormaic Offaly
11 J6 Kilcorney Cork
23 J9 Kilcotty Wexfd
6 H6 Kilcredan Cork
43 K10 Kilcroan Cross Roads Galway
3 L7 Kilcrohane Cork
12 G9 Kilcronat Cork
30 E3 Kilcullen/Cill Chuillinn Kildre
8 H2 Kilcummin Kerry
10 B5 Kilcummin Kerry
47 J2 Kilcurly Louth
47 J1 Kilcurry Louth
10 C2 Kilcusnaun Kerry
38 C2 Kildalkey Meath
29 Q3 Kildangan Kildre
30 C2 Kildare/Cill Dara Kildre
22 F5 Kildavin/Cill Damháin Carlow
14 B7 Kildermody Watfd
18 F4 Kildimo New Limrck
18 F4 Kildimo Old Limrck
12 B4 Kildorrery/Cill Dairbhre Cork
61 N7 Kildress Tyrone
66 B10 Kildrum Donegl
8 D4 Kildurrihy/Cill Ura Kerry
20 B9 Kilfeakle Tippry
17 F3 Kilfearagh Clare
25 J6 Kilfenora/Cill Fhionnúrach Clare
19 K10 Kilfinnane/Cill Fhionáin Limrck
18 F6 Kilfinny Limrck
16 F10 Kilflyn Kerry
10 C10 Kilgarvan/Cill Gharbháin Kerry
35 M5 Kilglass Galway
45 Q2 Kilglass Roscom
50 H4 Kilglass Sligo
9 N6 Kilgobnet Kerry
13 M7 Kilgobnet Watfd
30 E4 Kilgowan Kildre
18 E5 Kilgrogan Limrck
15 E7 Kilkea Kildre
21 N10 Kilkeasy Kilken
16 F2 Kilkee/Cill Chaoi Clare
47 Q1 Kilkeel Down
42 E5 Kilkelly/Cill Cheallaigh Mayo
21 N5 Kilkenny/Cill Chainnigh Kilken
21 N5 Kilkenny Castle Kilken
36 E4 Kilkenny West Wmeath
5 N5 Kilkerran Cork
35 J2 Kilkerrin Galway
32 G7 Kilkieran/Cill Chiaráin Galway
21 N4 Kilkieran Cross Roads Kilken
4 B8 Kilkilleen Cork
17 K10 Kilkinlea Lower Limrck
26 C10 Kilkishen/Cill Chisin Clare
45 P2 Kill Cavan
32 C3 Kill Galway
14 B8 Kill Watfd
29 G9 Kill/An Chill Kildre
36 F5 Killachonna Wmeath
12 C4 Killaclug Cork
18 F9 Killacolla Limrck
53 P3 Killadeas Ferman
35 N5 Killaderry Galway
40 F9 Killadoon Mayo
17 P3 Killadysert/Cill an Disirt Clare
26 C5 Killafeen Galway
15 M7 Killag Wexfd
17 N8 Killaghteen Limrck
13 J7 Killahaly Watfd
21 K5 Killahy Cross Roads Kilken
50 F5 Killala/Cill Ala Mayo
45 Q3 Killallon Meath
26 H10 Killaloe/Cill Dalua Clare
60 H1 Killaloo Lderry
21 K9 Killamery Kilken
26 D6 Killanena Clare
22 F8 Killann/Cill Anna Wexfd
16 H1 Killard Clare
52 G7 Killarga Leitrm
10 B6 Killarney/Cill Airne Kerry
36 H4 Killaroo Wmeath
45 J2 Killashandra/Cill na Seanrátha Cavan
44 D9 Killashee Longfd
42 D3 Killasser Mayo
33 L1 Killateeaun/Coill an tSiáin Mayo
28 D3 Killaun Offaly
41 N8 Killavally Mayo
12 F8 Killavarilly Cork
11 R9 Killavarrig Cork
51 P9 Killavil Sligo
34 H2 Killavoher Galway
11 Q5 Killavullen/Cill an Mhuilinn Cork
52 H5 Killea Leitrm
20 D2 Killea Tippry
14 F8 Killea Watfd
62 F6 Killead Antrim
6 H4 Killeagh/Cill la Cork
24 C3 Killeany/Cill Éinne Galway
22 D6 Killedmond Carlow
12 C4 Killee Bridge Cork
17 P9 Killeedy Limrck
26 C6 Killeen Galway
40 F8 Killeen Mayo
27 P4 Killeen Tippry
61 Q9 Killeen Tyrone
25 N1 Killeenaran Galway
20 C9 Killeenasteena Tippry
25 P2 Killeenavarra Galway
34 F10 Killeeneenmore Galway
4 C6 Killeenleagh Cork
8 H10 Killeenleagh/Cillín Liath Kerry
11 R9 Killeens Cross Cork
54 G8 Killeevan Monhan
35 P5 Killeglan Roscom
37 K10 Killeigh/Cill Aichidh Offaly
60 B6 Killen Tyrone
23 M6 Killenagh Wexfd
29 N3 Killenard Laois
27 P3 Killenaule Tippry
20 G7 Killenaule/Cill Náile Tippry
43 M4 Killerdoo Roscom
30 E9 Killerrig Cross Roads Carlow
37 M7 Killeshil Offaly
30 B9 Killeshin Laois
60 B6 Killeter Tyrone
34 H10 Killilan Bridge Galway
17 J4 Killimer Clare
27 K2 Killimor/Cill Íomair Galway
25 L6 Killinaboy/Cill Iníne Baoith Clare
11 L10 Killinardrish Cork
14 C4 Killinaspick Kilken
57 M1 Killinchy Down
23 M9 Killincooly Wexfd
9 J2 Killiney Kerry
39 P8 Killiney/Cill Iníon Léinín Dublin
15 P6 Killinick Wexfd
45 Q5 Killinkere Cavan
25 N3 Killinny Galway
38 B9 Killinthomas Kildre
31 P4 Killiskey Wicklw
10 H10 Killnamartery/Cill na Martra Cork
44 G8 Killoe Longfd
50 E3 Killogeary Mayo
36 E6 Killogeenaghan Wmeath
8 E10 Killoluaig/Cill Ó Luaigh Kerry
25 P3 Killomoran Galway
37 N8 Killoneen Offaly
35 M9 Killoran Galway
9 M5 Killorglin/Cill Orglan Kerry
35 J5 Killoscobe Galway
57 M6 Killough Down
33 P1 Killour Mayo
56 E10 Killowen Down
39 L4 Killsallaghan Dublin
37 P3 Killucan/Cill Liúcainne Wmeath
43 Q4 Killukin Roscom
37 J10 Killurin Offaly
15 M3 Killurin Wexfd
2 C1 Killurly/Cill Urlaí Kerry
20 G10 Killusty Tippry
62 D3 Killybegs Antrim
58 F7 Killybegs/Na Cealla Beaga Donegl
60 G8 Killyclogher Tyrone
44 H2 Killygar Leitrm
60 B4 Killygordon/Cúil na gCuirridín Donegl
67 L9 Killykergan Lderry
55 L5 Killylea Armagh
57 M3 Killyleagh Down
55 K6 Killyneill Monhan
28 D3 Killyon Offaly
6 F6 Kilmacahill Cork
31 N2 Kilmacanoge Wicklw
11 N3 Kilmaclenine Cross Roads Cork
14 D5 Kilmacow/Cill Mhic Bhúith Kilken
65 L8 Kilmacrenan/Cill Mhic Réanain Donegl
13 Q5 Kilmacthomas/Coill Mhic Thomáisín Watfd
43 N1 Kilmactranny Sligo
21 M10 Kilmaganny/Cill Mogeanna Kilken
34 B2 Kilmaine Mayo
46 D6 Kilmainham Wood Meath
25 L10 Kilmaley/Cill Mháile Clare
39 N10 Kilmalin Wicklw
19 J9 Kilmallock/Cill Mocheallóg Limrck
21 K6 Kilmanagh Kilken
17 K10 Kilmaniheen Kerry
35 Q3 Kilmass Roscom
30 C5 Kilmead Kildre
14 C6 Kilmeadan Watfd
38 D9 Kilmeage Kildre
18 D9 Kilmeedy/Cill Míde Limrck
38 F2 Kilmessan/Cill Mheasáin Meath
2 D6 Kilmichael Cork
4 G1 Kilmichael Cork
17 L2 Kilmihil/Cill Mhícíl Clare
11 Q8 Kilmona Cork
3 Q10 Kilmoon Cork
55 P3 Kilmore Armagh
19 J1 Kilmore Clare
57 K3 Kilmore Down
16 E7 Kilmore Kerry
42 B3 Kilmore Mayo
44 B5 Kilmore Roscom
15 M7 Kilmore Wexfd
38 F4 Kilmore Cross Roads Meath
15 M8 Kilmore Quay Wexfd
44 D9 Kilmore Upper Longfd
17 K8 Kilmorna Kerry
30 B7 Kilmorony Laois
42 G5 Kilmovee Mayo
23 M8 Kilmuckridge/Cill Mhucraise Wexfd
14 B9 Kilmurrin Watfd
24 F10 Kilmurry Clare
5 J1 Kilmurry Cork
18 E9 Kilmurry Limrck
30 F7 Kilmurry Wicklw
18 F1 Kilmurry/Cill Mhuire Clare
17 L3 Kilmurry McMahon Clare
24 B2 Kilmurvy/Cill Mhuirbhigh Galway
22 G6 Kilmyshall Wexfd
13 J8 Kilnacarriga Watfd
18 G1 Kilnacreagh Clare
44 C3 Kilnagross Leitrm
35 M8 Kilnahown Galway
45 L5 Kilnaleck/Cill na Leice Cavan
23 L8 Kilnamanagh Wexfd
25 L8 Kilnamona/Cill na Móna Clare
5 M3 Kilpatrick Cork
18 H5 Kilpeacon Cross Roads Limrck
31 P3 Kilpedder Wicklw
8 E3 Kilquane/Cill Chuáin Kerry
22 H2 Kilquiggin Wicklw
67 Q7 Kilraghts Antrim
15 Q6 Kilrane Wexfd
67 N10 Kilrea Lderry
58 G4 Kilrean Donegl
35 K9 Kilreekill Galway
34 C8 Kilroghter/Coill Uachtar Galway
24 C3 Kilronan/Cill Rónáin Galway
43 Q10 Kilroosky Roscom
19 N8 Kilross Tippry
16 H3 Kilrush/Cill Rois Clare
43 K10 Kilsallagh Galway
40 H7 Kilsallagh Mayo
47 K5 Kilsaran Louth
38 C6 Kilshanchoe Kildre
9 J1 Kilshannig Kerry
24 H6 Kilshanny Clare
13 N2 Kilsheelan Tippry
5 L5 Kilshinahan Cork
46 B9 Kilskeer Meath
53 Q3 Kilskeery Tyrone
42 C6 Kiltamagh/Caillte Mach Mayo
41 M8 Kiltarsaghaun Mayo
26 C3 Kiltartan Galway
22 F7 Kiltealy/Cill Téile Wexfd
38 H9 Kilteel Kildre
19 L6 Kilteely/Cill Tíle Limrck
43 Q10 Kilteevan Cross Roads Roscom
30 G8 Kiltegan Wicklw
23 J6 Kilthomas Cross Roads Wexfd
39 N9 Kiltiernan Dublin
25 P1 Kiltiernan Galway
37 K7 Kiltober Wmeath
36 B4 Kiltoom Roscom
45 L10 Kiltoom Wmeath
35 N9 Kiltormer Galway
34 H8 Kiltullagh/Cill Tulach Galway
53 J4 Kiltyclogher/Coillte Clochair Leitrm
21 J9 Kilvemnon Tippry
42 E10 Kilvine Mayo
12 H8 Kilwatermoy Watfd
63 K2 Kilwaughter Antrim
38 H7 Kilwoghan Kildre
12 D6 Kilworth/Cill Uird Cork
12 D5 Kilworth Camp Cork
36 H6 Kimalady Offaly
17 L5 Kinard Limrck
53 P7 Kinawley Ferman
64 C9 Kincaslough/Cionn Caslach Donegl
50 D5 Kincon Mayo
59 L1 Kingarrow/An Cionn Garbh Donegl
18 H3 King John's Castle Limrck
46 D4 Kingscourt/Dún an Rí Cavan
45 Q9 King's Cross Roads Meath
61 Q7 Kingsmill Tyrone
52 F2 Kinlough/Cionn Locha Leitrm
40 E9 Kinnadoohy Mayo
37 P4 Kinnegad/Cionn Átha Gad Wmeath
28 E3 Kinnitty/Cion Eitigh Offaly
5 P4 Kinsale/Cionn tSáile Cork
7 K4 Kinsalebeg Watfd
39 N5 Kinsaley Dublin
33 K7 Kinvarra/Cinn Mhara Galway
25 N2 Kinvarra/Cinn Mharra Galway
4 G5 Kippagh Bridge Cork
63 Q10 Kircubbin Down
67 P7 Kirkhills Antrim
57 P2 Kirkistown Down
10 G4 Kishkeam Cork
41 K7 Knappagh Mayo
8 E9 Knights Town Kerry
17 K4 Knock Clare
28 F7 Knock Tippry
42 D7 Knock/An Cnoc Mayo
25 L8 Knockacaurhin Clare
10 B5 Knockacullig Kerry
50 E7 Knockadangan Bridge Mayo
18 C7 Knockaderry Limrck
19 K7 Knockainy/Cnoc Áine Limrck
13 P3 Knockalafalla Watfd
43 M8 Knockalaghta Roscom
17 L2 Knockalough Clare
31 J8 Knockananna Wicklw
42 F8 Knockanarra Mayo
30 H6 Knockanarrigan Wicklw
4 H2 Knockane Cork
12 B3 Knockanevin Cork
50 E7 Knockanillaun Mayo
13 J9 Knockanore Watfd
17 K7 Knockanure Kerry
28 G7 Knockaroe Laois
54 G6 Knockatallan Monhan
12 E6 Knockatrasnane Cork
24 H8 Knockatullaghaun Clare
35 M10 Knockaun Galway
12 H6 Knockaunarast Watfd
17 J9 Knockaunbrack Kerry
9 L5 Knockaunnaglashy Kerry
9 K6 Knockaunroe Kerry
8 E4 Knockavrogeen/Cnoc an Bhróigín Kerry
17 M8 Knockawahig Limrck
13 M5 Knockboy Watfd
26 E9 Knockbrack Clare
60 B1 Knockbrack Donegl
16 F10 Knockbrack Kerry
46 B3 Knockbride Cavan
46 H3 Knockbridge Louth
20 F9 Knockbrit Tippry
5 L5 Knockbrown Cork
5 N1 Knockburden Cork
16 G9 Knockburrane Cross Roads Kerry
61 Q3 Knockcloghrim Lderry
35 Q2 Knockcroghery/Cnoc an Chrochaire Roscom
18 H8 Knockdarnan Limrck
37 L2 Knockdrin Wmeath
11 N6 Knockdrislagh Cork
10 G4 Knockeenadallane Cork
10 D1 Knockeencreen Kerry
10 B2 Knockeen Cross Roads Kerry
24 G5 Knockfin Cross Roads Clare
13 K2 Knocklofty Tippry
19 L8 Knocklong Limrck
25 P7 Knockmael West Clare
21 K2 Knockmannon Cross Roads Kilken
50 F9 Knockmore Mayo
12 F8 Knockmourne Cork
41 L4 Knockmoyle Bridge Mayo
17 N5 Knocknabooly Limrck
10 E4 Knocknaboul Cross Kerry
68 E6 Knocknacarry Antrim
30 D8 Knocknacree Cross Roads Kildre
5 M4 Knocknacurra Cork
17 K10 Knocknagashel/Cnoc na gCaiseal Kerry
26 G8 Knocknagower Clare
10 F5 Knocknagree Cork
9 N1 Knocknahaha Kerry
24 G10 Knocknahila Clare
5 M1 Knocknahilan Cork
48 G3 Knocknalina/Cnocán na Líne Mayo
48 G4 Knocknalower/Cnoc na Lobhar Mayo
6 G5 Knocknaskagh Cork
24 H7 Knockpatrick Clare
6 C4 Knockraha Cork
13 M7 Knockroe Watfd
9 J9 Knockroe/Cnocrua Kerry
5 J5 Knocks Cork
29 J4 Knocks Laois
5 J5 Knockskagh Cork
11 J2 Knockskavane Cork
21 N9 Knocktopher/Cnoc an Tóchair Kilken
15 L6 Knocktown Cross Roads Wexfd
43 P2 Knockvicar Roscom
5 M4 Knoppoge Bridge Cork
46 H9 Knowth Meath
11 Q6 Knuttery Cork
29 N6 Kyle Laois
26 G3 Kylebrack Galway
19 N4 Kylegarve Limrck
35 Q9 Kylemore Galway
32 H7 Kylesalia/Coill Sáile Galway

L

26 C2 Laban Galway
17 M4 Labasheeda/Leaba Shíoda Clare
60 C9 Lack Ferman
10 E10 Lackabaun/An Leaca Bhán Cork
29 Q2 Lackagh Kildre

19 M3 **Lackamore** Tippry
27 J9 **Lackamore** Tippry
21 Q4 **Lackan** Carlow
43 Q8 **Lackan** Roscom
31 J2 **Lackan** Wicklw
45 K10 **Lackan** Wmeath
35 P3 **Lackan Cross** Roscom
5 J2 **Lackareagh** Cork
10 D1 **Lackbrooder** Kerry
14 H3 **Lacken** Wexfd
12 B8 **Lackendarragh North** Cork
28 F6 **Lackey** Laois
6 G5 **Ladysbridge**/*Droichead na Scuab* Cork
15 Q7 **Lady's Island** Wexfd
67 Q4 **Lagavara** Antrim
20 C10 **Lagganstown** Tippry
55 M1 **Laghey Corner** Tyrone
59 K8 **Laghy**/*An Lathaigh* Donegl
11 M6 **Laharan Cross Roads** Cork
50 D9 **Lahardaun**/*Leathardán* Mayo
24 G7 **Lahinch**/*An Leacht* Clare
17 L4 **Lakyle** Clare
21 L10 **Lamoge** Kilken
44 C10 **Lanesborough**/*Béal Átha Liag* Roscom
26 D5 **Lannaght** Clare
38 E3 **Laracor** Meath
38 F6 **Laragh** Kildre
46 D1 **Laragh** Monhan
31 L5 **Laragh**/*Láithreach* Wicklw
11 L10 **Larchill Cross Roads** Cork
49 K6 **Largan** Mayo
43 Q6 **Largan** Roscom
51 J7 **Largan** Sligo
58 E7 **Largy** Donegl
52 E3 **Largydonnell** Leitrm
63 L2 **Larne** Antrim
54 H8 **Latnamard** Monhan
25 N10 **Latoon Bridge** Clare
19 N7 **Lattin** Tippry
46 B1 **Latton** Monhan
3 K3 **Lauragh**/*Láithreach* Kerry
56 B4 **Laurelvale** Armagh
35 P9 **Laurencetown**/*An Baile Mór* Galway
51 N7 **Lavagh** Sligo
56 C4 **Lawrencetown** Down
47 M9 **Laytown**/*An Inse* Meath
64 B9 **Leabgarrow**/*An Leadhb Gharbh* Donegl
6 D4 **Leamlara** Cork
4 F7 **Leap**/*An Léim* Cork
36 B3 **Lecarrow** Roscom
66 F4 **Leckemy** Donegl
32 H1 **Leenane**/*An Líonán* Galway
36 G1 **Legan or Lenamore** Longfd
44 G5 **Leggah** Longfd
63 J7 **Legoniel** Belfst
22 B3 **Leighlinbridge**/*Leithghlinn an Droichid* Carlow
38 B5 **Leinster Bridge** Kildre
32 H8 **Leitir Calaidh**/*Lettercallow* Galway
32 G9 **Leitir Mealláin**/*Lettermullan* Galway
58 H2 **Leitir Mhic an Bhaird**/*Lettermacaward* Donegl
32 H8 **Leitir Móir**/*Lettermore* Galway
17 K1 **Leitrim** Clare
56 H6 **Leitrim** Down
44 B3 **Leitrim**/*Liatroim* Leitrm
17 K6 **Leitrim East** Kerry
4 D5 **Leitry Bridge** Cork
39 J6 **Leixlip** Kildre
36 F8 **Lemanaghan** Offaly
13 P6 **Lemybrien**/*Léim Uí Bhriain* Watfd
14 F8 **Leperstown** Watfd
16 E10 **Lerrig** Kerry
59 J6 **Letterbarra** Donegl
53 N5 **Letterbreen** Ferman
32 H8 **Lettercallow**/*Leitir Calaidh* Galway
32 E2 **Letterfrack**/*Leitir Fraic* Galway
24 H9 **Letterkelly** Clare
65 M10 **Letterkenny**/*Leitir Ceanainn* Donegl
67 L7 **Letterloan** Lderry
58 H2 **Lettermacaward**/*Leitir Mhic an Bhaird* Donegl
41 K4 **Lettermaghera** Mayo
32 H8 **Lettermore**/*Leitir Móir* Galway
32 G9 **Lettermullan**/*Leitir Mealláin* Galway
34 G3 **Levally** Galway
41 Q10 **Levally** Mayo
14 C6 **Licketstown** Kilken
60 D3 **Lifford**/*Leifear* Donegl
60 F4 **Ligfordrum or Douglas** Tyrone
66 H8 **Limavady** Lderry
18 H3 **Limerick**/*Luimneach* Limrck
18 H3 **Limerick Hunt Museum** Limrck
19 P7 **Limerick Junction** Tippry
65 Q5 **Linsfort** Donegl
3 P10 **Lios Ó Móine**/*Lissamona* Cork
6 G4 **Lios Póil**/*Lispole* Kerry
63 M10 **Lisbane** Down
54 B5 **Lisbellaw** Ferman
45 N1 **Lisboduff** Cavan
62 H10 **Lisburn** Antrim
24 G7 **Liscannor**/*Lios Ceannúir* Clare

41 K8 **Liscarney** Mayo
11 M2 **Liscarroll**/*Lios Cearúill* Cork
38 B1 **Lisclogher Cross Roads** Wmeath
60 G2 **Liscloon** Tyrone
8 G4 **Lisdargan**/*Lios Deargáin* Kerry
24 H5 **Lisdoonvarna**/*Lios Dúin Bhearna* Clare
21 L2 **Lisdowney** Kilken
43 Q7 **Lisduff** Cavan
11 Q9 **Lisduff** Cork
28 E2 **Lisduff** Offaly
44 E9 **Lisduff Cross Roads** Longfd
27 M8 **Lisgarode** Tippry
6 E3 **Lisgoold** Cork
45 P5 **Lisgrea Cross Roads** Cavan
17 P1 **Lisheen** Clare
35 N10 **Lisheenaguile** Galway
43 L2 **Liskeagh** Sligo
45 K9 **Lismacaffry** Wmeath
11 K3 **Lismire** Cork
12 H7 **Lismore**/*Lios Mór* Watfd
35 P4 **Lismoyle** Roscom
55 N6 **Lisnadill** Armagh
19 K3 **Lisnagry** Limrck
14 C7 **Lisnakill Cross** Watfd
54 H10 **Lisnalong** Monhan
61 P3 **Lisnamuck** Lderry
53 N2 **Lisnarrick** Ferman
54 C7 **Lisnaskea** Ferman
5 P6 **Lispatrick** Cork
8 G4 **Lispole**/*Lios Póil* Kerry
25 K10 **Lisroe** Clare
13 M1 **Lisronagh** Tippry
45 J8 **Lisryan** Longfd
10 H10 **Lissacresig** Cork
43 L8 **Lissalway** Roscom
3 P10 **Lissamona**/*Lios Ó Móine* Cork
35 P10 **Lissanacody** Galway
43 K7 **Lissananny** Roscom
5 L4 **Lissaphooca Cross Roads** Cork
9 J9 **Lissatinnig Bridge**/*Droichead Lios an tSonnaigh* Kerry
4 H7 **Lissavard** Cork
16 G7 **Lisselton Cross Roads** Kerry
17 N1 **Lissycasey** Clare
9 N1 **Listellick** Kerry
14 E3 **Listerlin** Kilken
57 K3 **Listooder** Down
16 H8 **Listowel**/*Lios Tuathail* Kerry
19 N9 **Lisvarrinane** Tippry
6 C5 **Little Island** Cork
20 F6 **Littleton**/*An Baile Beag* Tippry
16 F9 **Lixnaw**/*Leic Snámha* Kerry
62 G6 **Loanends** Antrim
46 F7 **Lobinstown** Meath
64 E9 **Loch an Iúir**/*Loughanure* Donegl
45 J5 **Loch Gowna**/*Loch Gamhna* Cavan
17 M5 **Loghill** Limrck
12 H6 **Logleagh** Watfd
7 N2 **Loiscearán**/*Loskeran* Watfd
8 G4 **Lios Deargáin**/*Lisdargan* Kerry
2 H1 **Lomanagh** Kerry
11 M5 **Lombardstown** Cork
66 C9 **Londonderry** Lderry
66 C9 **Londonderry Tower Museum** Lderry
28 E4 **Longford** Offaly
44 E8 **Longford**/*An Longfort* Longfd
19 J3 **Longford Bridge** Limrck
20 G4 **Longfordpass Bridge** Tippry
38 C4 **Longwood** Meath
27 M4 **Lorrha**/*Lothra* Tippry
22 C5 **Lorum** Carlow
7 N2 **Loskeran**/*Loiscearán* Watfd
35 L7 **Loughaclerybeg** Galway
12 H2 **Loughacutteen** Tippry
37 J4 **Loughanavally** Wmeath
64 E9 **Loughanure**/*Loch an Iúir* Donegl
33 M9 **Loughaunbeg**/*An Lochán Beag* Galway
56 D5 **Loughbrickland** Down
45 K5 **Loughduff** Cavan
9 J3 **Loughgall** Armagh
55 P3 **Loughgall** Armagh
43 J6 **Loughglinn**/*Loch Glinne* Roscom
68 B7 **Loughguile** Antrim
57 K4 **Loughinisland** Down
61 J7 **Loughmacrory** Tyrone
20 E3 **Loughmore** Tippry
46 D1 **Loughmorne** Monhan
26 F1 **Loughrea**/*Baile Locha Riach* Galway
39 P2 **Loughshinny** Dublin
40 F3 **Louisburgh**/*Cluain Cearbán* Mayo
46 H3 **Louth**/*Lú* Louth
62 E9 **Lower Ballinderry** Antrim
3 M8 **Lowertown** Cork
56 G5 **Lowtown** Down
39 J6 **Lucan** Dublin
51 L4 **Lugdoon** Sligo
29 N7 **Luggacurren** Laois
31 J6 **Lugnaquilla Mountain** Wicklw
14 D3 **Lukeswell** Kilken
38 C8 **Lullymore** Kildre
42 F4 **Lurga** Mayo

56 C2 **Lurgan** Armagh
36 F6 **Lurgan** Offaly
43 M5 **Lurgan** Roscom
65 P6 **Lurganboy** Donegl
11 P7 **Lurganboy** Leitrm
39 N3 **Lusk**/*Lusca* Dublin
44 D10 **Lyneen Bridge** Longfd
16 H10 **Lyracrumpane** Kerry
11 P7 **Lyradane** Cork
11 L6 **Lyre** Cork
12 G9 **Lyre** Cork
10 D2 **Lyre** Kerry
12 F6 **Lyrenaglogh** Watfd

M

33 K4 **Maam Cross**/*An Teach Dóite* Galway
58 G3 **Maas** Donegl
41 M7 **Mace** Mayo
65 N3 **Machair Dromann**/*Magheradrumman* Donegl
65 L5 **Machair Loiscthe**/*Rosepenna* Donegl
53 P7 **Mackan** Ferman
67 L7 **Macosquin** Lderry
12 E6 **Macroney** Cork
11 J10 **Macroom**/*Maigh Chromtha* Cork
45 Q2 **Madabawn** Cavan
21 N6 **Maddockstown** Kilken
30 C8 **Maganey** Kildre
62 F10 **Maghaberry** Antrim
57 J7 **Maghera** Down
61 Q2 **Maghera** Lderry
25 P8 **Maghera Cross Roads** Clare
65 N3 **Magheradrumman**/*Machair Dromann* Donegl
61 Q4 **Magherafelt** Lderry
56 D2 **Magheralin** Armagh
66 B10 **Magheramason** Tyrone
63 L3 **Magheramorne** Antrim
54 E8 **Magheraveely** Ferman
62 A10 **Maghery** Armagh
58 F1 **Maghery**/*An Machaire* Donegl
54 B6 **Maguiresbridge** Ferman
18 C8 **Mahoonagh** Limrck
33 Q7 **Maigh Cuilinn**/*Moycullen* Galway
48 F4 **Maigh Raithin**/*Moyrahan* Mayo
32 F6 **Maighros**/*Moyrus* Galway
9 Q3 **Maine Bridge** Kerry
38 F7 **Mainham** Kildre
8 H10 **Máistir Gaoithe**/*Mastergeehy* Kerry
39 N4 **Malahide**/*Mullach Íde* Dublin
58 A6 **Málainn Bhig**/*Malin Beg* Donegl
58 B6 **Málainn Mhóir**/*Malin More* Donegl
66 D2 **Malin**/*Málainn* Donegl
58 A6 **Malin Beg**/*Málainn Bhig* Donegl
58 B6 **Malin More**/*Málainn Mhóir* Donegl
11 P5 **Mallow**/*Mala* Cork
62 H6 **Mallusk** Antrim
33 K1 **Mám Trasna**/*Maumtrasna* Mayo
4 G4 **Manch Bridge** Cork
36 D7 **Mannion's Cross Roads** Offaly
65 N10 **Manorcunningham**/*Mainear Uí Chuinneagain* Donegl
52 G6 **Manorhamilton**/*Cluainin* Leitrm
20 F4 **Manselstown** Tippry
47 J4 **Mansfieldstown** Louth
43 N6 **Mantua** Roscom
41 Q6 **Manulla** Mayo
20 G7 **Mardyke** Tippry
55 Q6 **Markethill** Armagh
13 L2 **Marlfield** Tippry
22 H7 **Marshalstown** Wexfd
68 C10 **Martinstown** Antrim
19 K9 **Martinstown** Limrck
46 C10 **Martinstown Cross Roads** Meath
46 D9 **Marty** Meath
8 H10 **Mastergeehy**/*Máistir Gaoithe* Kerry
20 C10 **Masterstown** Tippry
11 P9 **Matehy** Cork
4 E7 **Maulatrahane** Cork
4 C3 **Maulavanig** Cork
3 M8 **Maulawaddra** Cork
33 K3 **Maum**/*An Mám* Galway
33 K1 **Maumtrasna**/*Mám Trasna* Mayo
25 K8 **Mauricesmills** Clare
15 N6 **Mayglass** Wexfd
38 G6 **Maynooth**/*Maigh Nuad* Kildre
42 B8 **Mayo** Mayo
56 E8 **Mayobridge** Down
62 G10 **Mazetown** Antrim
68 C10 **McGregor's Corner** Antrim
67 N10 **McLaughlins Corner** Antrim
18 H6 **Meanus** Limrck
27 M2 **Meelick** Galway
10 H2 **Meelin** Cork
64 F6 **Meenaclady**/*Mín an Chladaigh* Donegl
58 C5 **Meenacross**/*Mín na Croise* Donegl
58 G1 **Meenacross**/*Mín na Croise* Donegl

58 D6 **Meenaneary**/*Mín an Aoire* Donegl
64 D9 **Meenbannad**/*Mín Beannaid* Donegl
10 D1 **Meenbannivane** Kerry
64 F6 **Meenlaragh**/*Mín Lárach* Donegl
10 F1 **Meennaraheeny** Cork
31 M8 **Meeting of the Waters** Wicklw
56 C9 **Meigh** Armagh
34 B8 **Menlough**/*Mionlach* Galway
35 J5 **Menlough**/*Mionlach* Galway
55 L6 **Middletown** Armagh
42 D5 **Midfield** Mayo
6 E5 **Midleton**/*Mainistir an Corann* Cork
22 H8 **Milehouse** Wexfd
30 F3 **Milemill** Kildre
19 Q3 **Milestone** Tippry
55 N5 **Milford** Armagh
18 E10 **Milford**/*Áth an Mhuilinn* Cork
63 K2 **Millbrook** Antrim
4 E7 **Milleen Bridge** Cork
65 M7 **Millford**/*Baile na nGallóglach* Donegl
63 P7 **Millisle** Down
12 E5 **Millstreet** Cork
13 L6 **Millstreet** Watfd
10 H6 **Millstreet**/*Sráid an Mhuilinn* Cork
62 E5 **Mill Town** Antrim
55 Q4 **Milltown** Armagh
45 J1 **Milltown** Cavan
28 H7 **Milltown** Donegl
65 M5 **Milltown** Donegl
39 J7 **Milltown** Dublin
34 E1 **Milltown** Galway
35 K3 **Milltown** Galway
38 D10 **Milltown** Kildre
14 C3 **Milltown** Kilken
67 K6 **Milltown** Lderry
67 M8 **Milltown** Lderry
37 J3 **Milltown** Wmeath
8 E4 **Milltown**/*Baile an Mhuilinn* Kerry
9 N4 **Milltown**/*Baile an Mhuilinn* Kerry
18 G10 **Milltown Cross Roads** Cork
24 G9 **Milltown Malbay**/*Sráid na Cathrach* Clare
37 N5 **Milltownpass**/*Bealach Bhaile an Mhuileann* Wmeath
58 D6 **Min an Aoire**/*Meenaneary* Donegl
64 F6 **Min an Chladaigh**/*Meenaclady* Donegl
6 B8 **Minane Bridge** Cork
64 D9 **Mín Beannaid**/*Meenbannad* Donegl
57 L6 **Minerstown** Down
64 F6 **Mín Lárach**/*Meenlaragh* Donegl
58 C5 **Mín na Croise**/*Meenacross* Donegl
58 G1 **Mín na Croise**/*Meenacross* Donegl
34 B8 **Mionlach**/*Menlough* Galway
12 D4 **Mitchelstown**/*Baile Mhistéala* Cork
12 F3 **Mitchelstown Caves** Tippry
16 H3 **Moanmore** Clare
19 M8 **Moanmore** Tippry
36 F6 **Moate**/*An Móta* Wmeath
44 G8 **Moat Farrell** Longfd
13 L7 **Modelligo** Watfd
11 M9 **Model Village** Cork
11 P10 **Model Village** Cork
27 N7 **Modreeny** Tippry
6 G4 **Mogeely** Cork
21 N4 **Mohil** Kilken
44 D4 **Mohill**/*Maothail* Leitrm
8 F10 **Moing Uí Dhúda**/*Muingydowda* Kerry
7 M2 **Móin na mBróthar**/*Monamraher* Watfd
56 D1 **Moira** Down
9 P9 **Moll's Gap** Kerry
23 J8 **Monagear** Wexfd
57 J7 **Monaghan**/*Muineachán* Monhan
55 J7 **Monaghan County Museum** Monhan
12 F8 **Monalour** Watfd
13 J6 **Monalour** Watfd
14 E7 **Monamintra Cross Roads** Watfd
23 L7 **Monamolin** Wexfd
7 M2 **Monamraher**/*Móin na mBróthar* Watfd
19 N6 **Monard** Tippry
23 K4 **Monaseed** Wexfd
18 G6 **Monaster** Limrck
43 K4 **Monasteraden** Sligo
47 J7 **Monasterboice** Louth
29 P2 **Monasterevin**/*Mainistir Eimhin* Kildre
53 N4 **Monea** Ferman
11 P6 **Monee Cross Roads** Cork
16 C5 **Moneen** Clare
34 D4 **Moneen** Cork
29 N9 **Moneenroe** Kilken
29 J1 **Monettia Bog** Laois
67 M9 **Moneycusker** Cork
27 P8 **Moneydig** Lderry
53 L7 **Moneygall**/*Muine Gall* Offaly
62 C4 **Moneyglass** Antrim
61 Q6 **Moneymore** Lderry
64 G8 **Money More**/*Muine Mór* Donegl

61 N3 **Moneyneany** Lderry
63 L9 **Moneyreagh** Down
56 F6 **Moneyslane** Down
37 M2 **Monilea** Wmeath
34 G6 **Monivea**/*Muine Mheá* Galway
63 J5 **Monkstown** Antrim
6 C6 **Monkstown** Cork
19 K1 **Montpelier** Limrck
14 C5 **Mooncoin**/*Móin Choinn* Kilken
30 D6 **Moone**/*Maoin* Kildre
7 K4 **Moord** Watfd
27 L1 **Moorfield Cross Roads**
62 F3 **Moorfields** Antrim
61 R1 **Moran's Cross Roads** Lderry
18 F7 **Morenane** Limrck
10 C9 **Morley's Bridge** Kerry
47 L8 **Mornington** Meath
19 Q6 **Morpeth Bridge** Tippry
19 K10 **Mortlestown** Limrck
5 L2 **Moskeagh** Cork
47 M10 **Mosney Camp** Meath
63 J6 **Mossley** Antrim
67 Q5 **Moss-Side** Antrim
13 Q3 **Mothel** Watfd
47 M2 **Mountain Bay** Louth
43 Q1 **Mountallen** Roscom
35 K4 **Mountbellew Bridge**/*An Creagán* Galway
28 F1 **Mountbolus** Offaly
6 C2 **Mountcatherine** Cork
59 J7 **Mountcharles**/*Moin Séarlas* Donegl
10 F1 **Mountcollins** Limrck
60 H7 **Mountfield** Tyrone
20 L7 **Mounthoward Cross Roads** Wexfd
60 F7 **Mountjoy** Tyrone
13 J6 **Mountmelleray** Watfd
29 L3 **Mountmellick**/*Móinteach Mílic* Laois
29 M4 **Mountmellick**/*Móinteach Mílic* Laois
55 Q7 **Mountnorris** Armagh
45 M6 **Mount Nugent** Cavan
29 J6 **Mountrath**/*Maighean Rátha* Laois
16 H1 **Mountrivers Bridge** Clare
26 H7 **Mountshannon**/*Baile Uí Bheoláin* Clare
63 P9 **Mount Stewart** Down
35 N3 **Mount Talbot** Roscom
52 C3 **Mount Temple** Sligo
36 F5 **Mount Temple** Wmeath
6 G3 **Mount Uniacke** Cork
56 G10 **Mourne Park** Down
16 F3 **Moveen** Clare
66 G5 **Moville**/*Bun an Phobail* Donegl
25 N3 **Moy** Galway
55 M2 **Moy** Tyrone
32 D2 **Moyard** Galway
16 H3 **Moyasta** Clare
20 E6 **Moycarky** Tippry
33 Q7 **Moycullen**/*Maigh Cuilinn* Galway
44 G10 **Moydow** Longfd
55 M1 **Moygashel** Tyrone
20 F8 **Moyglass** Tippry
22 D2 **Moyle** Carlow
22 G3 **Moylisha** Wicklw
35 J4 **Moylough** Galway
51 M9 **Moylough** Sligo
26 C9 **Moymore** Clare
46 C7 **Moynalty**/*Maigh nEalta* Meath
38 F4 **Moynalvy** Meath
44 G4 **Moyne** Longfd
43 J6 **Moyne** Roscom
20 F4 **Moyne** Tippry
31 J8 **Moyne** Wicklw
4 D5 **Moyny Bridge** Cork
48 F4 **Moyrahan**/*Maigh Raithin* Mayo
17 N6 **Moyreen** Limrck
32 F6 **Moyrus**/*Maighros* Galway
66 H9 **Moys** Lderry
38 C5 **Moyvally** Kildre
36 G3 **Moyvore** Wmeath
36 G5 **Moyvoughly** Wmeath
38 B6 **Mucklon** Kildre
10 B7 **Muckross** Kerry
10 B7 **Muckross House** Kerry
66 D8 **Muff**/*Magh* Donegl
64 G8 **Muine Mór**/*Money More* Donegl
10 C1 **Muinganear** Kerry
1 L6 **Muingaphuca** Kerry
9 Q1 **Muingnaminnane** Kerry
17 J10 **Muingwee** Kerry
8 F10 **Muingydowda**/*Moing Uí Dhúda* Kerry
39 K5 **Mulhuddart** Dublin
50 E5 **Mullafarry** Mayo
24 F10 **Mullagh** Clare
35 L10 **Mullagh** Galway
40 H8 **Mullagh** Mayo
38 G4 **Mullagh** Meath
46 B6 **Mullagh**/*An Mullach* Cavan
55 Q10 **Mullaghbane** Armagh
52 D2 **Mullaghmore** Sligo
43 K3 **Mullaghroe** Sligo
18 F1 **Mullan** Cork
67 P9 **Mullan Head** Antrim
51 K8 **Mullany's Cross** Sligo
47 K7 **Mullary Cross Roads** Louth
43 L6 **Mullen** Roscom
11 R6 **Mullenaboree** Cork
21 K10 **Mullennaglogh** Tippry
21 Q10 **Mullennakill** Kilken
22 H2 **Mullinacuff** Wicklw
21 J8 **Mullinahone**/*Muileann na hUamhan* Tippry

14 D4 **Mullinavat**/*Muileann an Bhata* Kilken
37 L3 **Mullingar**/*An Muileann gCearr* Wmeath
41 Q9 **Mullingar Bridge** Mayo
40 G4 **Mulrany**/*An Mhala Raithni* Mayo
37 L1 **Multyfarnham**/*Muilte Farannáin* Wmeath
18 G4 **Mungret**/*Mungairit* Limrck
17 K7 **Murher** Kerry
6 G2 **Murley's Cross Roads** Cork
15 N5 **Murntown** Wexfd
8 D3 **Murreagh**/*An Mhulríoch* Kerry
41 J7 **Murrisk** Mayo
19 L3 **Murroe** Limrck
24 H3 **Murroogh** Clare
40 D3 **Mweelin**/*An Mhaoilinn* Mayo
10 B2 **Mweennalaa** Kerry
4 F8 **Myross** Cork
6 C8 **Myrtleville** Cork
22 E4 **Myshall**/*Miseal* Carlow

N

38 F10 **Naas**/*An Nás* Kildre
11 L6 **Nad** Cork
65 L5 **Na Dúnaibh**/*Downies* Donegl
33 P9 **Na Forbacha**/*Furbo* Galway
37 P10 **Nahana** Offaly
58 F3 **Naran** Donegl
30 D4 **Narraghmore**/*An Fhorrach Mhór* Kildre
40 E4 **Na Sraithini**/*Sraheens Bridge* Mayo
39 L1 **Naul**/*An Aill* Dublin
46 F10 **Navan**/*An Uaimh* Meath
33 P2 **Neale**/*An Éill* Mayo
28 E6 **Nealstown** Laois
2 G3 **Nedanone** Kerry
27 L9 **Nenagh**/*An tAonach* Tippry
15 J4 **Newbawn** Wexfd
20 G6 **New Birmingham** Tippry
54 G9 **Newbliss**/*Cúil Darach* Monhan
35 L3 **Newbridge** Galway
18 C5 **Newbridge** Limrck
30 E2 **Newbridge**/*An Droichead Nua* Kildre
66 C10 **New Buildings** Lderry
57 J7 **Newcastle** Down
34 H7 **Newcastle** Galway
13 K4 **Newcastle** Tippry
39 J8 **Newcastle**/*An Caisleán Nua* Dublin
31 P4 **Newcastle**/*An Caisleán Nua* Wicklw
17 P8 **Newcastle West**/*An Caisleán Nua* Limrck
5 K3 **Newcestown** Cork
13 L1 **Newchapel** Tippry
37 K5 **Newell's Bridge** Wmeath
47 J9 **Newgrange Megalithic Passage Tomb** Meath
45 N4 **New Inn** Cavan
35 K8 **New Inn** Galway
29 M4 **New Inn** Laois
20 D10 **Newinn**/*Loch Ceann* Tippry
21 N9 **Newmarket** Kilken
11 J3 **Newmarket**/*Áth Trasna* Cork
10 D3 **Newmarket Cross Roads** Kerry
18 D1 **Newmarket-on-Fergus**/*Cora Chaitlín* Clare
4 H7 **Newmills** Cork
59 P1 **Newmills** Donegl
61 P9 **Newmills** Wmeath
19 L2 **Newport**/*An Port Nua* Tippry
41 K5 **Newport**/*Baile Uí Fhiacháin* Mayo
14 G3 **New Ross**/*Ros Mhic Thriúin* Wexfd
56 C8 **Newry** Down
35 L9 **Newtown** Galway
38 E6 **Newtown** Kildre
21 J5 **Newtown** Kilken
29 N9 **Newtown** Laois
19 K8 **Newtown** Limrck
41 P7 **Newtown** Mayo
46 G6 **Newtown** Meath
27 N2 **Newtown** Offaly
35 P7 **Newtown** Roscom
43 M9 **Newtown** Roscom
19 P9 **Newtown** Tippry
27 K8 **Newtown** Tippry
28 E8 **Newtown** Tippry
7 L3 **Newtown** Watfd
13 M8 **Newtown** Watfd
13 R5 **Newtown** Watfd
15 J7 **Newtown** Wexfd
15 M7 **Newtown** Wexfd
63 H6 **Newtownabbey** Antrim
13 J2 **Newtownadam** Tippry
63 M8 **Newtownards** Down
54 D8 **Newtownbutler** Ferman
36 C2 **Newtown Cashel** Longfd
50 F8 **Newtown Cloghans** Mayo
68 C9 **Newtown-Crommelin** Antrim
65 Q9 **Newtown Cunningham**/*An Baile Nua Chuinneagáin* Donegl
44 E8 **Newtown Forbes**/*An Lios Breac* Longfd
44 G1 **Newtown Gore** Leitrm

55 P8 **Newtownhamilton** Armagh
37 K6 **Newtownlow** Wmeath
25 M2 **Newtownlynch** Galway
31 P3 **Newtown Mount Kennedy**/*Baile an Chinnéidigh* Wicklw
17 K7 **Newtownsandes Moyvane**/*Maigh Mheáin* Kerry
18 F10 **Newtownshandrum**/*Baile Nua Sheandroma* Cork
60 F5 **Newtownstewart** Tyrone
11 N4 **New Twopothouse Village**/*Tigh Nua an Dá Phota* Cork
14 E5 **Nicholastown** Kilken
21 K10 **Ninemilehouse**/*Tigh na Naoi Míle* Tippry
46 E6 **Nobber**/*An Obair* Meath
6 B9 **Nohaval** Cork
28 E7 **Nore Bridge** Tippry
46 C3 **Northlands** Cavan
5 K6 **North Ring** Cork
25 K5 **Noughaval** Clare
25 N9 **Noughaval** Clare
30 C3 **Nurney** Kildre
22 C3 **Nurney**/*An Urnaí* Carlow
39 J4 **Nuttstown Cross Roads** Meath

O

16 G8 **Oaghley** Kerry
18 G1 **Oatfield** Clare
24 G7 **O'Brien's Bridge** Clare
19 K1 **O'Briensbridge**/*Droichead Uí Bhriain* Clare
26 D9 **O'Callaghansmills** Clare
35 P9 **Oghill** Galway
26 G8 **Ogonnelloe** Clare
23 J10 **Oilgate**/*Maolán na nGabhar* Wexfd
12 B9 **Old Bride Bridge** Cork
19 M5 **Old Bridge** Limrck
67 N4 **Old Bushmills Distillery** Antrim
45 P7 **Oldcastle**/*An Seanchaisleáin* Meath
38 G3 **Old Cross Keys** Meath
13 K3 **Oldgrange** Tippry
5 P6 **Old Head** Cork
30 E3 **Old Kilcullen** Kildre
29 Q8 **Oldleagh** Laois
22 B3 **Oldleighlin** Carlow
43 K5 **Old Lung Bridge** Roscom
47 J8 **Old Mellifont Abbey** Meath
6 E5 **Old Midleton Distillery** Cork
13 N7 **Old Pike Bridge** Watfd
14 H3 **Old Ross** Wexfd
39 L3 **Oldtown** Dublin
29 K8 **Old Town** Laois
35 Q8 **Old Town** Roscom
36 C6 **Oldtown** Roscom
22 E8 **Old Town** Wexfd
11 P4 **Old Twopothouse Cross Roads** Cork
60 G8 **Omagh** Tyrone
56 D10 **Omeath**/*Ó Méith* Louth
24 B2 **Onaght**/*Eoghanacht* Galway
19 N6 **Oola**/*Úlla* Limrck
34 D9 **Oranmore**/*Orán Mór* Galway
46 E8 **Oristown**/*Baile Órthaí* Meath
16 G7 **Orritor** Tyrone
36 G9 **Oughter** Offaly
33 N5 **Oughterard**/*Uachtar Ard* Galway
23 K8 **Oulart**/*An tAbhallort* Wexfd
13 J1 **Outeragh** Tippry
46 C2 **Ouvry Cross Roads** Monhan
11 N10 **Ovens** Cork
51 J4 **Owenbeg** Sligo
25 P2 **Owenbristy** Galway
41 J9 **Owenmore Bridge** Mayo
51 J5 **Owenykeevan or Tawnamaddoo** Sligo
33 Q4 **Ower** Galway
14 A3 **Owning** Kilken

P

41 M10 **Páirc an Teampaill**/*Churchfield* Mayo
22 E10 **Palace** Wexfd
30 D9 **Palatine** Carlow
19 M6 **Palatine Street** Limrck
35 L6 **Pallas** Galway
29 K5 **Pallas** Laois
37 L7 **Pallasboy** Wmeath
20 C4 **Pallas Cross** Tippry
35 L6 **Pallas Green** Limrck
19 M5 **Pallas Green New** Limrck
18 E4 **Pallaskenry**/*Pailís Chaonraí* Limrck
23 L3 **Pallis** Wexfd
39 K7 **Palmerstown** Dublin
61 J2 **Park** Lderry
41 Q4 **Park** Mayo
15 L7 **Park** Wexfd
12 B6 **Parkacunna** Cork
5 K3 **Parkbane** Cork
22 G4 **Park Bridge** Wicklw
52 E7 **Parks Castle** Leitrm
62 G5 **Parkgate** Antrim
25 N2 **Parkmore** Galway

3 J2 **Parknasilla** Kerry
18 H2 **Parteen** Clare
41 P9 **Partry**/*Partraí* Mayo
35 Q2 **Passage** Roscom
14 G6 **Passage East**/*An Pasáiste* Watfd
6 C6 **Passage West**/*An Pasáiste* Cork
18 G5 **Patrickswell**/*Tobar Phádraig* Limrck
22 B5 **Paulstown**/*Baile Phóil* Kilken
35 L9 **Peak** Galway
62 E4 **Peters Bridge** Antrim
26 D3 **Peterswell**/*Tobar Pheadair* Galway
59 P9 **Pettigo**/*Paiteagó* Donegl
6 A4 **Piercetown** Cork
15 N5 **Piercetown** Wexfd
3 Q4 **Pierson's Bridge** Cork
27 N3 **Pike** Tippry
38 F3 **Pike Corner** Wmeath
28 H7 **Pike of Rush Hall** Laois
14 B4 **Piltown**/*Baile an Phoill* Kilken
65 N10 **Pluck** Donegl
60 G4 **Plumbridge** Tyrone
25 N2 **Pollagh** Galway
36 F8 **Pollagh** Offaly
35 L9 **Pollatlugga** Galway
48 H3 **Pollatomish**/*Poll a' tSómais* Mayo
48 H3 **Poll a' tSómais**/*Pollatomish* Mayo
35 P8 **Pollboy** Galway
43 J10 **Pollshask** Galway
61 L8 **Pomeroy** Tyrone
41 Q3 **Pontoon** Mayo
41 Q3 **Pontoon Bridge** Mayo
19 P6 **Pope's Bridge** Tippry
47 L6 **Port** Louth
48 H2 **Port a' Chlóidh**/*Portacloy* Mayo
48 H2 **Portacloy**/*Port a' Chlóidh* Mayo
56 B3 **Portadown** Armagh
57 N7 **Portaferry** Down
66 E2 **Portaleen** Donegl
29 M2 **Portarlington**/*Cúil an tSúdaire* Laois
57 Q2 **Portavogie** Down
67 N4 **Portballintrae** Antrim
49 J2 **Port Durlainne**/*Porturlin* Mayo
62 B2 **Portglenone** Antrim
27 L3 **Portland** Tippry
29 L5 **Portlaoise**/*Port Laoise* Laois
14 B5 **Portlaw**/*Port Lách* Watfd
8 D10 **Portmagee**/*An Caladh* Kerry
39 N5 **Portmarnock**/*Port Mearnóg* Dublin
63 M2 **Portmuck** Antrim
65 J5 **Portnablaghy**/*Port na Blaiche* Donegl
40 D7 **Portnakilly** Mayo
37 L1 **Portnashangan** Wmeath
58 F3 **Portnoo**/*Port Nua* Donegl
39 P3 **Portraine**/*Port Reachrainn* Dublin
27 J8 **Portroe**/*An Port Rua* Tippry
67 M5 **Portrush** Antrim
65 N5 **Portsalon**/*Port an tSalainn* Donegl
67 L5 **Portstewart** Lderry
27 L4 **Portumna**/*Port Omna* Galway
49 J2 **Porturlin**/*Port Durlainne* Mayo
5 J1 **Poulanargid** Cork
10 D8 **Poulgorm Bridge** Kerry
13 K1 **Poulnamucky** Tippry
12 B8 **Powers Bridge** Cork
31 N1 **Powerscourt Gardens** Wicklw
31 M2 **Powerscourt Waterfall** Wicklw
27 J4 **Power's Cross** Galway
56 C6 **Poyntz Pass** Armagh
12 B8 **Prap** Cork
14 G5 **Priesthaggard** Wexfd
60 E7 **Priest's Bridge** Tyrone
13 L5 **Priesttown** Tippry
38 E8 **Prosperous**/*An Chorrchoill* Kildre
27 K7 **Puckaun** Tippry

Q

5 K2 **Quarry Cross Roads** Cork
62 E1 **Quarrytown** Antrim
25 L2 **Quay** Galway
6 C6 **Queenstown Story** Cork
16 G4 **Querrin** Clare
66 E6 **Quigley's Point**/*Rinn Uí Choigligh* Donegl
24 F10 **Quilty**/*Coillte* Clare
25 P10 **Quin**/*Cuinche* Clare
28 D8 **Quinlisk's Cross Roads** Tippry

R

21 N4 **Radestown** Kilken
57 L2 **Raffrey** Down
51 N2 **Raghly** Sligo
45 P8 **Rahaghy** Meath
36 H8 **Rahan**/*Raitheán* Offaly
37 Q3 **Raharney**/*Ráth Fhearna* Wmeath
30 G9 **Raheen** Carlow
5 M2 **Raheen** Cork

10 D6 **Raheen** Kerry
12 H2 **Raheen** Tippry
15 J3 **Raheen** Wexfd
36 G5 **Raheen** Wmeath
23 M8 **Raheenlusk** Wexfd
3 N7 **Raheenroe** Cork
57 M4 **Raholp** Down
50 D8 **Rake Street** Mayo
14 G6 **Ramsgrange** Wexfd
26 H2 **Ranamackan** Galway
62 D4 **Randalstown** Antrim
28 C2 **Rapemills** Offaly
60 C2 **Raphoe**/*Ráth Bhoth* Donegl
10 G3 **Rascalstreet** Cork
67 P10 **Rasharkin** Antrim
59 P1 **Rashedoge** Donegl
43 N4 **Ratallen Cross Roads** Roscom
28 D3 **Rath** Offaly
38 B10 **Rathangan**/*Ráith Iomgháin* Kildre
9 Q2 **Rathanny** Kerry
44 H10 **Rathaspick** Wmeath
27 N3 **Rathcabban** Tippry
38 D1 **Rathcarran**/*Ráth Chairn* Meath
38 D1 **Ráth Chairn**/*Rathcarran* Meath
38 F7 **Rathcoffey** Kildre
43 N9 **Rathconor** Roscom
37 J3 **Rathconrath** Wmeath
11 J6 **Rathcool** Cork
39 J8 **Rathcoole**/*Ráth Cúil* Dublin
38 D4 **Rathcore** Meath
12 D8 **Rathcormack**/*Ráth Chormaic* Cork
43 M7 **Rathcroghan Cross Roads** Roscom
25 K10 **Rathcrony** Cork
39 K3 **Rath Cross Roads** Meath
30 H7 **Rathdangan**/*Ráth Daingin* Wicklw
28 G9 **Rathdowney**/*Ráth Domhnaigh* Laois
31 M7 **Rathdrum**/*Ráth Droma* Wicklw
36 H1 **Rathduff** Longfd
17 P9 **Ratheenagh** Limrck
38 D9 **Rathernan** Kildre
47 J6 **Rathescar Cross Roads** Louth
39 J1 **Rathfeigh** Meath
6 C3 **Rathfilode** Cork
56 E7 **Rathfriland** Down
22 F9 **Rathfylane** Wexfd
29 L9 **Rathgar** Dublin
13 P3 **Rathgormuck** Watfd
34 B1 **Rathgranagher** Mayo
19 N8 **Rathkea** Tippry
18 D6 **Rathkeale**/*Ráth Caola* Limrck
46 F8 **Rathkenny** Meath
43 N8 **Rathkeva** Roscom
13 L2 **Rathkevin** Tippry
43 M6 **Rathkineely** Roscom
50 E3 **Rathlackan**/*Ráth Leacáin* Mayo
50 H3 **Rathlee** Sligo
30 F9 **Rathlyon** Carlow
13 Q5 **Rathmaiden** Watfd
65 N8 **Rathmelton**/*Ráth Mealtain* Donegl
46 D10 **Rathmore** Meath
10 F6 **Rathmore**/*An Ráth Mhór* Kerry
38 H10 **Rathmore**/*An Ráth Mhór* Kildre
14 F9 **Rathmoylan** Watfd
38 D4 **Rathmoylon** Meath
65 P7 **Rathmullan**/*Ráth Maoláin* Donegl
31 P5 **Rathnew**/*Ráth Naoi* Wicklw
22 E9 **Rathnure** Wexfd
50 E5 **Rathoma** Mayo
6 F3 **Rathorgan** Cork
45 J10 **Rathowen**/*Ráth Eoghainn* Wmeath
50 F6 **Rathreedan** Mayo
3 P7 **Rathruane** Cork
16 E9 **Rathscannel** Kerry
22 E2 **Rathtoe** Carlow
30 F8 **Rathvilly**/*Ráth Bhile* Carlow
37 P3 **Rathwire** Wmeath
39 J3 **Ratoath**/*Ráth Tó* Meath
3 M8 **Ratooragh** Cork
47 K1 **Ravensdale** Louth
56 G1 **Ravernet** Down
65 P7 **Ray** Donegl
4 C7 **Rea Cross Roads** Cork
46 G4 **Reaghstown** Louth
7 M3 **Reanaclogheen**/*Ré na gChoichín* Watfd
25 J10 **Reanagishagh** Clare
10 B1 **Reanagowan Cross Roads** Kerry
10 G10 **Reananerree**/*Ré na nDoirí* Cork
4 G6 **Reanascreena** Cork
19 N3 **Rearcross** Tippry
36 C10 **Reask** Galway
4 F6 **Reavouler Bridge** Cork
32 H4 **Recess**/*Sraith Salach* Galway
61 L10 **Reclain** Tyrone
66 F6 **Redcastle** Donegl
31 N8 **Redcross**/*An Chrois Dhearg* Wicklw
25 J10 **Redgate** Wexfd
54 D10 **Redhills**/*An Cnoc Rua* Cavan
27 M3 **Redwood** Tippry
3 N2 **Releagh Bridge** Kerry
7 M3 **Ré na gChoichín**/*Reanaclogheen* Watfd

10 G10 **Ré na nDoirí**/*Reananerree* Cork
32 D1 **Renvyle** Galway
3 J6 **Rerrin** Cork
67 N5 **Revallagh North** Antrim
37 N7 **Rhode**/*Ród* Offaly
55 P4 **Richhill** Armagh
55 P4 **Riesk** Cork
6 C7 **Ringaskiddy**/*Rinn an Scidigh* Cork
67 L8 **Ringsend** Lderry
23 J5 **Ringstown** Laois
13 N9 **Ringville**/*An Rinn* Watfd
64 D8 **Rinnafarset**/*Rinn na Feirste* Donegl
24 G8 **Rinneen** Clare
4 E8 **Rinneen** Cork
64 D8 **Rinn na Feirste**/*Rinnafarset* Donegl
34 D9 **Rinville** Galway
23 M5 **Riverchapel** Wexfd
5 Q3 **Riverstick** Cork
6 B5 **Riverstown** Cork
27 P4 **Riverstown** Tippry
52 D9 **Riverstown**/*Baile Idir Dhá Abhainn* Sligo
9 Q3 **Riverville Cross Roads** Kerry
24 G5 **Roadford** Clare
38 D8 **Robertstown**/*Baile Riobaird* Kildre
38 E1 **Robinstown** Meath
15 L6 **Robinstown** Wexfd
14 C4 **Rochestown** Kilken
14 F5 **Rochestown** Kilken
13 J2 **Rochestown** Tippry
37 M5 **Rochfortbridge**/*Droichead Chaisleán Loiste* Wmeath
10 G1 **Rockchapel** Cork
54 H10 **Rockcorry**/*Buíochar* Monhan
31 N7 **Rocketstown** Wicklw
18 G9 **Rockhill** Limrck
12 B5 **Rockmills** Cork
20 D8 **Rock of Cashel** Tippry
43 G5 **Rodeen** Roscom
34 E10 **Roevehagh** Galway
27 N1 **Rooaun** Galway
42 H3 **Roosky** Mayo
44 C6 **Roosky**/*Rúscaigh* Roscom
35 Q7 **Rooty Cross Roads** Roscom
33 K8 **Ros an Mhíl**/*Rossaveel* Galway
14 G3 **Rosbercon** Wexfd
4 G1 **Roscat** Carlow
35 P1 **Roscommon**/*Ros Comáin* Roscom
28 D7 **Roscrea**/*Ros Cré* Tippry
48 H3 **Ros Dumhach**/*Ross Port* Mayo
20 E9 **Rosegreen** Tippry
36 G5 **Rosemount** Wmeath
29 J3 **Rosenallis** Laois
65 L5 **Rosepenna**/*Machair Loiscthe* Donegl
33 J7 **Ros Muc**/*Rosmuck* Galway
33 J7 **Rosmuck**/*Ros Muc* Galway
20 C5 **Rosmult** Tippry
65 M5 **Rosnakill** Donegl
45 M7 **Ross** Meath
19 Q9 **Rossadrehid** Tippry
10 B4 **Rossanean** Kerry
33 K8 **Rossaveel**/*Ros an Mhíl* Galway
58 E3 **Rossbeg** Donegl
9 J6 **Ross Behy** Kerry
3 P8 **Rossbrin** Cork
33 P6 **Rosscahill** Galway
4 G7 **Ross Carbery**/*Ros Ó gCairbre* Cork
51 P3 **Rosses Point**/*An Ros* Sligo
52 H4 **Rossinver**/*Ros Inbhir* Leitrm
15 Q6 **Rosslare**/*Ros Láir* Wexfd
15 Q6 **Rosslare Harbour**/*Calafort Ros Láir* Wexfd
54 F7 **Rosslea** Ferman
3 J5 **Rossmackowen** Cork
4 G1 **Rossmore** Cork
4 H5 **Rossmore** Cork
22 B2 **Rossmore** Laois
20 B6 **Rossmore** Tippry
29 N4 **Rossmore Cross Roads** Laois
3 M3 **Rossnagrena** Cork
59 J9 **Rossnowlagh** Donegl
48 H3 **Ross Port**/*Ros Dumhach* Mayo
41 P4 **Ross West** Mayo
6 E6 **Rostellan** Cork
56 E10 **Rostrevor** Down
40 H4 **Rosturk** Mayo
42 B10 **Roundfort** Mayo
32 E6 **Roundstone**/*Cloch na Rón* Galway
31 M4 **Roundwood**/*An Tóchar* Wicklw
61 K9 **Rousky** Tyrone
25 M7 **Ruan** Clare
57 P1 **Rubane** Down
39 P3 **Rush**/*An Ros* Dublin
11 K9 **Rusheen** Cork
13 L3 **Russellstown** Watfd
34 G6 **Ryehill** Galway
11 L8 **Rylane** Cork

S

39 J8 **Saggart** Dublin
66 C9 **St Columb's Cathedral** Lderry

57 K2 **Saintfield** Down
60 D1 **St Johnston**/*Baile Suingean* Donegl
39 L5 **St Margaret's** Dublin
22 C9 **St Mullin's** Carlow
6 E6 **Saleen** Cork
8 G10 **Sallahig** Kerry
38 F9 **Sallins**/*Na Solláin* Kildre
6 B4 **Sallybrook** Cork
20 B2 **Sallypark** Tippry
34 B9 **Salthill**/*Bóthar na Trá* Galway
14 H7 **Saltmills** Wexfd
61 N8 **Sandholes** Tyrone
39 M8 **Sandyford** Dublin
39 M5 **Santry** Dublin
21 L4 **Sart Cross Roads** Kilken
57 M4 **Saul** Down
10 E2 **Scalp Bridge** Kerry
35 P2 **Scardaun** Roscom
42 C10 **Scardaune** Mayo
23 N3 **Scarnagh Cross Roads** Wexfd
26 F8 **Scarriff**/*An Scairbh* Clare
38 C3 **Scarriff Bridge** Meath
10 C4 **Scartaglin**/*Scairteach an Ghlinne* Kerry
13 M6 **Scart Bridge** Watfd
56 C5 **Scarva** Down
3 N8 **Schull**/*An Scoil* Cork
55 K8 **Scotch Corner** Monhan
55 Q2 **Scotch Street** Armagh
54 E10 **Scotshouse** Monhan
54 H6 **Scotstown**/*Baile an Scotaigh* Monhan
10 D5 **Scrahanfadda** Kerry
44 B8 **Scramoge** Roscom
12 B6 **Scrarour** Cork
23 K10 **Screen** Wexfd
36 H9 **Screggan** Offaly
66 H10 **Scriggan** Lderry
46 C9 **Scurlockstown** Meath
57 K5 **Seaforde** Down
56 D4 **Seapatrick** Down
13 N2 **Seskin** Tippry
60 G10 **Seskinore** Tyrone
4 E3 **Shanacrane** Cork
6 G6 **Shanagarry** Cork
25 P5 **Shanaglish** Galway
17 P5 **Shanagolden**/*Seanghualainn* Limrck
29 J7 **Shanahoe** Laois
24 H9 **Shanavogh East** Clare
35 J7 **Shanballard** Galway
6 C7 **Shanbally** Cork
35 K1 **Shanbally** Galway
13 P7 **Shanbally** Watfd
19 N3 **Shanballyedmond** Tippry
42 F10 **Shanballymore** Galway
12 A5 **Shanballymore**/*An Seanbhaile Mór* Cork
38 C3 **Shanco Bridge** Meath
26 H2 **Shangarry** Galway
39 P9 **Shankill** Dublin
4 G3 **Shanlaragh** Cork
46 G6 **Shanlis Cross Roads** Louth
17 N4 **Shannakea** Clare
18 D2 **Shannon** Clare
18 E2 **Shannon**/*Sionainn* Clare
36 B8 **Shannonbridge**/*Droichead na Sionainne* Offaly
36 C10 **Shannon Harbour**/*Caladh na Sionainne* Offaly
29 P7 **Shanragh** Laois
12 G4 **Shanrahan Cross Roads** Tippry
18 C9 **Shanrath** Limrck
46 C1 **Shantonagh** Monhan
46 C2 **Sharavogue** Offaly
46 C2 **Shercock**/*Searcóg* Cavan
13 Q2 **Sheskin** Watfd
20 B5 **Shevry** Tippry
22 H3 **Shillelagh**/*Síol Éalaigh* Wicklw
28 C6 **Shinrone**/*Suí an Róin* Offaly
57 M3 **Shrigley** Down
16 H6 **Shrone** Kerry
19 N7 **Shronell** Tippry
16 H6 **Shronowen** Kerry
34 B3 **Shrule**/*Sruthair* Mayo
4 E4 **Sillahertane** Cork
55 Q10 **Silver Bridge** Armagh
27 K10 **Silvermines**/*Béal Átha Gabhann* Tippry
55 K6 **Silver Stream** Monhan
60 D4 **Sion Mills** Tyrone
18 F1 **Sixmilebridge**/*Droichead Abhainn Ó gCearnaigh* Clare
61 J9 **Sixmilecross** Tyrone
63 N7 **Six Road Ends** Down
4 B4 **Skahanagh** Cork
6 C2 **Skahanagh North** Cork
6 C3 **Skahanagh South** Cork
4 C7 **Skeagh** Cork
36 H3 **Skeagh Beg** Wmeath
26 C3 **Skehanagh** Galway
34 H5 **Skehanagh** Galway
12 E4 **Skeheen** Cork
11 Q4 **Skenakilla Cross Roads** Cork
39 P1 **Skerries**/*Na Sceirí* Dublin
4 D8 **Skibbereen**/*An Sciobairín* Cork
38 H1 **Skreen** Meath
51 M4 **Skreen** Sligo
14 G9 **Slade** Watfd
46 H9 **Slane**/*Baile Shláine* Meath
57 J8 **Slieve Donard** Down
35 L2 **Slievemurry** Galway
4 H2 **Slieveowen** Cork
14 E6 **Slieverue** Kilken

5 Q2 **Sligga Bridge** Cork
52 C6 **Sligo**/*Sligeach* Sligo
52 C6 **Sligo Abbey** Sligo
46 H6 **Smarmore** Louth
8 C3 **Smerwick**/*Ard na Caithne* Kerry
54 G7 **Smithborough** Monhan
21 P2 **Smithstown** Kilken
2 H1 **Sneem**/*An tSnaidhm* Kerry
52 D9 **Sooey** Sligo
9 M1 **Spa** Kerry
25 N8 **Spancehill** Clare
24 F9 **Spanish Point**/*Rinn na Spáinneach* Clare
61 K4 **Sperrin** Tyrone
33 N9 **Spiddal**/*An Spidéal* Galway
29 M8 **Spink Bridge** Laois
36 H6 **Spittaltown** Wmeath
66 C9 **Spring Town** Lderry
31 M3 **Sraghmore** Wicklw
41 N9 **Srah**/*An tSraith* Mayo
48 F5 **Srah**/*An tSraith* Mayo
28 F5 **Srahanboy** Laois
49 K2 **Srahataggle**/*Sraith a' tSeagail* Mayo
42 B5 **Sraheens** Mayo
40 E4 **Sraheens Bridge**/*Na Sraithíní* Mayo
48 H6 **Srahmore** Mayo
48 H8 **Srahnamanragh Bridge** Mayo
49 K2 **Sraith a' tSeagail**/*Srahataggle* Mayo
32 H4 **Sraith Salach**/*Recess* Galway
13 J6 **Sruh** Watfd
47 J5 **Stabannan** Louth
46 G9 **Stackallan** Meath
62 C5 **Stafford** Antrim
47 M10 **Stamullin** Meath
38 E7 **Staplestown** Kildre
39 M9 **Stepaside** Dublin
61 Q8 **Stewartstown** Tyrone
39 M8 **Stillorgan** Dublin
54 F8 **Stone Bridge** Monhan
19 J5 **Stonepark** Limrck
62 G8 **Stonyford** Antrim
21 N8 **Stonyford**/*Áth Stúin* Kilken
63 L8 **Stormont** Down
60 D3 **Strabane** Tyrone
8 H2 **Stradbally** Kerry
29 N5 **Stradbally**/*An tSráidbhaile* Laois
13 Q7 **Stradbally**/*An tSráidbhaile* Watfd
42 B4 **Strade** Mayo
45 N3 **Stradone**/*Sraith an Domhain* Cavan
38 G8 **Straffan**/*Teach Srafáin* Kildre
22 H6 **Strahart** Wexfd
63 J4 **Straid** Antrim
17 N9 **Strand** Limrck
51 P3 **Strandhill**/*An Leathros* Sligo
57 N4 **Strangford** Down
67 Q6 **Stranocum** Antrim
59 P3 **Stranorlar**/*Srath an Urláir* Donegl
30 F6 **Stratford**/*Áth na Sráide* Wicklw
36 H5 **Streamstown** Wmeath
34 J9 **Street** Wmeath
20 F2 **Strogue Cross Roads** Wexfd
43 Q7 **Strokestown**/*Béal na mBuillí* Roscom
43 Q7 **Strokestown Park** Roscom
66 H4 **Stroove** Donegl
11 M8 **Stuake** Cork
5 Q5 **Summer Cove** Cork
38 E4 **Summerhill**/*Cnoc an Linsigh* Meath
30 D3 **Suncroft** Kildre
29 N8 **Swan** Laois
53 N8 **Swanlinbar**/*An Muileann Iarainn* Cavan
54 H9 **Swan's Cross Roads** Monhan
61 Q1 **Swatragh** Lderry
42 D4 **Swinford**/*Béal Átha na Muice* Mayo
39 M4 **Swords**/*Sord* Dublin

T
35 P6 **Taghmaconnell** Roscom
15 L5 **Taghmon**/*Teach Munna* Wexfd
15 Q6 **Tagoat** Wexfd
3 J1 **Tahilla** Kerry
39 K8 **Tallaght** Dublin
46 H4 **Tallanstown** Louth
12 G8 **Tallow**/*Tulach an Iarainn* Watfd
12 H8 **Tallowbridge** Watfd
53 Q5 **Tamlaght** Ferman
61 R1 **Tamlaght O'Crilly** Lderry
55 N1 **Tamnamore** Tyrone
56 B4 **Tandragee** Armagh
38 E3 **Tang** Wmeath
18 H9 **Tankardstown** Limrck
38 G2 **Tara** Meath
36 H7 **Tara** Meath
17 K5 **Tarbert**/*Tairbeart* Kerry
13 K4 **Tar Bridge** Tippry
17 K3 **Tarmon** Clare
11 L1 **Tarrant's Cross Roads** Cork

55 N6 **Tassagh** Armagh
10 G3 **Taur** Cork
65 M5 **Tawny** Donegl
42 F4 **Tawnyinah** Mayo
52 G8 **Tawnylea** Leitrm
27 P2 **Taylor's Cross** Offaly
3 P5 **Tedagh** Kerry
54 H6 **Tedavnet** Monhan
58 C7 **Teelin**/*Teileann* Donegl
54 B9 **Teemore** Ferman
8 G2 **Teer**/*An Tír* Kerry
8 E10 **Teeravanagh**/*An Trian Iarach* Kerry
8 C4 **Teeravane**/*Tíorabháin* Kerry
4 H1 **Teerelton** Cork
25 M10 **Teermaclane** Clare
33 K3 **Teernakill Bridge**/*Tír na Cille* Galway
8 H8 **Teeromoyle** Kerry
46 C5 **Teevurcher** Meath
58 C7 **Teileann**/*Teelin* Donegl
51 L4 **Templeboy** Sligo
19 Q1 **Templederry** Tippry
13 N1 **Templeetney** Tippry
20 E2 **Templemore**/*An Teampall Mór* Tippry
3 L1 **Templenoe** Kerry
37 L6 **Templeoran** Wmeath
14 B3 **Templeorum** Kilken
62 G5 **Templepatrick** Antrim
22 F7 **Templeshanbo** Wexfd
20 F2 **Templetouhy**/*Teampall Tuaithe* Tippry
14 H8 **Templetown** Wexfd
6 B4 **Templeusque** Cork
54 C4 **Tempo** Ferman
15 N7 **Tenacre Cross Roads** Wexfd
65 L8 **Termon**/*An Tearmann* Donegl
44 D8 **Termonbarry** Roscom
47 L7 **Termonfeckin**/*Tearmann Feichín* Louth
27 L4 **Terryglass**/*Tír Dhá Ghlas* Tippry
37 N2 **Tevrin** Wmeath
62 B7 **The Battery** Tyrone
47 M2 **The Bush** Louth
21 Q3 **The Butts** Carlow
66 D10 **The Cross** Lderry
62 E7 **The Diamond** Antrim
62 A7 **The Diamond** Tyrone
37 N3 **The Downs** Wmeath
68 B7 **The Drones** Antrim
39 M2 **The Five Roads** Dublin
24 H9 **The Hand Cross Roads** Clare
23 K7 **The Harrow** Wexfd
15 K3 **The Leap** Wexfd
61 R6 **The Loup** Lderry
36 E3 **The Pigeons** Wmeath
27 N5 **The Pike** Tippry
6 H2 **The Pike** Watfd
13 P7 **The Pike** Watfd
61 N8 **The Rock** Tyrone
22 C10 **The Rower** Kilken
62 G1 **The Sheddings** Antrim
61 M4 **The Six Towns** Lderry
57 J4 **The Spa** Down
14 B4 **The Sweep** Kilken
57 J1 **The Temple** Down
19 K10 **Thomastown** Limrck
46 D7 **Thomastown** Meath
20 B9 **Thomastown** Tippry
21 P8 **Thomastown**/*Baile Mhic Andáin* Kilken
21 M4 **Threecastles** Kilken
54 H7 **Three Mile House** Monhan
31 L8 **Threewells** Wicklw
20 E5 **Thurles**/*Durlas* Tippry
43 K5 **Tibohine** Roscom
16 B8 **Tiduff** Kerry
13 M2 **Tikincor** Watfd
38 D7 **Timahoe** Kildre
29 M6 **Timahoe**/*Tigh Mochua* Laois
5 L6 **Timoleague**/*Tigh Molaige* Cork
30 E6 **Timolin** Kildre
23 J2 **Tinahely**/*Tigh na hÉille* Wicklw
36 F7 **Tinamuck** Offaly
23 J8 **Tinnacross Cross Roads** Wexfd
15 M3 **Tinnakilla** Wexfd
22 C2 **Tinryland** Carlow
47 J7 **Tinure Cross Roads** Louth
8 C4 **Tíorabháin**/*Teeravane* Kerry
19 P7 **Tipperary**/*Tiobraid Árann* Tippry
61 P2 **Tirkane** Lderry
33 K3 **Tír na Cille**/*Teernakill Bridge* Galway
5 L6 **Tirnanean** Cork
25 J6 **Tirnaneill** Monhan
25 P4 **Tirneevin** Galway
53 J8 **Tober** Cavan
36 G6 **Tober** Offaly
30 F5 **Toberbeg** Wicklw
51 M8 **Tobercurry**/*Tobar an Choire* Sligo
26 D2 **Toberelatan** Galway
61 P3 **Tobermore** Lderry
11 J2 **Tobernaclougha Cross Roads** Cork
38 B2 **Tobernadarry** Mayo
52 C9 **Toberscanavan** Sligo
19 P5 **Toem** Tippry
47 F3 **Togher** Cork
47 L6 **Togher** Louth
38 D4 **Togher** Meath
37 N7 **Togher** Offaly
31 J4 **Togher** Wicklw
16 D9 **Togherbane** Kerry

34 B8 **Tóin na Brocaí**/*Tonabrocky* Galway
40 F3 **Tóin re Gaoth**/*Tonregee* Mayo
15 N7 **Tomhaggard** Wexfd
34 B8 **Tonabrocky**/*Tóin na Brocaí* Galway
41 M8 **Tonlegee** Mayo
40 F3 **Tonregee**/*Tóin re Gaoth* Mayo
45 Q3 **Tonyduff** Cavan
4 G3 **Toom** Cork
25 J4 **Toomaghera** Clare
35 K3 **Toomard** Galway
32 F5 **Toombeola** Galway
62 B4 **Toome** Antrim
4 H1 **Tooms** Cork
27 N9 **Toomyvara**/*Tuaim Uí Mheára* Tippry
19 N2 **Toor** Tippry
13 L5 **Tooraneena** Watfd
17 M6 **Tooraree** Limrck
11 R6 **Tooreen** Cork
19 N2 **Tooreenbrien Bridge** Tippry
10 E4 **Tooreencahill** Kerry
10 H2 **Tooreendermot** Cork
12 A8 **Toorgarriff** Cork
41 N10 **Toormakeady**/*Tuar Mhic Éadaigh* Mayo
3 M8 **Toormore** Cork
17 N10 **Toornafulla** Limrck
37 K6 **Torque** Wmeath
14 D7 **Towergare** Watfd
6 D7 **Trabolgan** Cork
6 B8 **Tracton** Cork
3 L5 **Trafrask** Cork
9 N2 **Tralee**/*Trá Lí* Kerry
14 D8 **Tramore**/*Trá Mhór* Watfd
34 H3 **Trasternagh** Galway
2 G5 **Travara Bridge** Cork
4 B5 **Trawlebane** Cork
33 M1 **Trean**/*Tréan* Mayo
33 M1 **Tréan**/*Trean* Mayo
65 L9 **Treantagh** Donegl
45 M1 **Treehoo Cross Roads** Cavan
9 J2 **Trench Bridge** Kerry
43 J8 **Trien** Roscom
54 B2 **Trillick** Tyrone
38 E2 **Trim**/*Baile Átha Troim* Meath
38 E2 **Trim Castle** Meath
35 L7 **Trust** Galway
34 E3 **Tuam**/*Tuaim* Galway
26 F8 **Tuamgraney**/*Tuaim Gréine* Clare
41 N10 **Tuar Mhic Éadaigh**/*Toormakeady* Mayo
25 P6 **Tubber** Galway
21 J4 **Tubbrid** Kilken
12 H3 **Tubbrid** Tippry
26 C8 **Tulla**/*An Tulach* Clare
48 G7 **Tullachán Dubh**/*Tullaghanduff* Mayo
4 E2 **Tullagh** Cork
25 J10 **Tullaghaboy** Clare
52 E10 **Tullaghan** Leitrm
48 G7 **Tullaghanduff**/*Tullachán Dubh* Mayo
21 Q10 **Tullagher** Kilken
21 L10 **Tullaghought** Kilken
21 P7 **Tullaherin** Kilken
9 K10 **Tullagneal** Kerry
37 J8 **Tullamore**/*Tulach Mhór* Offaly
9 J2 **Tullaree** Kerry
21 K5 **Tullaroan** Kilken
25 L9 **Tullassa** Clare
16 D4 **Tullig** Clare
9 L5 **Tullig** Kerry
16 G9 **Tullig** Kerry
22 F2 **Tullow**/*An Tulach* Carlow
33 L9 **Tully**/*An Tulaigh* Galway
47 J8 **Tullyallen** Louth
15 L6 **Tullycanna** Wexfd
52 F8 **Tullycoly** Leitrm
32 E1 **Tully Cross** Galway
61 P8 **Tullyhogue** Tyrone
11 K1 **Tullylease** Cork
45 P1 **Tullyvin** Cavan
42 F9 **Tulrohaun** Mayo
43 N7 **Tulsk**/*Tuilsce* Roscom
3 K2 **Tuosist** Kerry
37 N2 **Turin** Wmeath
25 L3 **Turlough** Clare
41 Q5 **Turlough** Mayo
34 G6 **Turloughmore** Galway
4 E1 **Turnaspidogy** Cork
11 Q3 **Turnpike Cross** Cork
44 C10 **Turreen** Longfd
15 P6 **Twelveacre Cross Roads** Wexfd
20 D6 **Twoford Bridges** Tippry
20 F5 **Twomileborris** Tippry
29 K2 **Twomile Bridge** Laois
27 J2 **Tynagh** Galway
55 L5 **Tynan** Armagh
61 P10 **Tyrone Crystal** Tyrone
37 L6 **Tyrrellspass**/*Bealach an Tirialaigh* Wmeath

U
60 F7 **Ulster American Folk Park** Tyrone
4 F8 **Unionhall**/*Bréantrá* Cork
62 F9 **Upper Ballinderry** Antrim
20 B4 **Upperchurch** Tippry
61 Q2 **Upperlands** Lderry
5 M3 **Upton** Cork
42 G5 **Urhin** Cork
42 G6 **Urlaur** Mayo

20 H4 **Urlingford**/*Áth na nUrlainn* Kilken

V
30 H3 **Valleymount** Wicklw
8 D4 **Ventry**/*Ceann Trá* Kerry
29 P4 **Vicarstown** Laois
60 E4 **Victoria Bridge** Tyrone
13 K8 **Villierstown**/*An Baile Nua* Watfd
45 Q6 **Virginia**/*Achadh an Iúir* Cavan

W
37 N9 **Walsh Island** Offaly
6 E3 **Walshtown** Cork
38 H1 **Walterstown** Meath
39 L4 **Ward** Dublin
56 D2 **Waringstown** Down
5 P2 **Warner's Cross Roads** Cork
56 D10 **Warrenpoint** Down
30 G1 **Watch House Cross Roads** Kildre
22 G4 **Watch House Village** Wexfd
5 P1 **Waterfall** Cork
14 E8 **Waterford** Watfd
14 E6 **Waterford**/*Port Láirge* Watfd
14 D6 **Waterford Crystal** Watfd
6 C3 **Watergrasshill**/*Cnocán na Biolraí* Cork
2 E1 **Waterville**/*An Coireán* Kerry
59 N3 **Welchtown** Donegl
15 K6 **Wellingtonbridge**/*Droichead Eoin* Wexfd
5 J6 **West Cork Model Railway Village** Cork
41 L7 **Westport**/*Cathair na Mart* Mayo
41 K7 **Westport Quay** Mayo
14 D9 **Westtown** Watfd
64 F3 **West Town**/*An Baile Thiar* Donegl
15 N4 **Wexford**/*Loch Garman* Wexfd
30 D1 **Wheelam Cross Roads** Kildre
63 K6 **Whiteabbey** Antrim
11 Q8 **Whitechurch** Cork
13 L7 **Whitechurch** Watfd
14 G5 **Whitechurch** Wexfd
55 Q7 **Whitecross** Armagh
26 H7 **Whitegate**/*An Geata Bán* Clare
6 D7 **Whitegate**/*An Geata Bán* Cork
9 M4 **White Gate Cross Roads** Kerry
44 D8 **Whitehall** Roscom
45 M10 **Whitehall** Wmeath
63 M4 **Whitehead** Antrim
A4 A4 **White's Cross** Cork
62 D3 **Whitesides Corner** Antrim
47 N2 **Whites Town** Louth
31 Q6 **Wicklow**/*Cill Mhantáin* Wicklw
46 F8 **Wilkinstown**/*Baile Uilcín* Meath
25 K7 **Willbrook** Clare
43 J10 **Williamstown** Galway
21 L10 **Windgap**/*Bearna na Gaoithe* Kilken
38 C7 **Windmill Cross Roads** Kildre
29 N8 **Wolfhill** Laois
63 K5 **Woodburn** Antrim
31 M9 **Woodenbridge** Wicklw
26 D10 **Woodfield Bridge** Cork
26 H4 **Woodford**/*An Chráig* Galway
35 K7 **Woodlawn**/*Móta* Galway
14 F7 **Woodstown** Watfd

Y
46 G9 **Yellow Furze** Meath
27 J8 **Youghal** Tippry
7 K4 **Youghal**/*Eochaill* Cork